DEVELOPMENT AND UNDERDEVELOPMENT

Series editors: Ray Bromley and Gavin Kitching

Socialism and Underdevelopment

In the same series

Socialism and Underdevelopment

Ken Post
and Phil Wright

Routledge

LONDON and NEW YORK

First published in 1989 by
Routledge
11 New Fetter Lane, London EC4P 4EE
29 West 35th Street, New York NY 10001

© 1989 Ken Post and Phil Wright

Typeset by LaserScript Ltd, Mitcham, Surrey
Printed and bound in Great Britain by
Biddles Ltd, Guildford and King's Lynn

British Library Cataloguing in Publication Data

Post, Ken
    Socialism and underdevelopment.—
    (Development and underdevelopment).
    1. Developing countries. Socialism
    I. Title II. Wright, Phil III. Series
    335'.009172'4

    ISBN 0-415-01627-4
    ISBN 0-415-01628-2 Pbk

Library of Congress Cataloging in Publication Data

Post, Ken 1935- .
    Socialism and underdevelopment / Ken Post and Phil Wright.
        p.   cm. — (Development and underdevelopment)
    Bibliography: p.
    Includes index.
    ISBN 0-415-01627-4   ISBN 0-415-01628-2 (pbk)
    1. Communism--Developing countries. 2. Developing countries—
    Economic policy. 3. Communism. 4. Economic development.
    I. Wright, Phil. II. Title. III. Series.
    HX517.8.P67 1988
    335.43'091724—dc19   88-19909
                                                                CIP

Contents

List of figures

Series editors' preface

Development studies is a complex and diverse field of academic research and policy analysis. Concerned with the development process in all the comparatively poor nations of the world, it covers an enormous geographical area and a large part of the modern history of the world. Such a large subject area has generated a varied body of literature in a growing number of journals and other specialist publications, encompassing such diverse issues as the nature and feasibility of industrialization, the problem of small-scale agriculture and rural development in the Third World, the trade and other links between developed and developing countries and their effects on the development prospects of the poor, the nature and causes of poverty and inequality, and the record and future prospects of 'development planning, as a method of accelerating development. The nature of the subject matter has forced both scholars and practitioners to transcend the boundaries of their own disciplines whether these be social sciences, like economics, human geography or sociology, or applied sciences such as agronomy, plant biology or civil engineering. It is now a conventional wisdom of development studies that development problems are so multi-faceted and complex that *no* single discipline can hope to encompass them, let alone offer solutions.

This large and interdisciplinary area and the complex and rapidly changing literature pose particular problems for students, practitioners and specialists seeking a simple introduction to the field or some part of the field with which they are unfamiliar. The Development and Underdevelopment series attempts to rectify these problems by providing a number of brief, readable introductions to important issues in development studies written by an international range of specialists. All the texts are designed to be readily comprehensible to students meeting the issues for the first time, as well as to practitioners in developing countries, international agencies and voluntary bodies. We hope that, taken together, these books will bring to the reader a sense of the main preoccupations and problems in this rich and stimulating field of study and practice.

RAY BROMLEY
GAVIN KITCHING

Foreword and Acknowledgements

The first sentence of this book was written as long ago as 1977, but it has certainly lost none of its import. Our progress has been slow, for in the meantime one of us moved back to Britain and had to cope with the inevitable hassles of a new job as well as being separated from the other (which meant a voluminous correspondence, now almost as long as the book itself!), and we have both been involved in other work. This joint project therefore became something of a side-line which we have picked up and dropped as time and mental equilibrium have permitted.

On the other hand, we feel that our tardiness has had an important positive side which has helped to enrich the book. First of all, some of the other work in which we have been involved has concerned countries engaged in socialist transformation, namely Viet Nam (K. Post) and Yugoslavia (P. Wright), and this has provided us with new insights. Indeed, originally this book was conceived of as an introductory theoretical text which would guide our work on 'case-studies', but in the event it has been rather the other way round. Second, our work would have been impoverished without the benefit of the flowering of critical and creative writing about socialist transformations which began in the 1970s but has continued over the last few years. Here we wish to single out the inspiring work of Janos Kornai whose fascinating elaboration, in the *Economics of Shortage*, of a working micro-economics for a planned economy must surely rank as the foremost achievement of post-war economic theory.

Nevertheless, we hope not to be judged derivative. We have tried to relate our work and that of others to a different problematic, the key one for the twentieth century inscribed in our title. We have tried, thus, to show key issues as a continuum, from the original Soviet case to the most recent ones. And we have tried more systematically than is usual to combine political and economic analysis.

Reference to the writings of others draws special attention to our own sources. After some thought, we decided not to include a separate bibliography. The point is that, even to pretend to adequate coverage, a list of theoretically relevant works in the *two* major fields embraced by our title would fill a volume as long as this one, and selection would be an invidious task. As for titles related to our concrete reference points, a similar situation would prevail, at least for the USSR and China. Thus we decided to give full reference in relevant notes and leave it at that.

At a personal level, writing this book has been an odyssey out of the fog of dogma towards a greater tolerance of eclectic views of the world. The book has served us as a sort of political psychoanalysis, exposing our hang-ups and limitations. However, during the added trials and tribulations which this involved, one of us at least had the support of Stoya and Alexander, the latter having progressed from baby to schoolboy while we were writing.

As is usual we have also accumulated other debts. Michael Ellman read and commented on Chapter 3, as did George Irvin who led us to devote more attention to the problems faced by smaller, more open state socialist economies. Andrew Gamble also read Chapter 3 and said it was new to him, which was encouraging. Part of Chapter 5 benefited from a discussion with Tony Burke although, as an *aficionado* of one-party states, he will probably not agree with our conclusions. We are also particularly grateful to our anonymous referees and to Gavin Kitching, one of the series editors: their painstaking comments were both testing and valuable. Finally, we would like to thank the Institute of Social Studies in The Hague for providing support services and particularly those of Lyske Schweigman, Aïda Jesurun, and Barbara Kennedy, who put the manuscript into its final physical shape after a frustrating experience when technological change demanded a shift from one computer system to another, a trauma which caused one of us at least to look back to the days of his youth, when typing was all that was needed.

KEN POST	PHIL WRIGHT
Institute of Social Studies	University of Sheffield
The Hague	Sheffield
Holland	England

Socialism and underdevelopment

In the last quarter of the twentieth century Rosa Luxemburg's famous alternative, 'socialism or barbarism', still seems as relevant as it did in the first quarter. During the 1970s capitalism in the advanced industrial countries moved into its deepest and longest recession since the 1930s, leaving in its wake a fast-growing pool of wasted humans. As the world enters the late 1980s right-wing governments have proliferated, international tensions have mounted, and with the 'INF agreement' affecting at most 5 per cent of total destructive capacity and President Reagan's enthusiasm for taking the arms race into space continuing, the spectre of nuclear holocaust hangs heavily over the world. Moreover, the alternative is now perhaps just as stark as it was at the beginning of the century – despite attempts to resuscitate it, the reformist Keynesian-inspired middle ground has disappeared as the system is no longer able to generate the rates of growth of both output and employment which provided the cement for the post-war alliance between labour and capital. Indeed, in spite of its self-proclaimed capacity for eliminating capitalist crises, 'Keynesianism' proved not to be up to the task of coping with the concurrent problems of inflation and unemployment afflicting increasingly open and interdependent economies. In its place the rise of 'monetarism' has reflected the consolidation of a new era of domination by international finance capital and the imperative of creating conditions under which the self-regulating mechanisms of capitalism (the destruction of inefficient capital and the disciplining of the labour force through mass unemployment) could assert themselves more freely.

As for the underdeveloped countries, the so-called Third World which emerged historically as a result of the expansion of western capitalism throughout the globe and the restructuration which it imposed for its own purposes, their prospects seem even more uncertain. It is, of course, necessary to recognize how diverse the over one hundred countries of this 'World' are, ranging as they do from Argentina and South Korea to Chad. Yet there is a crucial economic parameter which limits their diversity, and that is their interpenetration with advanced capitalism. All of them, therefore, have been caught up to one degree or another in the repercussions of the crisis of the latter, a crisis characterized by a far-reaching restructuring of the world economy the implications of which are as yet unclear. However, the economic and social problems which will beset them vary greatly, ranging from massive debt burdens to the drought, mass starvation, and destitution which have afflicted the poorest, above all in Africa. In these circumstances, another common feature which serves as a kind of political parameter to their diversity is authoritarianism in response to the need to allow their own versions of the self-regulating mechanisms to take effect.

On the other hand, and despite this acute instability and uncertainty in the world economy, it is also true that the socialist alternative no longer seems to offer the obvious solace which it did at the beginning of the century. It is this paradox which motivates us to write this book. While socialist ideas have been important to national liberation struggles in peripheral capitalist countries since the Second World War, workers in advanced capitalist countries have, by and large, judged socialism by its concrete practice in the so-called socialist countries and, justifiably, found it an unattractive alternative. Indeed, as Polish workers and peasants have most conspicuously shown, Rosa Luxemburg's alternative applies just as much to the 'socialist' bloc as to western capitalism. Moreover, while the impact of socialist ideology on national liberation struggles in peripheral capitalist countries may have been substantial since the Second World War, at the present time it is being challenged by Islamic fundamentalism.

This state of affairs leaves the labour movement and all kinds of working people in a dangerous limbo – the possibilities for introducing reforms are severely circumscribed and, just at a time when a confident socialist alternative is more necessary than ever, socialist ideas have lost much of their mass appeal. Similarly, they have been judged and condemned on the basis of their practical implementation in a number of underdeveloped countries. As we see it, therefore, central to moving out of this limbo is the development of new insights into why the implementation of socialist ideas has led to the emergence of societies which appear unattractive to ordinary people living in all parts of the capitalist world, and which, with a few exceptions, are certainly not held in very high esteem by most of the people who actually live in them. This is the main objective of this short book.

THE PROBLEMATIC

In this book we are concerned to begin to unravel the 'laws of motion' of 'state socialist societies'.[1] Its title is *Socialism and Underdevelopment* because all of the socialist revolutions of the twentieth century have occurred in underdeveloped peripheral capitalist countries (a secondary objective of the book is to consider why this has been so) and, more importantly, because the problems created by conditions of socio-economic underdevelopment have clearly had a decisive, but not fully recognized bearing on the emergence of the main characteristics of contemporary state socialist societies. In this respect it is very unfortunate that socialist ideas in general have been judged and condemned on the basis of their practical implementation in a number of underdeveloped countries, including the original USSR. It would surely be more reasonable first of all to extricate these ideas from the quagmire of circumstances under which they were put into practice. If this can be done it would certainly represent a step towards the possibility of real debate about socialist ideas, in turn making the elaboration of a viable socialist alternative that much more attainable.

The problematic of this book is therefore the relationship between socialism and underdevelopment, and that in three senses. First, because that is historically what came to be the case; it seems to us of decisive importance that after about 1920, and certainly since 1945, both the debate about the building of socialism and the attempts to do so shifted from capitalism's advanced centre to its underdeveloped periphery. Second, as a result, the relationship between socialism and underdevelopment has now become the key issue for the future of the former, given that it is the only potential alternative to barbarism for a human race most of whom do not enjoy the privileges of living in the central countries (which can now be taken to include Japan, Canada, Australia, and New Zealand). After all, it should always be borne in mind that socialist ideas originally emerged as a critique of industrial capitalism, not as a programme for dealing with the socio-economic problems of peripheral capitalist countries. The possibility that they cannot, in fact, become the latter without deformation must still be left open as a matter for discussion. The historical shift may well have been into a terrible dead end. In face of that possibility the relationship between socialism and underdevelopment is part of our problematic in a third sense, namely the question of whether a socialism, which has no developed industrial base 'inherited' from capitalism, can provide a way forward.

Following from the above issues we may state our proposed laws of motion of state socialism as follows:

1. State socialist systems have an innate economic tendency to underproduction and shortage which is reciprocally related to a series of macro- and micro-economic conflicts over the distribution of resources.

2. State socialist systems are marked by an innate political tendency to the assertion of state control, eradicating all autonomous elements in civil society.

It should be noted that we do not put these forward as absolute 'scientific' laws which *have* to be realized; that would be in the worst traditions of Stalinist theorizing. Rather, we see them as 'laws of tendency' which may never be fully realized, certainly not in every concrete case. Moreover, it is one of their innate characteristics that their very operation serves to create countervailing tendencies, either within the given system itself or introduced from outside. Thus we have a dialectical situation in which specific elements brought into combination generate certain processes which in turn shape those elements in such a way as to modify or even block the processes.

The issues raised here will be theorized (though, it must immediately be pointed out, unevenly) in the rest of this book. In the remainder of this chapter we shall sketch out some of the main elements of the socialism-underdevelopment relationship which we feel have been neglected in previous discussion and to which we shall give special attention later.

The problematic of socialism and underdevelopment as it has emerged in the second half of the twentieth century encompasses for us the interplay between three elements: underdevelopment, the form and nature of the seizure of power, and the 'received ideas' of socialism. Underdevelopment is an 'objective' element contributing the material conditions which both nurture the possibility of a revolutionary seizure of power and circumscribe the options open to the revolutionary leadership once the seizure of power has taken place. The form and nature of the seizure of power is also an 'objective' element which leaves an indelible imprint on post-revolutionary history, although it is itself determined by both objective factors (particular material conditions) and 'subjective' factors (the political perceptions upon which the revolutionary leadership acts). The 'received ideas' of socialism constitute a purely 'subjective' element. Derived above all from Soviet experience, they provide the main substance of what the revolutionary leadership thinks it is about once the seizure of power has taken place. Although these elements may differ in content, according to time and place, theorizing them and the interplay between them provides general insights into the 'laws of motion' of all state socialist societies – as we shall be seeking to demonstrate, though obviously not exhaustively, in our companion studies.

Underdevelopment

The 'socialist' revolutions of the twentieth century (including the 'induced' ones in eastern Europe, except perhaps Czechoslovakia) have all occurred in underdeveloped, peripheral capitalist countries.[2] The necessity for socialism is, of course, an issue wherever capitalism exists, but our chosen focus is this phenomenon. This means that the potential 'catchment area' for this study of experience to date includes some twenty-four countries, if we exclude the Soviet Union itself. As we shall explain at the beginning of the second chapter, eight in eastern Europe (Albania, Bulgaria, Czechoslovakia, East Germany, Hungary, Poland, Rumania, and Yugoslavia) may be seen as belonging to one historical bloc. They are significant for us because they offer the longest experience of attempting to build systems on the Soviet model, or of reacting against it. Angola, Benin, Congo, China, Cuba, Ethiopia, Cape Verde, Guinea-Bissau, Kampuchea, North Korea, Laos, Mongolia, Mozambique, Somalia, Viet Nam and South Yemen are successors to the Soviet Union in describing themselves as 'Marxist–Leninist' or 'scientific' in their socialism (though Somalia with less emphasis since 1977). This distinguishes them from the others, like contemporary Tanzania or Burma, which style themselves 'socialist'; these bear many of the characteristics we shall analyse, but are not fully committed to the dominant model which is our concern. Nicaragua is potentially a key case, with a leadership genuinely committed to socialism but not to the Marxist–Leninist model we are analysing. In that sense it could provide a future alternative model, though there is also the possibility that, especially under the pressure of external aggression, the regime may swing more in a state socialist direction.[3]

Given that the second group of sixteen listed above has historically more in common with possible future cases (South Africa? the Philippines?) than the eastern European countries, the main weight of our discussion, at least in terms of implications, is meant to rest there. However, our basic starting point is that in all twenty-four the particular form of peripheral capitalism which gave rise to revolutionary possibilities was broadly similar (again, possibly excepting Czechoslovakia).

1. All the countries concerned had been integrated into the world division of labour as primary commodity-exporting economies during the stage of the expansion of western capitalism when the search for food and raw materials began in earnest on a world scale and the periphery was being increasingly spatially reorganized for capitalist purposes, sometimes involving the creation of units which never existed before (for example, the colonies created by the 'grab for Africa').

2. They were all largely agrarian economies with a low absolute level of development of the productive forces and exhibiting a combination of forms of production and surplus extraction.

3. Corresponding to their importance as suppliers of food and raw materials to western capitalist countries, the strategic sectors of their economies were under the control of foreign capital.

4. Significant local initiatives in the direction of industrialization, if there were any, were generally being carried out under the auspices of the state or foreign capital, rather than by a 'domestic bourgeoisie'.

This form of peripheral capitalism was also related to a particular class structure including a weak domestic capitalist class, a small working class, a large peasantry and petty bourgeoisie, and a small range of middle strata.

That these features of peripheral capitalism were crucially important to revolutionary prospects in Russia was recognized by Trotsky as early as 1906 – from them he derived the 'law of uneven and combined development' and the 'theory of permanent revolution'.[4] However, neither he nor any of the other critics of state socialist societies who we shall discuss later really integrate the particular problems of underdevelopment generated by this peripheral capitalism into their analytical conceptualizations of post-revolutionary society, or only do so at a very general level. Trotsky himself uses underdevelopment to explain bureaucratic degeneration, but he only sees the causal link between the two in terms of a scarcity of consumption goods: the role of underdevelopment in the emergence of specific production relations is nowhere in the picture. At one point Mandel has a potentially interesting insight:

> It is, therefore, at least possible, if not probable, that what today seem to be 'general' features of this transitional society are in reality peculiarities having less to do with the internal logic of such a society than with the conditions of socio-economic under-development.[5]

But his conceptualization does not incorporate his remark: underdevelopment is an exogenous nuisance factor which generates deviations from a 'normal' transition to socialism.

Similarly, Cliff writes that, 'Russia presents us with the synthesis of a form of property born of proletarian revolution and relations of production resulting from a combination of backward forces of production and the pressure of world capitalism.'[6] However, backwardness is then related to the development of state capitalism only in a very abstract way - the bureaucracy has to fulfil the 'historic tasks of the bourgeoisie'.

In contrast, our method involves appreciating the importance of a specific pattern of underdevelopment to an understanding of state socialist societies: underdevelopment is a basic element in our problematic which, in conjunction with the other two, fashions the laws of motion and contradictions of such societies. In other words, we are concerned to investigate the *concrete* relationships between underdevelopment and the specific historical paths followed by these societies in order to develop a theoretical abstraction which has explanatory power with reference to the history of these societies as a kind. We shall argue that the condition of underdevelopment clearly imposes the objective necessity of industrialization, and its specific form then confronts industrialization with particular constraints and harsh choices, which in turn are the engine of contradictions which shape the structure of the emerging society. Isolation in a hostile capitalist environment only serves to render the constraints more rigid and the choices harsher. Moreover, the specific nature of the laws of motion of state socialist societies will also be related to the form of the original seizure of power and to the 'socialist methods' which are employed to launch the industrialization drive.

The seizure of power

In introducing the seizure of power as an element in the problematic of socialism and underdevelopment, we shall be theorizing why and how it is that 'socialist' revolutions have been produced within these specific features of peripheral capitalism rather than within more advanced formations. On the other hand, we must also explain the widely differing forms of seizure of power in these twentieth century revolutions, and must indicate the conditioning effects which the different forms have had on post-revolutionary society. In fact, despite general similarities in socio-economic structure, socialist revolutions produced within peripheral formations have shown wide variations in politico-military terms, while each different seizure of state power involved considerable variation even though upon a common pattern of class alliance. This has been a particularly crucial element after the coming to power of the revolutionaries, as we shall see.

In addition to a systematic examination of the above factors, we feel that our work can be innovative in opening two other dimensions of the seizure of power. First, there is the question of violence and the armed struggle. With the single exception of the Unidad Popular in Chile, no political movement openly dedicated to socialist transformation along lines inspired by Marxism has ever come to power at the national level without armed struggle against foreign invaders, colonial liberation war, civil war, urban insurrection, or at least a coup. In fact, most often the struggle has combined more than one of these forms. It also seems clear that adequate theorization of the role of violence would take us beyond the confines of the social formations themselves, and thus cause us to locate at least part of our explanation at the level of the contradictions of capitalism on a world scale.

Second, nationalism in one guise or another proved to be an important lever of political mobilization, particularly for those revolutions which followed the Second World War. The gestation of 'socialist nationalism' therefore constitutes an important (and neglected) avenue of enquiry for explaining different forms of seizure of power. Understanding socialist nationalism is, in fact, integrally related to examining how the international contradictions of capitalism contribute to the creation of revolutionary possibilities.

Further discussion in Chapter 2 will show why we see the form of the seizure of power as extremely relevant to the development of post-revolutionary societies – for example, coming to power at the head of an 800,000 strong, largely peasant national liberation army whose leading cadres came from heterogeneous urban social groups (as the Communist Party of Yugoslavia did) surely holds out the prospect of different patterns of conflict and change from those which ensue after coming to power at the head of a limited urban insurrection in which the main actors are workers and the leading cadres largely intellectuals (the Bolsheviks)? Nevertheless, it is also true that the imprint of different seizures of power upon what happens subsequently tends to be partly modified by the fact that all revolutionary leaderships, at least initially, have subscribed to the same 'received ideas of socialism'.

The received ideas of socialism

Ideas are enormously important in shaping human action, even though that may find its origins in material circumstances and the social relations which spring from them. People do not act socially in blind instinctive reactions, but with the mediation of pictures in their heads, however blurred and inaccurate. The point in the underdeveloped countries is that, as we shall argue in Chapter 2, in certain circumstances a group of revolutionary organic intellectuals may be formed which comes through particularly strongly as the bearer of Marxist–Leninist received ideas – at least in a simplified form – to discontented workers, peasants, youth, women, ethnic minorities, and others. In that way ideas become a material force, because human actions shaped by them are capable of changing material conditions.

In a broadly similar way, though with very different consequences, ideas based on the twentieth-century experience of state socialism have become a material force in the developed countries. There, as a sort of critical reflex to what has happened on the periphery, intellectuals, even progressive ones, have raised doubts and, sustained if only against their will by capitalist propaganda, have disseminated these very widely, including into the labour movement. This process has undoubtedly played a major part in inhibiting the development of socialist revolution at the centre. The more academic side of this trend, reinforced by the work of dissident east European intellectuals, will be surveyed in the next section. The problem has been the overwhelming negativity of their ideas, coupled often with a lack of realism. This book has been written partly in order to begin to make a break with this.

As for the application of socialist doctrine in the context of the capitalist periphery, the implication of classical Marxist ideas, of course, was that such would be impossible, since there the victory of socialism was predicated upon the development of capitalist industrialization and the growth of the working class, the only one which would find no other emancipation but through the revolution. Historically, what has actually happened under advanced capitalism suggests strong arguments that a developed working class finds a more comfortable political home in the ranks of social democracy, which also includes in effect the local communist party. However, here is not the place to discuss this. Our intention is rather to argue that peripheral capitalist formations are potentially fertile grounds for socialist blossomings, though not that they are the only ones.

Here let us note, therefore, that, faced with that other supremely awkward historical fact that the 'socialist' revolutions came first in Russia, then Outer Mongolia (of all places – a sort of periphery of the periphery) and then eastern Europe, Viet Nam, Korea, and China, the Marxist–Leninists had to fall back on a range of arguments. The most important of these was to transfer the doctrine of struggle against capitalism, via the concept of imperialism, to a world level, thus permitting the Stalinist formulation of the concept of the 'weak links' in the overall imperialist chain. This could go far in explaining why the revolutions actually occurred. The possibility of building socialist systems thereafter could then be made dependent upon successful revolutions in developed capitalist countries (Lenin's and Trotsky's view) or, when that proved chimerical, upon an ability to do so drawing only on the resources of the Soviet Union, mobilized through forced collectivization of agriculture and rapid industrialization (Stalin's 'socialism in one country'). At a later stage, after the Second World War, the essential predicate became help from the Soviet Union and then also China.

Lenin and Trotsky continued to be proved wrong. Stalin at least had the support of realism, and also of the necessity of defending the Bolshevik revolution in a hostile world, but the other moment of the contradiction in his doctrine was widespread suffering and repression, and the consolidation of party rule, in effect the abandonment of democratic socialism. The application of Marxist–Leninist received ideas along with dependence on aid from the USSR and People's China has as a result become a major factor in reinforcing similar trends in other countries, as well as reducing freedom of action in external relations. A reformulation of the possibilities of class and other social struggle resulting in socialist liberation for peripheral countries is therefore overdue. At this stage, however, our discussion must stick with the already established received ideas.

The conventional wisdom about what constituted socialism, which was inherited by the leaders of twentieth century socialist revolutions, came originally from Marx and Engels. Socialism may thus be taken as corresponding to Marx's lower stage of communism, the precursor of 'full communism' and the 'withering away of the state', and it was synonymous with the political form of a 'dictatorship of the proletariat'. This is not to say that Marx and Engels provided future generations with a blueprint for a socialist society – blueprints were the wares of nineteenth century 'utopian socialists' with whom Marx would have no truck – but they did identify a number of the necessary features of the lower stage of communism as a partial negation of capitalism. The lower stage of communism would simultaneously exhibit features which were the antithesis of capitalism and others which reflected the imprint of the old society (the origins of the concept of 'transition'). These features of the lower stage of communism can be distilled from a series of scattered remarks in the 'Critique of the Gotha Programme', 'Civil War in France' and the *Communist Manifesto.*[7] Here is a list of the main 'received ideas of socialism' which may be said to have come from Marx and Engels. 'Socialism' involves:

1. The establishment of a 'dictatorship of the proletariat' under which the political power of the people is assured via a system of elected and mandated delegates extending from local to national level.

2. The nationalization of the banks, transportation, communications, and the commanding heights of industry and commerce.

3. The nationalization of land and the collectivization of agriculture.

4. The rapid development of productive forces in an effort to eliminate relative scarcity and prepare the way for the establishment of full communism.

5. The introduction of planning to allocate resources (what kind of planning was not specified).

6. Income distribution according to labour rather than need (i.e. the continuation of 'bourgeois' norms of distribution reflecting the imprint of the old society).

7. The continuation of a division of labour between mental and

manual tasks (again reflecting the imprint of the old society).

8. The gradual abolition of the distinction between town and country.

9. Free education for all children.

10. Although Marx and Engels elaborated their remarks with reference to the lower stage of communism in one country, they envisaged that socialism would, and would have to, spread rapidly to encompass the whole world; internationalism is therefore an integral feature of socialism.

Behind all these points must be taken to lie the assumption of industrialization, that is, that socialism could only have been put upon the historical agenda by a full development of industrial capitalism and the crucial revolutionary class to which it gives birth, the proletariat.

By the time of the Russian revolution the intervening experiences of working-class struggles had probably added three other items to the list, namely:

11. Elected factory/workplace workers' councils as the basic units of the new political order; the concept of 'Soviet power' was a development from the experience of the Paris Commune and workers' control had become an important socialist slogan.

12. The creation of conditions for women, above all equal legal rights and access to employment outside the family household, which would achieve equality between the sexes.

13. A vanguard party should play the leading role in constructing socialism and preparing the way for full communism.[8]

The theoretical debates within the Second International between 1889 and 1914 had also established three other ideas, which were at a more general level than the sort of tactical and programmatic statements which we have listed above, but were very influential in creating the whole body of received ideas and the sort of thinking which accepted them. Thus, history and all human social development was seen as being determinable by 'scientific' laws which were as discoverable as those of, say, physics. Second, history was taken as progressing in stages, which were determined ineluctably to follow one from another. Last, in this process economic factors (the base) were primary and the 'superstructure' of politics and ideology secondary and subordinate. Though Lenin gave a higher status to politics, especially by his vitally important concept of the vanguard party, these broad theoretical positions passed down to his successors and became sanctified as part of Stalinism.[9] In a similar way Lenin himself 'fathered' a further general theorization of imperialism, which became part of the framework within which the received ideas were set.

In addition, the experience of the Russian revolution and the years immediately thereafter added four more received ideas.

14. The right of national self-determination was an integral part of socialist doctrine.

15. If socialists came to power in a country which was not already industrialized, this must be undertaken as a priority task.

16. Socialism could be built even without a full prior development of capitalism, provided already established socialist states gave help. This postulate (by Lenin) was a particularly important addition.

17. So was Lenin's other major proposition, that in the above circumstances the revolution would have to be conducted in two stages. The first 'national democratic' one would build an independent economy and destroy feudalism, the second would actually involve building socialism.

It is immediately apparent that even if Marx and Engels never intended their illustrative remarks to be constituted into a socialist blueprint, this is what they became – sooner or later after the seizure of power the leaderships of all the socialist revolutions of the twentieth century have attempted to introduce the socialist package originally outlined by Marx and Engels and further developed up to the early 1920s. Indeed, after Lenin's death in January 1924 we see that the package soon came, under the sponsorship of Stalin, to have a new label, 'Marxism-Leninism'.[10]

This 'fixity' of socialist ideas lends specificity to the problematic of socialism and underdevelopment – the interplay between the received ideas of socialism and the problems of underdevelopment gives rise to specific contradictions which cannot be identified by conceiving state socialist societies as transitional or as a variant of capitalism. The analysis of these contradictions forms a basis for uncovering the tendential laws of motion of such societies as a type in themselves which we have already specified as our approach.

However, we have to recognize that our ideas are inevitably situated within a debate which has been going on for at least sixty years. A major problem here is that this has been almost entirely based on the experience of the Soviet Union, and latterly of the eastern European systems modelled most closely on it. The last part of setting up our own problematic, therefore, must be to indicate what we feel to be shortcomings in some of the main contributions to the debate concerning what has come to be called the 'transition to socialism'.

THE 'TRANSITION' ACCORDING TO SOME OTHERS[11]

In embarking upon what can only be a summary discussion, we would make a preliminary point which applies to most of these contributions. It seems to us that previous writers have always had in their minds some image, usually not made explicit, of what a socialist society ought to be, have applied this to state socialist societies, and have naturally enough found them wanting. This is an essentially idealist method, in which concrete historical phenomena have been weighed against a future condition which is only postulated and does not exist anywhere. Since what does exist is questionably socialist, some label has to be found for it. As a result, much of the discussion of these societies has tended to become an exercise in 'premature labelling' which imposes stereotypes and imputes characteristics in advance of any real analysis. In contrast to most of the authors now to be discussed, we wish to come to grips with the laws of motion of these societies on their own terms. Only by doing this, we believe, can we come to grips with what 'socialism' has in fact meant in terms of underdevelopment; only when this is done can there be any real basis for a future projection of the kind which is, of course, involved in the 'socialism or barbarism' alternative.

Soon after October 1917 the leaders of the Russian revolution faced a difficult dilemma. Although the opportunity to seize power had been successfully grasped, they believed that the ultimate success of their revolution was predicated on the spread of revolution throughout Europe. Building socialism in a backward, largely agrarian country like Russia was inconceivable without help from the proletariats of the advanced industrial countries of western Europe, Germany in particular. The Russian revolution was the first outpost and its role was simply that of a catalyst. However, the German revolution failed, counter-revolution beset Europe, and the young Soviet republic was left isolated and besieged. What next? Clearly the Bolshevik Party was not going to relinquish power because socialism could not be on the historical agenda in an isolated, backward Russia. Instead, Stalin changed that agenda, proclaiming that it was indeed possible to build socialism in one country. All that was required for the achievement of socialism in Russia was to raise the level of development of the productive forces: most of the other required changes had been or could be realized by administrative fiat (nationalization, central planning, etc.).

Stalin's perspective was appealingly simple and simplifying and, indeed, large sections of the European labour movement became romantically mesmerized by the achievements of the Five-Year Plans, by the marvel of the Dneiper dam, the output of tractors from Stalingrad.[12] Essentially socialism became reduced to planned industrialization and this became the model, at least initially, for the revolutions which followed the Second World War. Any unfortunate by-products of the process could be put down to the low level of development of the productive forces, to bad harvests and the machinations of counter-revolutionaries. Although it was soon apparent that what was happening in the Soviet Union contravened the spirit of socialism, and that while planned industrialization might have been a suitable response to the problems of underdevelopment it had not brought about the triumph of socialist ideals, critical reactions from socialists were slow to emerge. There were good reasons for this: there was a strong emotive compulsion to show solidarity with the first 'socialist' country; the Soviet bureaucracy was unlikely to initiate any debate because it had a vested interest in the status quo and was able to use the levers of power to present Soviet reality in a favourable light; the revolutions which followed the Second World War initially gave greater legitimacy to the Soviet regime by emulating its practices; the Cold War forced a sharp choice between the two sides, leaving little room in the middle for detached theoretical speculation.[13]

Before the Second World War Leon Trotsky had already broken the silence, claiming, in *The Revolution Betrayed*, that the Soviet Union had become a 'degenerated workers' state'. He thus founded the first major school of critics from the left.

The Trotskyist tradition

The Revolution Betrayed is Trotsky's main work on what had gone wrong in the Soviet Union. It is a rather controversial book whose message is sometimes ambivalent. Nevertheless, the main core of his conceptualization of Soviet reality is clear enough.

In the first instance Trotsky conceives of the Soviet Union as a 'transitional' society: 'It would be truer, therefore, to name the present Soviet regime in all its contradictoriness, not a socialist regime, but a *preparatory* regime *transitional* from capitalism to socialism.'[14] However, the isolation of the revolution and the low level of development of the productive forces meant that the 'transition' in the Soviet Union had assumed the form of a 'degenerated workers' state'. The 'degeneration' was represented by the emergence of a parasitic bureaucracy enjoying numerous consumption privileges. The emergence of this bureaucracy was partly related to the consequences of isolation and backwardness.

> The basis of bureaucratic rule is the poverty of society in objects of consumption, with the resulting struggle of each against all. When there are enough goods in a store, the purchasers can come whenever they want to. When there is little goods, the purchasers are compelled to stand in line. Where the lines are very long, it is necessary to appoint a policeman to keep order. Such is the starting point of the power of the Soviet bureaucracy. It 'knows' who is to get something and who has to wait.[15]

In addition were the factors of generalized chaos and the exhaustion of the masses in the aftermath of world war and civil war. The bureaucracy had since maintained itself through the application of bourgeois norms of income distribution (to each according to their work), which meant that the state they controlled was defending the interests of a (better paid) minority by creating a social base for itself among that minority, in the rich collective farms and, in certain instances, by itself creating new additions to that minority (e.g. the best workers of the 'Stakhanovite' (piece-work) movement).

Trotsky heaps abuse upon the reactionary, bourgeois characteristics of the bureaucracy: at one point he even refers to it as 'the bourgeois organ of a workers' state', and yet he still maintains that the Soviet Union is essentially a workers' state.[16] The reason for this was that the means of production had been nationalized:

> The nationalization of the land, the means of production, transport and exchange, together with the monopoly of foreign trade, constitute the basis of the Soviet social structure. Through these relations, established by proletarian revolution, the nature of the Soviet Union as a proletarian state is for us basically defined.[17]

This is in fact all part and parcel of Trotsky's conception of the Soviet Union as a 'transitional society' which has two possible historical directions before it, either the realization of socialism or the restoration of capitalism. Since the bureaucracy had not restored private property rights (and thus did not constitute a 'class'), nor achieved socialism, the Soviet Union was 'transitional' and the development of Soviet society could be conceptualized as a struggle between socialist property relations, supported by the workers, and the forces of bourgeois counter-revolution represented by the bureaucracy. The ultimate end point of bureaucratic degeneration was the restoration of capitalism, because the bureaucracy would not be satisfied with less than the restoration of private property relations, for otherwise it would be unable to transmit its property rights to its offspring.

These, then, are the main points in Trotsky's analysis of Soviet society and they are still retained by Ernest Mandel, a latter-day Trotskyist and leader of the Fourth International. Nevertheless, Mandel does develop certain important refinements and illustrations. First among these comes an attempt to demonstrate that while a transitional society does not embrace a distinct mode of production, it does display specific production relations. The production relations specific to the transitional society are thus a hybrid combination of essentially non-capitalist economic planning and the elements of commodity production (with their drive towards private appropriation and private enrichment), which arise from basically still bourgeois relations.[18] These production relations can be subjected to analysis in terms of a struggle between two antagonistic laws: the logic of the plan (conscious allocation of resources according to the priorities of society) and the logic of the market (allocation of resources according to the law of value). The logic of the plan corresponds to the interests of the proletariat, while the logic of the market corresponds to the interests of the bourgeoisie 'and of the classes and strata working on the basis of private enterprise and private property'.[19] It will be apparent that this formulation represents a step beyond Trotsky, who did not discuss the nature of *production* relations in the Soviet Union or really characterize the transitional society in terms of a particular relationship between planning and commodity production. Trotsky, as we have seen, tended to couch his characterization in terms of *property* relations and class, in terms of a struggle between the proletariat, supporting socialist property relations, and the bureaucracy which represented the forces of bourgeois counter-revolution.

Second, by way of an illustration of why the concept of transition is an appropriate one, Mandel draws a parallel between the 'transition to socialism' and the path followed by the bourgeois revolutions. The bourgeois revolutions, he points out, started in the sixteenth and seventeenth centuries with a breaking of the 'political and social class power of the feudal nobility', but did not result in the direct exercise of power by the bourgeoisie; the latter only came about once capitalism, in the form of the industrial revolution, had fully undermined the economic basis of feudalism. Mandel therefore concludes that there is every justification for conceptualising a transition from capitalism to socialism because history shows us that the passage from one mode of production to a superior mode has always involved a rather lengthy transitional period. Furthermore, the relations of production of these transitional periods have corresponded neither to those of the old mode of production nor to those of the new.[20]

Mandel introduces further refinements of Trotsky's analysis when he comes to identify the contradictions in the Soviet transition. At some points he systematizes ideas which can be distilled from Trotsky, while at others he introduces new ones. For example, according to Mandel, the Soviet bureaucracy does not represent the proletariat and yet it has to rely on an ideology (Marxism) which does: the bureaucracy has no ideology of its own because it was born out of a proletarian revolution; it cannot acknowledge its own power. As a result, while in effect being devoid of all political rights, workers in the Soviet Union have considerable *de facto* rights and powers.[21] This contradiction was also identified by Trotsky, but seemingly only in passing.[22]

On the other hand, Mandel identifies a contradiction in Soviet society which Trotsky did not: he suggests that the bureaucracy differs fundamentally from a capitalist class because, unlike the latter with respect to the capitalist system, there exists no correspondence between the interests of the bureaucracy and the internal logic of a planned economy. There is therefore a contradiction, according to Mandel, between the potential performance of a planned economy and the interests of the bureaucracy. *Individual* bureaucrats are indifferent to optimization in the planning system and are only really interested in maximizing their own consumption. This leads to a great deal of wastage of resources and an economic performance which is below potential. Yet the bureaucracy has to manage the economy at least adequately, and therefore cannot give entire priority to its own material interests. This contradiction has been manifest in the introduction of various economic reforms in the Soviet Union, designed to link the material interests of individual bureaucrats with the performance of the planning system and the economy.

However, Mandel sees this contradiction as insurmountable for the bureaucracy:

> There is no way to find the philosopher's stone that would permit simultaneous satisfaction of both the private interests of the bureaucrats and the needs and requisites of a socialized and planned economy.[23]

Thus the reforms have only served to create different forms of wastage and new contradictions.

State capitalism

An alternative conceptualization and critical analysis of state socialist systems comes from those who suggest that the Soviet Union is a 'state capitalist' rather than a 'transitional' social formation. While being aware that this was in effect the view of the leaderships of both the Yugoslav and the Chinese Communist Parties when their turns came to fall out with the Soviet Union, we have chosen to review only the work of Tony Cliff and Charles Bettelheim in this section, both for the sake of brevity and because Cliff and Bettelheim offer comprehensive and contrasting expositions of the concept of 'state capitalism'.

Cliff begins making his case for conceptualizing the Soviet Union as 'state capitalist' with an empirical investigation of the prevailing relations of production. This approach differs from Trotsky, whom he criticizes for considering forms of property in the Soviet Union independently of the relations of production; for Cliff, Trotsky's approach constitutes a 'metaphysical abstraction' and a 'conservative attachment to formalism, which by its nature is contradictory to Marxism that subordinates form to content'.[24] Cliff's investigation reveals three main features of Soviet production relations. First of all, consumption is subordinate to accumulation. Second, the bureaucracy is exploiting the rest of the Soviet population because its own income exceeds that of the value which it produces.[25] Third, workers' control has ceased to exist and thus there is no longer any socialist counterbalance to the necessary evils (in this lower stage before communism) of a division of labour between mental and manual tasks and the use of bourgeois norms of distribution.

Cliff then moves on to explain, theoretically, why these relations of production are those of 'state capitalism'. His argument contains four main points. First, in 'personifying' capital and subordinating consumption to accumulation the bureaucracy is fulfilling the historic tasks of the bourgeoisie. Second, the bureaucracy can indeed be defined as a class because it has all the characteristics of a class as defined by Lenin, Bukharin, and Engels.[26] Third, the behaviour of the economy in the Soviet Union is subordinate to the 'law of value', not especially in the sphere of internal economic relationships, but through the relationship between the Soviet economy and the world economy. The Soviet economy is subordinate to the 'law of value' as it operates on a world scale, not through trade but through the arms race: according to Cliff's data armaments production completely dominates the Soviet economy.

The last of Cliff's four main points is designed to refute Trotsky's stipulation that the bureaucracy could only become a class, and the Soviet Union capitalist, through a violent counter-revolution to restore private property rights. Cliff, in contrast, asserts that the Soviet Union could degenerate into state capitalism without violent counter-revolution because the particular social structure of Soviet state capitalism meant that the bureaucracy could look after its material interests in other ways without resort to private property relations.

It should not be understood from the above, however, that Cliff views the Soviet Union as having been 'state capitalist' since the October revolution. In fact, he refers to the Soviet Union as the 'workers' state of Lenin and Trotsky' between 1917 and 1923.[27] State capitalism really emerged with the inauguration of the First Five-Year Plan in 1928 because it was from that point onwards that the above-mentioned features of Soviet production relations became pronounced. One has to presume, therefore (and Cliff is not very clear on this point), that the bases of state capitalism were evolving during the period of Lenin's New Economic Policy. The following quotation would appear to support such an interpretation:

> The gradual evolutionary divorce of the bureaucracy from the control of the masses, which continued until 1928, reached the stage of a revolutionary qualitative change with the First Five-Year Plan.[28]

Turning to Bettelheim, it is in a purely theoretical work that he conceptualizes the Soviet Union as 'state capitalist'.[29] His argument has two essential aspects. On the one hand, economic calculation in the Soviet Union is monetary calculation, which cannot reflect the 'useful effects of the various articles compared with one another'. Instead it implies the persistence of commodity production, for exchange rather than use, something which inevitably continues to exist during a transitional period between capitalism and socialism. In fact, according to Bettelheim, the extent to which monetary calculation and commodity production continue to exist in a transitional society measures the extent to which that society has progressed towards socialism.

On the other hand, the kind of property relations which exist in the Soviet Union place the continued use of monetary calculation in quite a different light. Here Bettelheim distinguishes between 'property' and 'possession'. 'Property' in the Soviet Union is, in a *juridical* sense, vested in the state. At the level of production, however, 'possession' is vested in enterprise managers as a consequence of the persistence of commodity production. The latter means that ordinary workers are separated from their labour power and thus, although property vested in the state should reflect a control over the transitional process exercised by workers, it does not, because these same workers are dispossessed at the level of production. State property has therefore become the property of the bureaucracy, of a 'state bourgeoisie':

> The real significance of state property depends on the real relations existing between the mass of the workers and the state apparatus. If this apparatus is really and concretely dominated by workers (instead of being situated above them and dominating them), then state property is the legal form of workers' social property; on the other hand, if the workers do not dominate the state apparatus, if it is dominated by a body of functionaries and administrators, and if it escapes the control and direction of the working masses, then this body of functionaries and administrators effectively 'becomes the proprietor' (in the sense of a relation of production) of the means of production. This body then forms a 'social class' (a state bourgeoisie) because of the relation existing between itself and the means of production, on the one hand, and the workers on the other.[30]

A new mode of production

Castoriadis, Bahro and, more recently, Feher, Heller, and Markus are all advocates of the view that existing 'socialist' societies in the world can be conceptualized neither as capitalist nor socialist, neither as transitional nor state capitalist, but as a specific mode of production in their own right, governed by their own specific laws.

Castoriadis labels this new mode of production the bureaucratic society.[31] The specific characteristics of this mode of production were first of all created in the Soviet Union, by a revolution which only involved a partial break with the capitalist system and a revolutionary party which was completely ill-prepared for the task of building a socialist society.

The Russian revolution only broke partially with the capitalist system because it inherited capitalist 'rationality' and copied centralizing forms of capitalist technology. This meant that the Soviet Union reproduced capitalist forms of organization and, in particular, a division of labour between those who command (les dirigeants) and those who carry out orders (les exécutants). Les dirigeants became the bureaucracy, and the bureaucracy can be considered a class because it has access to the means of production and this allows it to appropriate, for its own consumption, surplus value produced by others, to 'exploit' the rest of the population. Here Castoriadis asserts that private property relations are not a necessary precondition for the bureaucracy to be defined as a class because they are not necessary for it to have access to the means of production. Under capitalism, on the other hand, private property relations are necessary because it is only through them that the capitalist class can have access to the means of production, while denying the same privilege to the mass of the population.

The Bolshevik Party played an important part in the development of bureaucratic power because it came to power completely ill-equipped for the tasks ahead of it: prior to 1917 the Bolsheviks had only been prepared (by Lenin) to accomplish bourgeois democratic tasks and not to build socialism. Thus the party of the revolution did nothing to combat the pervasive influence of capitalist technology; indeed, it was in charge of the 'copying' process and the very organizational structure of the party itself reflected the authoritarian imprint of 'capitalist rationality'.

As well as expounding his own views, Castoriadis is concerned to elaborate a critique of Trotsky's conceptualization of the Soviet Union. He pours scorn on the way in which Trotsky sought to divorce distribution from production and to equate socialism with nationalization. In particular, though, he singles out Trotsky's attribution of the degeneration of the revolution to its isolation and the low level of development of productive forces in Russia. Revolution, claims Castoriadis, was never likely to spread rapidly on an international scale because of the law of uneven and combined development formulated by Trotsky himself; it would inevitably spread in *isolated* stages and the first stage would influence subsequent stages. If, therefore, a period of isolation is supposed to guarantee the degeneration of the first stage, there is no reason to suppose that degenerated revolutions will not proliferate all over the world. Equally well, backwardness cannot be made into a culprit, because the problem to which it gives rise, relative scarcity, is one which will have to be faced by all revolutions wherever they may break out: needs are always relative to the level of development under capitalism. In any event revolution is only a likely possibility in more backward countries, because the working class is more likely to be reformist than revolutionary in advanced industrial countries. Finally, Castoriadis asserts that isolation and backwardness are mutually contradictory as causes of degeneration: if, as Trotsky would have wished, revolution had spread rapidly all over the world after 1917, most of the countries involved would have been far more backward than Russia.

The East German dissident, Bahro, conceptualizes what he terms 'actually existing socialism' as non-capitalist industrialization. However, he is more concerned to describe and analyse the existing social structure in eastern Europe than to explain how that social structure came into being. Nevertheless, from what he does say about the latter, two basic ingredients can be distilled. First, 'non-capitalist industrialization' was initially born out of a break with the world capitalist system under circumstances of semi-Asiatic under-development which excluded a socialist perspective:

> For Russia, therefore, the abolition of capitalist private property could not have a great positive significance, since there was little private property there, and economic life was affected by it only at certain points. The tragedy of the Russian socialist vanguard was that they found a different task to fulfil in practice from that which the influence of their west European models suggested to them. The October revolution was to introduce a completely different process from the socialist revolution anticipated in western Europe.[32]

A revolutionary situation had been engendered 'more by the external contradictions of world imperialism than by capitalism's "normal" internal contradictions'. Thus the new society which came into being was only able to win its 'autonomy' from the capitalist system, to proceed along a 'non-capitalist' path of industrialization, but not to realize any loftier ideals. The basic impulse to the new society was given by 'the pressure of the industrial productive forces created by capitalism'.[33]

Second, the social structure of 'actually existing socialism' (hierarchy, subordination, stratification by function, despotism) arises out of the division of labour. In fact, Bahro holds a view similar to that of Castoriadis:

> The historical root still showing its effects today, for all its modifications, is the antithesis between predominantly manual or executive work, and predominantly mental work – work of planning and command. 'Those who work with their hands carry others; those who work with their heads are carried by others', so the Chinese philosopher Mencius taught more than 2,000 years ago.[34]

Compartmentalization into many spheres of competence means that the state rises to become a unifying instance over all of them.

This conceptualization of the nature and roots of the social structure of 'actually existing socialism' later leads Bahro to reject the application of the concepts of 'the working class' or a polarization between 'the masses and the state apparatus' to the societies of eastern Europe and the future course of struggles there.[35]

For the Hungarian dissident Rakovski (actually two people), the concept of a 'transition to socialism' as applied to what 'he' terms 'soviet societies' precludes their analysis *sui generis*, and thus denies from the outset that they may have historical aims different from socialism.[36] If it is obvious that 'soviet societies' have not realized socialism, then the concept of transition to socialism leaves only two possibilities: either they are capitalist or partially socialist, in other words 'transitional'. Moreover, the concept contains a logical flaw:

> A transitional society is one in which basic institutions both presuppose and exclude each other at the same time; they are grouped around antagonistic power centres whose relations are regulated not by mechanisms accepted as legitimate by all of society, but by more or less open class war. In order to locate soviet societies among the class of transitional societies, it is not enough to point to, for example, the simultaneous existence of central planning and something similar to the capitalist market. It must also be shown that the former is the incarnation of the power of the producers, while the latter is the incarnation of the power of

enterprise directors, and that the legitimate co-operation of the two is inconceivable in the long term. We have only to pose the problem in this way to see that the concept of transitional society is not applicable to soviet societies.[37]

Rakovski therefore prefers to analyse soviet societies *sui generis*, and he proceeds by comparing them with a capitalist society as portrayed by Marx. He concludes that

> the soviet type of modern development is distinguished by a lack of formally autonomous organization. Functional and social organisations are all subordinated to the same global management and power system. In this system the working of the economy is not controlled by self-regulating market mechanisms. In the same way, the exercise of power is not controlled by democratic mechanisms involving the confrontation of opposed social interests. The possible decentralization of the system cannot change this situation.[38]

These aspects of 'soviet societies' make them fundamentally different from capitalism which does allow 'autonomous organizations'. According to Rakovski, they also mean that the conventional Marxist concept of class becomes redundant to their analysis. Instead, it is again the division of labour which generates antagonisms.

> The fundamental antagonisms are determined solely by the position of social groups *vis-à-vis* the power hierarchy: on the one hand, that part of the population which undertakes real activities, and on the other, that part which controls and directs. The former can be termed the 'producing class', and the latter the 'class in power'.[39]

Like Bahro, Rakovski's formulation is similar to the polarization between *les dirigeants* and *les exécutants* identified by Castoriadis.

Finally, complex and densely argued as it is, the work of Feher, Heller and Markus is perhaps most difficult to summarize in the sense that key arguments are not easily divorced from the rest of the text. However, the title of their book, *Dictatorship Over Needs*, provides a starting point for it, indeed encapsulates the essence of their view of state socialist societies, namely, that their characteristics derive from the fact that needs are or have been 'dictated' at different times by either an 'aristocratic', an 'autocratic', or an 'oligarchic' bureaucratic apparatus. In this sense, and in contrast to the views of the other authors discussed in this section, Feher, Heller, and Markus see the shortcomings of state socialist societies as a function of a particular manner of exercising power. Their work is therefore centrally concerned with the detailed mechanics of bureaucratic domination. From this point it is perhaps best to focus on their Chapter 2 which is entitled 'Corporate property and command economy' and, in our view, maps out their central analytical theses. Here, in conventional Marxist fashion, their approach is to seek out the character of property relations in state socialist societies and they conclude:

> So the fundamental economic relations in eastern European societies are determined by the fact that the nationalized means of production in effect constitute the property of the unified apparatus of power as a corporative entity.[40]

This notion of 'corporate property', although its connotations may be different from those with which it is associated in the completely different environment of a capitalist economy, reflects for Feher, Heller, and Markus the essence of bureaucratic rule as a 'trusteeship' of the 'general interest of the state'. The economic relations to which corporate property gives rise are, in line with their general view of a political 'dictatorship over needs', in fact political relations. This economy functions through an 'uninterrupted process of conscious political decision-making taking the form of central plan-commands'.[41] Although the authors are prepared to admit that even this kind of political domination over the economy cannot eliminate what they term the 'spontaneity of economics', it flows logically from this position that they should see bureaucratic domination as the ultimate cause of shortage and waste in state socialist societies.

Nevertheless, the existence of a corporate ruling group does not mean that Feher, Heller and Markus take the crude view that the 'general interest of the state' is synonymous with the material interest of production being the 'goal-rationality' of the system, with the ruling class ensuring that this only takes place on its own terms.

> The total system of social domination is not directed here at securing an expanded appropriation of surplus by one class of society, but this appropriation of surplus constitutes only the material basis for the expropriation and monopolization (in principle) of all means of socialization and social organization by a single apparatus of power.[42]

As is implicit in this statement, Feher, Heller and Markus also later dismiss the application of concepts of class and class analysis to state socialist societies.

An overview

If, for a moment, we detach details of the above analyses of state socialist societies from their respective conceptual frames of reference, they all offer interesting empirical insights into why such societies behave as they do. Among these insights figure the roles of underdevelopment, isolation, external pressure from the capitalist world, technology, the division of labour, commodity production, and the structure of the revolutionary party and its forms of intervention. Moreover, the fact that the Soviet Union is the laboratory from which most of these insights are derived does not, in principle, mean that they have no general applicability in the analysis of other societies.[43] Indeed, understanding the Soviet Union is an important key to understanding other state socialist societies because of the influence which it has had over their establishment and development. However, at least as far as the theorists of the 'transition' and of 'state capitalism' are concerned, their theoretical conceptualizations are like foreign objects in relation to the empirical insights. It is therefore the overall theoretical conceptualizations with which we would, first of all, like to take issue. Later we shall point out some empirical blind-spots which have scarcely been theorized at all.

It will already be clear that applying the concept of 'a transition from capitalism to socialism' to these societies is extremely questionable. Rakovski's comments alone are enough to refute the validity of this theoretical framework. The concept of 'transition' prevents and precludes an analysis of state socialist societies as a distinct form. It also superficially assumes socialist content from a particular form of prevailing property relations. Cliff and Bettelheim also say as much in their different ways. Mandel appears to improve on Trotsky's original formulation by introducing the notion of 'transitional production relations', but the basic postulate that state property necessarily embraces a socialist dynamic remains. Moreover, Mandel's depiction of transitional production relations as a 'hybrid combination', itself actually contradicts the concept of 'transition': a 'hybrid combination', as Mandel points out, is surely a *specific combination* corresponding neither to the production relations of socialism nor to those of capitalism. Why, therefore, should we assume that the 'laws' associated with this 'hybrid combination' are those of a transition from capitalism to socialism, and not peculiar to themselves?

At root, the scientific straitjacket which Trotsky and Mandel seek to place on the analysis of state socialist societies can probably be traced back to subjective factors. As one of the leaders of the Russian revolution, whose fighting revolutionary optimism did not desert him even in exile, Trotsky could not bring himself to deny the heritage of October completely. The Cold War gave this practice a pragmatic basis and Mandel continues to repeat it. In consequence, the analyses offered in the Trotskyist tradition are *partial*: they subsist within the problematic of a critique of 'Stalinism' and thus cannot come to grips with the total historical experience of state socialist societies. The objective of the critique pushes objectivity aside and there is always a powerful implication running through their work that a different subjective element in such societies (i.e. 'Trotskyism' rather than 'Stalinism') would have resulted in a fundamentally different (and superior) outcome. Historical idealism is the ever present companion of the concept of 'transition to socialism'.

The concept of 'state capitalism' is no more helpful than the concept of 'transition to socialism'. From what has gone before, it is clear that we sympathize with Cliff's critique of Trotsky: property relations cannot be considered independent of production relations, content should not be made subordinate to form. Nevertheless, we do not see a necessary correlation between Cliff's description of the production relations in the Soviet Union after 1928 and the concept of 'state capitalism'. Cliff's exercise consists of an *a priori* application of the concepts developed by Marx for analysing capitalism to a social formation which differs fundamentally from capitalism. Even Cliff himself admits that the 'law of value' does not regulate the relationships between producers inside the Soviet Union. Effectively the only justification which Cliff offers for employing the concept of state capitalism boils down to the assertion that the bureaucracy has been fulfilling the historic tasks of the bourgeoisie. What does this mean? Simply that the bureaucracy was concerned to develop the forces of production. Given that developing the forces of production will usually be the concern of any regime whatsoever in an underdeveloped – or, for that matter, developed – country, Cliff's assertion is meaningless and it would seem that he also is subordinating content to form. Moreover, the concept of 'state capitalism' does not enable Cliff to explain why and how production relations in the Soviet Union began to assume ever more retrogressive forms after 1928: the Soviet Union simply 'became' state capitalist. In this respect the concept of 'state capitalism' is particularly exposed as nothing more than a label.

Similarly with Bettelheim, it may well be that workers in the Soviet Union are dispossessed at the level of production but why, we may ask, does this necessarily mean that the Soviet Union is state capitalist? The problem with the theorists of state capitalism is that they feel a compulsion to relate the retrogressive aspects of Soviet society to an all-embracing variant of a system which, as socialists, they know to be 'bad', that is, capitalism.

The methodology which Bettelheim employs in his empirical analysis of Soviet history appears to be potentially more fruitful. Nevertheless, we feel unconvinced that it is legitimate to use the orthodox Marxist concept of 'class' in the analysis of state socialist societies. Certainly, Bahro and Rakovski categorically reject it. The problem for us is that the concept of the 'working class', for example, was developed by Marx in his analysis of capitalism, and its existence in that system is dialectically defined by its antithesis, the capitalist class. How, therefore, can the working class continue to exist as an analytical concept once the capitalist class has been irrevocably destroyed by revolution? We agree that in a post- revolutionary society the working class will continue to have particular characteristics which differentiate it from other groups in the population, such as the peasantry. However, if the concept of class is to be used at all, it needs to be redefined in the light of the particular production relations of state socialist society. Bettelheim fails to do this, or even to see it as a problem.

Castoriadis, Bahro, and Rakovski make a significant advance over the offerings of the Trotskyist tradition and the theorists of state capitalism in so far as they do not foist external concepts onto the historical reality of state socialist societies. At the same time, however, they only really begin the task of conceptualizing them in terms of a distinct mode of production. In particular, their analyses are rather 'cross-sectional' in character and they are limited to a discussion of specific aspects of the social superstructure in these societies. The laws of motion of the economy are consequently treated peripherally or in very general terms and they thus fall short of offering a political economy of state socialist societies. Some of these points also apply to Feher, Heller and Markus. Despite the detailed insights which they offer, their analysis remains within the realm of a mainly ahistorical political sociology, and when they do delve into history this is restricted to elaborating a political typology of different stages in the development of state socialist societies. Indeed, the concept of 'dictatorship over needs' excludes the possibility of political economy and means that they are unprepared to admit that the experience of state socialism reveals anything other than the usurpation of power by a corrupt corporate ruling group.

OUR BASIC APPROACHES

Earlier we referred to some empirical blind-spots which affect all three of the conceptual schools. These blind-spots concern the tendency to see the history of state socialist societies as starting after the seizure of power, as if history stopped before the revolution and began again with a clean sheet afterwards. This habit excludes any consideration of the form of the seizure of power (and there have been many different forms) and its subsequent importance to the political economy of these societies. This means that there is not merely an empirical but also a theoretical gap.

Pursuing our tendential laws of motion of state socialist societies, therefore, we shall begin in Chapter 2 with the seizure, arguing that it is not an historical accident that this has occurred on the periphery. Rather, it follows from the basic conditions of underdevelopment that large sections of the population may for different reasons be brought to see socialism as a liberating force. Moreover, prevalent conditions of economic and social crisis make it possible for Marxist–Leninist revolutionaries to bring on political crises for the existing regime. At the same time, it is one of our major concerns in Chapter 4 to show that the very conditions in which people are mobilized against it go far to explaining what we shall characterize as the swallowing up of civil society by the state after the revolution.

Shifting to the post-revolutionary situation with Chapter 3, our basic propositions concerning economic change revolve around outlining the nature of what, following Janos Kornai, we see as a resource-constrained economy. Further, we posit that this has an innate tendency, if not arrested by special internal and external factors, to go through three stages, of initial reconstruction, implementation of received ideas, and then deconcentration and decentralization in an attempt to rectify the problems thus induced. This is the working out of the tendential law of motion of the economy, which cannot be reduced, as is so often the case in commentary, to the simplistic dichotomy of swings between central planning and the market. We further argue in Chapter 5, in the context of decentralization and democracy, that planning is essential to socialism, but that if decentralization is contemplated, to be meaningful it must be accompanied by a form of collective property other than that of the state.

In Chapter 4 we raise above all the issue of democracy in state socialist systems, again trying to show that the undoubted tendency for this to be absent follows from the complex interaction between the nature of the seizure of power, the conditions of underdevelopment and the received ideas which imbue the leadership. Attempting to show how the new regimes operate as systems of distribution creating new divisions and hierarchies, we cast doubt on the ability to use the usual concepts of surplus, exploitation and class to explain their social nature. We postulate them as certainly not some version of capitalism or deformed workers' states, but as not marked by the presence of a new ruling class either.

It follows from this, as we try to show in Chapter 5, that state socialist systems have indeed to be taken seriously as socialist in nature, will be with us for the indefinite future, and new cases of which may well emerge. The issue for critical Marxists and other socialists is that the received ideas which give them doctrinal foundations and policies for transformation have as yet no effective challengers, by which we mean alternatives. Moreover, we feel it extremely important to draw up a careful balance sheet based on our analysis, which we attempt in Chapter 5, weighing the economic and political trade-offs associated with particular policy stances, including the fundamental choice between capitalism and state socialism on the periphery. It has to be kept in mind that the point of comparison here is underdeveloped capitalism, not the developed industrial centre which sustains itself to a considerable degree from the periphery. Nevertheless, this does not in any way mitigate the point that democracy and basic human rights remain the achilles heel of state socialist systems, with an apparently innate tendency to override them.

Lastly, two questions of methodology should be made clear to the reader before she/he goes any further. Our general approach is to combine a sustained level of theoretical and analytical discussion with concrete historical examples. However, in Chapter 3 we do allow the latter to fall away somewhat. Theorization of the resource-constrained economy is so basic to our enterprise that we have felt it better to expose its contours very sharply, at risk of appearing somewhat abstract. Chapter 4 has something of the same qualities but, above all, it, in combination with Chapter 3, is marked by the second methodological issue, namely that the weight of theorising has to fall on the experience of the more advanced cases of state socialism, the Soviet Union and eastern Europe. This is because, slightly to paraphrase Marx's comment in the Preface to the first German edition of *Capital*, Volume I, the more developed cases hold up to the newer ones the image of the future.

2

The seizure of power

Revolutionary struggle inspired by Marxism–Leninism has been a process spread over more than eighty years and a very wide variety of circumstances. The crucial question here is that already raised as one of three basic ones in the last chapter: why is it that ever since 1917 successful revolutions claiming socialist inspiration have always occurred on the underdeveloped periphery of capitalism, never at its heart, as Marx and Engels supposed? Further to this, why have socialists come to power in such diverse ways and, more importantly, in such diverse circumstances? And why have these other two questions had such a profound effect on what happened after the revolution? All three are, of course, closely intertwined, and their answers, indeed, will all be seen to stem from the same historical situation.

Seen in terms of the creation of new revolutionary regimes, five groupings, which are also in a sense 'generations' born over time, may be discerned. First, in 1917 came the crucial breach in the wall of world capitalism, the October Revolution in Russia. This pulled Outer Mongolia along with it, in 1924, a telling exception to the rule that the world revolution failed to spread, in particular at the capitalist centre where orthodoxy expected it. The Second World War gave the chance to the Soviet Union to sponsor and/or enforce revolutions in a second bloc of east European countries, in the period 1945-8, namely Bulgaria, Czechoslovakia, East Germany, Hungary, Poland and Rumania, and to support those in Albania and Yugoslavia which had more indigenous dynamics. (Already, in 1948, the Yugoslav leadership was breaking with the Soviet.) Basically in the same period, in faraway Asia, successful revolutions put Marxist–Leninist leaderships into power in China and two colonial countries, Viet Nam and North Korea, the last again with direct Soviet sponsorship. The two smaller Asian cases provide a bridge to our fourth grouping, countries which have experienced revolution based ideologically on a fusion of national liberation struggle against imperialism with Marxism- Leninism. Cuba was another landmark at the end of the 1950s. Angola, Mozambique, Guinea-Bissau, Cape Verde, South Yemen, (South) Viet Nam, Laos and Kampuchea were added in the 1960s and 1970s. Those years also saw a fifth group of cases (to which Cuba, Laos and Kampuchea also provide a bridge) in which crisis conditions were created by developments after the gaining of formal independence. These were Benin, Congo, Ethiopia, and Somalia, in which regimes describing themselves as Marxist-Leninist or 'scientific' socialist were established.

These last cases in particular raise a point which must be made explicit. As indicated in Chapter 1, because of our concern with state socialist systems and their dynamics, we take as our catchment area only those cases in which the leaderships claim to be inspired by Marxism–Leninism. This begs a number of important questions which we shall have to take up later, such as the origins of such regimes in military coups, but enables us to begin to focus on cases which are doctrinally most significant, most numerous, and most clearly and most often associated with revolution.

The first task, however, is to introduce one of our basic terms of reference, underdevelopment. Our basic proposition is deceptively simple: in the late nineteenth and early twentieth centuries, roughly between 1880 and 1914, capitalism, which was already worldwide in scope, decisively consolidated its hold on the world outside its original heartland and the comparatively new (one hundred-year-old) USA. It did so by extending its investment in the periphery, above all in productive enterprise as compared with the previous concentration on trade and loans to states (though these remained very important), and, on the political level, by creating a range of colonial territories and by forcing other regimes to 'modernize' themselves to suit its needs.[1]

On the surface this proposition seems to repeat the basic analysis by Lenin of imperialism as the 'highest stage of capitalism', and it is indeed necessary to acknowledge his work, and that of others like Nikolai Bukharin, Rosa Luxemburg, and J.A. Hobson. Nevertheless, we must distance ourselves from the conventional Leninist position in two major respects. First, it is now apparent that the imperialism of the late nineteenth and early twentieth centuries was not the last stage of development of world capitalism, nor was it a product of that system's decay, as Lenin asserted but never really proved.[2] In terms of this book, however, that proposition is rather less important than a second one, namely that the famous image which grew out of Lenin's work and which purported to explain the apparent contradiction of a revolution in underdeveloped Russia in 1917, that of the 'weak link in the capitalist chain', is indeed only that, a metaphor, not a theorization which explains causality. Trotsky's concept of uneven and combined development, intended to explain the same phenomenon, remained only a sketch. More than sixty years after the publication of Lenin's work, and eighty after Trotsky's – such is the paralysing power of received ideas – that task remains to be accomplished.

TOWARDS A THEORY OF THE CAPITALIST PERIPHERY

To present a full exposition of the concept of the capitalist periphery would require more space than can possibly be allowed here. Reduced to its essentials, it implies a particular structure of unequal relationships on a global scale which emerged as a result of a process lasting in all some four centuries. The constant element in this process was its dynamic, the need for western capitalism to expand the geographical sphere and scale of its accumulation. This need had effects far beyond an extension of geographical spread or quantities of capital involved, however, since in order to ensure the continuation of that accumulation changes had to be secured both in patterns of class formation and relations, and in state forms.[3] It was these cumulative changes that produced the conditions now commonly termed 'underdevelopment', which in that sense can be said to have been actually created historically, since without the process of capitalist expansion they would not have existed.[4]

It is possible, thus, to speak of a 'capitalist world system' which had emerged in an almost complete form by 1914 and has continued to develop since then, notably by shifting since 1945 from the old colony–metropolis relationship to one of hierarchies of sovereign states and supra-national bodies. We may then hypothesize three basic historical forms in which peripheral social formations have been integrated into that system. The obvious reservation must be made that they are in no sense 'pure', but overlap both in time and structurally.[5]

'Integration', obviously the crucial variable for us, is here, then, the penetration of capitalism from its base in the advanced industrial countries in ever-more massive and complex forms. The first, which we would designate 'primitive integration', in fact no longer really exists anywhere, since it was associated with the phase of western mercantile capitalism from the fifteenth to the late eighteenth centuries. Its typical expression was the trading fort or, at its most highly developed, the slave plantation. The further development of western capitalism, taking us into its manufacturing phase, with new and increased demands for raw materials, labour power, markets and investment outlets to ensure its accumulation and reproduction, brought with it the phase of 'intermediate integration' of the peripheral formations, which at this point were increasingly being spatially reorganized for capitalist purposes, sometimes involving the creation of units which never existed before. These were often colonies, like those created by the 'grab for Africa', for example, but could be technically sovereign, like those in eastern Europe. This was typically a phase of investment for extraction, so that the major productive enterprises of this form were plantations and mines, using labourers pressured off the land in one way or another. Peasant agriculture was structured round these to provide subsistence for rural and urban labourers, or directed towards cash crops where capitalist accumulation found this more efficient (for instance, cocoa in the Gold Coast (Ghana)).

Most recently, with manufacturing capitalism in its monopoly stage, we have entered a phase in which cases are emerging of 'advanced integration', in which direct capitalist production is spreading in the rural areas of the periphery and the manufacturing sector is growing and even becoming dominant. Both phenomena are associated with the direct investment of capital by western transnationals, sometimes in collaboration with local capitalists, and the initial impetus is often related to the ability to adopt import-substitution or export-expansion policies.[6] All this occurs, of course, in the name of capitalist 'development' ideology.

The purpose of this discussion is basically to underline the point already touched upon in Chapter 1, namely that, at first realization surprisingly, all the attempted socialist transformations have occurred in countries which are cases of only intermediate integration. Russia in 1917 and Cuba in the late 1950s might be argued to have been embarking on the transition towards advanced status, though still with a long way to go.[7] On the other hand we have cases like Laos or Cambodia (Kampuchea), where the degree of even intermediate capitalist integration was low, and the generalization is obviously historically valid.

Whether it will remain so is an open question and one to which we shall return in Chapter 5. Immediately we must emphasize the importance of the changing context of world capitalism which, despite the fact that all our cases stem from intermediate integration, was responsible for distributing them into the five phases distinguished at the beginning of this chapter. Thus, the collapse of the old imperial capitalist system, which had partially incorporated the Hapsburg, Romanov, and Ottoman empires, during the First World War directly produced the Bolshevik Revolution. It also swept away the old empires and laid the foundations for some subsequent revolutions. The Second World War, stemming from the great capitalist depression, fascism, and the rivalry among the powers, had even more far-reaching effects. From it resulted the sponsoring of revolution in Eastern Europe by the Soviet Union, the new world power, the first anti-colonial cases, and People's China. It also gave a major impetus to the later anti-colonial revolutions, as did the sponsorship of the new 'socialist camp', even after its unity disappeared with the Sino–Soviet dispute. In the same post-war period, up to the early 1970s, the long capitalist economic upswing also helped to relegate the colonial form of political control to the past, though at the same time it implied an even deeper economic penetration of the periphery and an extended movement towards advanced integration. The effects of these last phenomena, however, seem to have inaugurated the shift towards our fifth group of cases, for which the Cuban revolution seems to be particularly significant. In these, as noted above, crisis conditions have resulted not from worldwide events like general wars, or from fusions of Marxism–Leninism with nationalism (though that element may still be present), but from the incapacities of local ruling groups in alliance with international capital. The revolutions seem likely to take one of two forms, either militarized mass movements – civil war – or coups by radical officers. The implications of this latest phase, which seems likely to continue into the indefinite future, may best be taken up in Chapter 5. Here, while recognizing that overall conjunctures which necessarily involve international factors determine which actual cases have occurred and will occur, we intend to focus upon the more general historical characteristics of peripheral capitalism in its intermediate forms in an attempt to theorize crisis through examining class and state formation and social struggle.

CLASSES IN PERIPHERAL CAPITALISM

The decisive factor in the evolution of classes and state forms in the peripheral countries has been the intervention from outside of capitalism, causing a massive – though by no means absolute –

discontinuity in processes of indigenous class formation. Typically, the social formation becomes structured around the concentration of foreign capital to be found in the whole category of countries in which we are most interested.

Western mercantile capitalism, as it first of all surrounded its new sources of commodities and outlets with a web of trading relations and then penetrated inland by the rivers and trade paths, had to have reliable contacts and agents and, beyond them, producers and consumers. At this stage it was at first not necessary to extend political control in a colonial form in Africa and Asia (Latin America was different, since there British merchants from the early eighteenth century were penetrating the colonies of the first European imperial powers, Spain and Portugal). The Ottoman state already held sway as a more ancient empire, Russia was a feudal imperial state expanding south and east, partly at the expense of a third old empire, China. Gradually, however, interference with traders and the missionaries who sometimes even preceded them by local potentates brought about political intervention and in the end direct rule; Mammon and the Christian God were accompanied by Caesar. Even more important, Mammon came to take the form of investment capital destined for productive enterprises, not just trade. For a long time mines and plantations were the focus of investment, then, ultimately, factories were added, though this not till the twentieth century in any significant way. By that time integration was much further advanced in terms of a truly global economy; the growth and consolidation of capitalist production in western Europe, the USA, and Japan demanded it. Britain, France, Germany, Italy, Belgium, the Netherlands, the USA, Portugal and Spain (still hanging on), and even the newcomer Japan, had by 1914 seen fit to carve up most of the globe among themselves, demarcating the boundaries of direct colonial rule and coming to understandings, as in China, concerning spheres of influence elsewhere (though not well enough to avoid this factor contributing to the outbreak of the so-called First World War). Direct political rule in its colonial form had thus become widespread though by no means universal.

The impact of this gradual creation of the periphery (for such it was) upon class formation there was enormous. Old classes and strata were given new shapes, new ones created, but in no case did this exactly parallel the western experience; we are now in the realm of 'underdevelopment'. Indeed, that is how that phenomenon took its characteristic shape, an interpenetration and hybridization of non-capitalist forms of production, distribution and exchange with capitalist modes, the latter of course dominant and determining (at least ultimately) the ability of the others to reproduce themselves. Forms and modes of production mean people in social relations with one another, and structured into classes and other social groups. Those relations in turn mean exploitation and oppression, contradictions and class struggle. To give substance to our analysis of underdeveloped formations on the periphery and the 'socialist' revolutions which they generate, we must at least sketch out the main lines of these phenomena there. This is not easy, not the least because it cannot have escaped notice that the category of intermediately integrated countries is far larger than that of advanced, while it is our hypothesis that the seizures of power with which we are concerned occur in the former, not the latter.

Capitalism has become the dominant mode of production without the need to create uniformly capitalist relations. In the technical language of Marx, all other forms of labour are subsumed to capital's direct reproduction of itself through wage labour and the creation of surplus value. On the other hand, in these formations all non-capitalist forms of labour are not reduced to work for wages, as Marx apparently supposed they would be. By being bound into a capitalist market peasants and other petty producers contribute part of capitalist surplus, even though they continue to be incorporated into non-capitalist relations of production. This is the basic feature which has distinguished the capitalist periphery from its centre.

Also typical is the process of 'modernization' through which the local capitalist class passes by virtue of its association with foreign enterprise and its increasing incorporation into wider regional and world markets. Nevertheless, it remains highly divided internally, among the usual sectors of finance, agriculture, industry, trade and so on, and stratified by levels of wealth. Moreover, these strata tend to associate closely with foreign capital; in particular, only local small businessmen have to function without that support and even in competition.

At its lower, less affluent margins the capitalist class merges into the petty bourgeoisie of self-employed manufacturers and traders, struggling always for survival as they compete with foreign products, the capitalists above them, and one another. For the most part close to them in incomes and attitudes, but distinct in class terms, are the middle strata – at the top affluent professionals closer to the capitalists, then fading down through various grades of bureaucrats, teachers, and clerks until one reaches genteel poverty and even worse. Distinguished from the petty bourgeoisie proper by the fact that they sell their labour power directly to live (in this resembling rather the working class), these strata have a tendency to proliferate as the state apparatus grows and capitalism demands even more services as it expands its production and marketing.[8] This is especially the case if a movement towards advanced integration begins.

Beyond the petty bourgeoisie, the basic mass of working people remain peasants, subjected to various pressures. These partly stem from incorporation into market relations, which enclose even those who do not have old-style landlords or capitalists squatting on their backs. Those thus burdened have to face various forms of demand for rent or labour services. Capitalist 'modernization' may involve expelling them from the land, and the same effect may follow even when a new peasantry is supposedly created by 'Green Revolution' policies, marking an attempt at the transition to an 'advanced' status. These displacements contribute to a slow formation of a working class, though only very partially a classical factory proletariat; most wage-earners are agricultural labourers, construction workers, porters and dockers. Seasonal labour keeps the working class close to the peasantry, with much movement from one class to the other and back. Rates of unemployment and underemployment are high. The large 'reserve army of labour' is kept in being by the rural linkages and the slums and shanty towns full of those who scratch a living by all conceivable – and some almost unimaginable – exercises of human ingenuity.

It clearly follows from the above sketch that in countries of the capitalist periphery, especially those we have termed intermediately integrated, the processes of class formation induced by many years of capitalist penetration have been complex and the situation fluid. Classes and strata are internally divided and overlap and interpenetrate one another, people move readily and frequently among them and simultaneously hold such positions as poor peasant and rural wage worker. Contradictions among and within classes are thus multiple.

More than that, class contradictions based on the material circumstances of division of labour and above all control of means of production and extraction of surplus (exploitation) are supplemented by and interwoven with others which stem from different kinds of social relations. It is extremely important to remember the antagonisms which follow from the relations between men and women, youth and their elders, and minority and majority national, ethnic, and religious groups. These cannot simply be absorbed for analytical purposes into the 'class struggle', since their contradictions are heavily shaped by material and ideological factors other than those of class, such as women's exploitation through 'family' labour.

All this is very far from the classical Marxist picture of polarization between working class and capitalists, who gradually absorb the rest, and the growing size, solidity and self-consciousness of the proletariat. Yet, as we shall go on to show, *this situation of multiple class and other contradictions provides the basic reason why revolutions led by Marxist–Leninist socialists have taken place in countries intermediately integrated into the capitalist periphery.*

STATE AND CLASS ON THE PERIPHERY

For a revolution to have full meaning, in the sense that the process of transformation of the old society can be set in train, the state apparatus has to be seized. However much it will be changed subsequently itself, it will serve as one of the crucial instruments for that general transformation, and recognition of this fact has been the main element marking off socialism from the other current of modern revolutionary thought, anarchism. Marx and Engels held out a vision of the eventual 'withering away' of the state after socialism had been consolidated. It is evident, however, that the old order is most unlikely to yield to the new with grace, that the old power bloc and dominant class will seek to keep power if they can, even after the initial loss of the state apparatus. Central to the beginnings of any attempted socialism, therefore, must be a seizure and consolidation of power in a double, but closely related, movement: first, seizure from the dominant class and its power bloc of the state, which in fact represents the most developed concentration of power at the disposal of that class and bloc; and then consolidation, in part through control of the state.

Already the above paragraph opens up conceptual and historical problems. What are meant by 'dominant class', 'power bloc' and 'state apparatus'? Why should the last concentrate so much power? Can we not see many ways of seizing power in the twentieth century, legal and illegal, violent and non-violent, and in most cases not even by 'socialists'? All of these issues will have to be faced, if only briefly, in this chapter.

In the literature on underdevelopment the state has occupied a prominent place in recent years, as both Marxist and other writers have come to see it as playing a decisive interventionary role. Both have therefore spoken of the 'autonomous' or at least 'semi-autonomous' state, acting as an independent force 'above' class or other social interests, because its perspectives are wider and its resources much greater than theirs. The problem is that such an approach tends, first, to personify the state as if it were a sort of conscious force in itself, or at least as if it were the expression of some group (the military?) who could transcend class interests. Second, and more seriously, time and again the literature fails to make clear what exactly is meant by 'the state' in any given context, what precisely it is that is supposed to be doing something.

For us the problem lies in the fact that subsumed in the concept of 'the state' are in fact at least five aspects, so that at any given moment the reference may be to one or more of these. Thus, what is most often referred to is the state apparatus, the complex of institutions, specialized to some degree or other, which together ensure the formulation and execution of a government's policies. These are, of course, staffed by a professional bureaucracy, including armed forces, which thus frequently becomes a crucial social force, not in itself a class but forming a self-conscious collectivity. Second, the state represents a concentration of economic and political power, often, in fact, the biggest single such concentration in the particular social formation. (Though it may command less resources than the total commanded by the bigger transnational corporations which have branches there.) It also represents a concentration of another vital political resource, authority, in the ideological sense of being able – or at least claiming – to give legitimacy to the deeds of those who act in its name. We would suggest that these three aspects are what are usually conveyed in speaking of the state. Often, however, two more things are implied. Because the state by definition overarches all social interests (its apparatus is intended to ensure a generalized application of policy), it is often looked at in terms of a sort of arena within which those interests meet and come to some accommodation. Too often, however, such a portrayal, while bringing out an important aspect, fails to make it clear that the rules of this arena are not impartial and the referee is an active partisan. That viewpoint does come through more clearly in a fifth portrayal of the state, the classical Marxist one of the 'ruling committee of the bourgeoisie'.

It is now commonly recognized, even by Marxists, that this last position is far too simplistic. This is partly because of the range of things which we have suggested are included in the concept of the state. Even more important for our analysis of peripheral capitalism, however, is that such a characterization of the state apparatus/ power/authority in terms of direct instrumentality is misleading if we are to understand the role of the state (taken as embracing all five aspects) in peripheral capitalism, and especially in terms of the socialist seizure of power.

The challenge, then, is to find a different mode of analysis. In attempting this, let it immediately be clear that we would not suggest some neutral role for the state apparatus.[9] Evidently there are such things as dominant classes which have a disproportionate share of economic and political power and hence much freer access to the state-as-arena and the ability to direct the game in their own favour. But to speak of them as 'dominant' is less misleading than to use the more time-honoured expressions 'ruling' or 'governing', which again imply too direct a relationship to the state apparatus. Even in the advanced capitalist countries the position is more complex than this. In the capitalist periphery, where the historical origins and formation of the state are different, the relationship of the dominant classes to the state apparatus is certainly even more nuanced, mediated by a power bloc which gives a particular shape to that relationship.

The origins of the state in the capitalist periphery are basically colonial, or where they are not (in Siam, Russia, China, or Turkey, for example) are to be found in a conscious attempt to 'modernize' on a European model. (Latin American states are both, being nineteenth-century 'modernizations' of very old colonial structures.) This means that these states were essentially imports. They did not evolve organically – better, dialectically – with the internal class struggle, as did those of western Europe, but were injected into it and immediately became a factor of great influence on the new patterns of class formation which followed capitalist penetration. Above all, in the colonial cases, their points of reference were thus the interests not of local classes but of the dominant class in the metropolis.

Formal independence changed this position by directing the state inwards towards its own civil society, as it were, and this probably represents the biggest real shift, at the point when flags and national anthems are changed. This is not to suggest that the external interest disappeared, but it did now have to deal with a local politically (if not yet economically) dominant class. That class in turn, however, was now operating through a state apparatus which in its original form had assumed a quite different posture towards local classes, less directly aligned in particular with those which now became dominant.

The point may be extended and consolidated by looking more closely at the concept of the power bloc, introduced above. Theorizing the existence of such a bloc, and demonstrating its existence in actuality, provide a better explanation for certain features of peripheral capitalism (though the general analysis applies also to the developed variant) than postulating a state which is in some way 'autonomous' or 'semi-autonomous' from civil society. In particular, the feature with which we are concerned is the way in which the state apparatus at times intervenes in ways counter to the interests of some part of the capitalist or another dominant class. This is more readily comprehensible if we see that mediating between dominant class(es) and state apparatus there is always a bloc of elements selectively drawn from the dominant class but also including others, such as senior bureaucrats, which have direct access to policy formation, and thus to the use of state resources. If some fraction of the local capitalist class, the agrarian for example, is excluded from the power bloc or inadequately represented (perhaps only by one regional group), then it may well find itself seriously disadvantaged. The exact composition of the power bloc in a given formation at a given time is thus of great importance in understanding its distribution of power and the dynamics of its class formation at the upper levels. In this way we may explain an apparent state autonomy from class relations, especially where classes are also complexly divided internally, without postulating the freedom of action of an ill-defined 'state' which is not even represented in terms of human actors, but as an abstraction from them.

Let us take pre-revolutionary Nicaragua as a concrete example. Evidently the power bloc there had one very special – though by no means unique – feature, the presence at its centre of the Somoza family, which gave it a particular coherence. Beyond them were their immediate business associates, top officers of the national guard, and certain leading bureaucrats (though some of these were also extended family members, like the head of the National Power Company and the National Development Institute). It could well be argued that successive US ambassadors also directly belonged to the bloc, since they gave advice on a virtually day-to-day basis.[10] Obviously the way in which policies were formulated and executed was mediated and determined by the composition of the bloc, and conversely not to belong or to have direct entry was a manifest disadvantage.

The Somozist state apparatus was thus not some semi-autonomous entity. Indeed, quite the reverse, it was very firmly in the grip of a minority even of the dominant capitalist class, and any apparent freedom of action which it might have had was precisely a result of counter-pressures by a variety of complex contradictions (such as the Somoza group *v.* other capitalists, foreign *v.* national business, big businessmen *v.* small), not of an absence of such direct determinations.

It is not only the case that state apparatuses on the periphery are not 'autonomous' from their civil societies. A second crucial feature is that *though they may represent the biggest single concentration of power within their territory, they are usually unstable and fragile.* Particularly in terms of colonial origins, it has become common to term them 'overdeveloped states', seen thus as swollen bureaucratic apparatuses with excessive coercive capacity.[11] Whether they are necessarily proportionately more inflated than the state apparatuses of advanced industrial capitalism itself requires proof; certainly colonial origins could not account for this, since those apparatuses were quite simple structures until their last decades.

Of course contemporary state apparatuses can coerce, but this is a two-edged sword; if in the end coercion provokes resistance on a massive scale, that ability is worse than useless. Witness the fate of the Shah of Iran's regime, which possessed a repressive apparatus any European dictator might envy. Moreover, concentrated power does not automatically ensure concentrated authority; indeed, as batons are wielded and crowds fired on, legitimacy flees before the resisters do. Nor is size alone a protection, or giants from the brontosaurus to the blue whale would not have faced extinction. Less poetically, large bureaucracies are expensive and unwieldy, can provide multiple opportunities for corruption, and certainly do not guarantee effective execution of policies. This is a point also made, of course, by those who speak of 'overdeveloped' state apparatuses, and we agree with them that there is a sort of bureaucratic dropsy which swells and distends on the periphery as it has at the centre of capitalism, where the state apparatus has had to be called in more and more to ensure its reproduction. Given that this is a general phenomenon, however, it is not enough in itself to serve as an explanation for political instability in peripheral formations. Rather, it is part of a much more complex constellation of reasons which must be seen occurring in combination, having as the outcome in certain cases a socialist-led seizure of power. We must now begin to point the argument more firmly in that particular direction.

CLASS STRUGGLE ON THE PERIPHERY

It is our next task, therefore, to look at class struggle in relation to the socialist seizure of power. In doing so we shall, of course, be coming much closer to a theorization of that seizure itself, since Marxist debate concerning the revolution has centred upon class struggle. Contemporary peripheral formations are characterized by particularly complex class structures with multiple contradictions which interpenetrate one another. It follows that the class struggle there must be equally complex. In other words, there is a multiplicity of interests, those of classes, of groupings of various kinds within classes, and of social groups not definable as classes (women, youth, national, and ethnic minorities), which in some degree or other are organized and self-conscious. In the case of the relatively privileged they are attempting to maximize advantages and in the case of the subordinated they are trying to win something for themselves. The direct continuity from the existence of classes etc. to social and political struggle follows from the fact that on the periphery external relations in particular, along with a relatively low development of productive forces linked with those relations, make the pool of locally-held resources for which to compete quite small. In certain circumstances (and quite quickly, as we shall argue) the competition becomes one not just for available resources but for state power in general. Once it reaches that level, of course, the system has passed into a condition of crisis.

The 'received idea' on the seizure of power noted by us in Chapter 1 was established in the April 1925 Theses of the Comintern's Executive Committee. These formulated three basic principles, upon a foundation first laid by experience in Russia during the aborted revolution of 1905-6 and theoretically by Lenin, which provided the framework within which the member parties of the Comintern approached their individual strategies.[12] Moreover, through the agency of the Soviet Union these in effect continued to be reproduced unchanged to this day, influencing every national experience of the seizure.[13] These principles were: (1) that social formations on the periphery (in the original language, 'colonial and semi-colonial' countries) could not be immediately ready for the socialist revolution, since they were without highly developed working classes; (2) that, following from this, the revolution would have to go through stages, the first of which would be 'national', 'democratic', and 'anti-feudal', and only the second socialist; (3) that each stage would require forming a different bloc of classes to carry it through. With these in mind, let us look more closely at the question of the shaping of class struggle.

It follows from the points just made that in the Comintern tradition (within which, let it be emphasized, every successful revolutionary socialist leadership has been more or less formed to date) one part at least of the local capitalists, the so-called 'national bourgeoisie', could even be included in the revolutionary bloc (our term) in the first stage. This was because it was opposed in its interests to both foreign capital, its competitor, and to the 'feudal' landlords, the traditional enemy of the bourgeoisie. This point was established in the famous exchange between Lenin and the Indian communist M.N. Roy at the Second Congress of the Comintern in 1920.[14] By the time of the Sixth Congress in 1928, however, emphasis upon the possible contribution of the national bourgeoisie had diminished, and in the 'Programme' adopted there 'national reformism' was described as 'vacillating and inclined to compromise'.[15]

We would suggest that the basic problem was and remains that of *finding* a national bourgeoisie, that is, it must be remembered, *a part* of the total class, which has a sufficiently clear separate existence for its interests to be distinguishable and organizable. This might in some cases be possible for a brief period, as with the Wafd in Egypt, or even over a longer term, as with the Indian National Congress, particularly where there was mass pressure from below, but these were unusual cases and in the end the tendency was always to slide towards making a deal with foreign capital. (Though, as in the Indian case, this could take the form of an actual move to political independence.) Local capital is rarely as strong as the Egyptian Misr group, or the Tatas and Birlas of Bombay; usually its functioning is strictly determined by international sources of technology and other inputs over which it has no control, while local sources of capital and markets permit only a certain degree of expansion. In order to cross that threshold the local bourgeoisie finds it necessary to link with foreign enterprises, thus becoming what the Comintern called a 'compradore bourgeoisie', indissolubly linked with external interests. Conversely, the national bourgeoisie is the more inclined to do this because it can never bring itself to form a genuine alliance with the workers, peasants and poor petty bourgeoisie.

Both the petty bourgeoisie (including what we have termed the middle strata) and the peasantry were included by the 'Leninism' of the Comintern among the potential members of the revolutionary bloc in the national democratic stage. In theory it remains clear that they have interests in getting rid of foreign domination and the landlords who are its supporters. The intellectuals are marked, however, according to the 1928 'Programme' which represented a radical turn in strategy, by their 'hesitating and irresolute' ideology.[16] Like the national bourgeoisie, the 'mass movement may draw them in, but may also push them into the camp of extreme reaction, or encourage the spread of utopian reactionary tendencies in their ranks'.[17]

By 1928 the Comintern view of the peasants was somewhat more sanguine. Along with the working class they were held to be 'a driving force of the revolution'. Indeed, the 'peasantry can only achieve its emancipation under the leadership of the proletariat, while the proletariat can only lead the bourgeois-democratic revolution to victory in union with the peasantry'.[18] This finally established the theoretical central place which the 'worker-peasant alliance' was to occupy in the bloc of revolutionary classes. The proletariat remained the leading class, of course, as the historical bearer of socialism, but it was recognized that it was small and that most of its members were only recent recruits, squeezed by capitalism and feudalism in combination out of 'the pauperized village' or 'ruined artisans driven from the decaying handicrafts'.[19] Thus, though the working class was to give the lead, it needed the peasants to provide weight and bulk for the drive for state power.

Already during the 1920s, therefore, Marxist–Leninist theory, more especially in its Stalinist formulation, had established that it was not the workers alone upon whom the revolution would rest but rather that in the conditions of peripheral capitalism a broader range of class elements must be brought together. This was realistic, but also in our opinion decisive for the future 'socialist' seizures of power. To formulate a proposition in line with our previous analysis: *in the conditions of multiple class and other social contradictions which prevail on the periphery, the revolutionary bloc is bound to include a wide range of dissident elements.* The implications of this for the nature of the revolution are very great. In terms of the seizure of power, they are that the revolutionary bloc cannot be integrated on a basis of any one class interest, because of its essential heterogeneity. Particularly if capitalist elements are present in the bloc, interests will be very different and even opposed. With a small and underdeveloped working class, it will be impossible automatically to extend its interests into a hegemonic 'socialist' ideology of transformation.

CREATING THE REVOLUTIONARY BLOC

We are now at a pivotal point in our analysis, with the issue before us of how class and other social struggles in peripheral capitalist countries are in fact given shape by Marxist–Leninist strategists. Our basic propositions are these: *the condition of relatively complex and multiple social contradictions which prevails at the periphery, along with the frequently insecure rooting of the state apparatus, have created opportunities for the successful application of strategies based on Marxism in its latter-day 'Leninist' variant, which the original doctrine would not have permitted.* However, the hugely ironic contradiction then emerges that the very conditions and circumstances of success are a major obstacle to the socialist transformation. In the remainder of this chapter we shall focus primarily on the first proposition, since the other is better developed in our later analysis of the post-revolutionary situation on the periphery.

In order to explain the seizure of power by socialists in peripheral capitalist countries we need to theorize three concepts, which we term 'war of position', 'war of manoeuvre', and 'crisis of the regime'. The first two we take from Antonio Gramsci, the Comintern's most original theorist, who used these military terms, suitably enough, to enter the problem of the seizure of power. We shall depart significantly from him in our usage, but his approach is important because of the distinction he draws between conditions for the seizure in the 'East' (Russia) and in the 'West' (the advanced industrial countries).[20] Thus he characterizes civil society in the former as 'primordial', as we speak of an incomplete (from the point of view of the capitalist centre) and complex class formation. He emphasizes the importance of the state apparatus, and feels that a protracted war of manoeuvre will be required there gradually to bring about conditions for the seizure of power. This kind of delayed frontal attack is not necessary in developed formations (to use our terminology), where power may be won by a taking of position through political struggle in a civil society with well-defined classes and with a state apparatus which is only part of the defences of the dominant class.[21]

Behind Gramsci's discussion, of course, lay the whole debate which had rent the Second International from 1899 to 1914 concerning 'reform' and 'revolution', pitting Eduard Bernstein against Karl Kautsky, Luxemburg and Lenin, and this adds a dimension to the conceptualization additional to that of 'East' and 'West'.[22] Thus Perry

Anderson is correct to warn that the 'mere counter position of 'war of position' to 'war of manoeuvre' in any Marxist strategy in the end becomes an opposition between reformism and adventurism'.[23] This is not how we intend to use these ideas. On the other hand, Anderson accepts the view of the revolution taking place in stages when he counterposes the idea of integrating the two 'wars' in a 'correct theoretical and temporal order'.[24] As we have already noted, this view has the status of a received idea, but that does not necessitate its acceptance. More important for us, however, is the fact that in his discussion Anderson is concerned only with the seizure of power in developed capitalist formations. Our reformulation of the Gramscian problematic can apply to all parts of the world system. Thus we suggest that the struggle to overthrow capitalism everywhere involves *both* a war of position and a war of manoeuvre, and that these have to be fought whether one takes a revolutionary position of the need for illegal and probably violent action to seize the state apparatus, or the social democratic or 'Eurocommunist' line on the electoral road to power. Moreover, the two 'wars' overlap in time and activity (and thus theoretically).

The war of position for us, then, is the process whereby the party or other organization (such as the 26th July Movement in Cuba) which is to lead the socialist revolution puts itself at the head of a bloc of dissident class and other elements, and in doing this roots itself so deeply that it cannot henceforth be eradicated by the power bloc and its state apparatus. The war of manoeuvre is the politico-military process by which that party/organization actually seizes power. We may now go on to look more closely at various issues involved in these definitions.

A number of problems for the organization of class struggle follow directly from the above propositions on revolutionary strategy. First, the need to combine a wide variety of alienated elements into one movement means finding suitable forms of organization. It is obvious that the Comintern's concern with vanguards implied creating as close a replica of the Russian Bolshevik Party in 1917 as was possible, or perhaps more accurately, a replica of what it was supposed to have been. 'Iron proletarian discipline' would mark such parties, which 'should from the very outset demarcate themselves in the most clear-cut fashion, both politically and organizationally, from all petty-bourgeois groups and parties'.[25] A special problem in the 'colonial and semi-colonial countries' was for them to 'become genuinely communist parties in their social composition' by combining the 'best elements of the revolutionary intelligentsia' with 'strengthening the party organization in the factories and mines, among transport workers, and among the semi-slaves in the plantations'.[26] These injunctions of 1928 were faithfully carried out, for example by Ho Chi Minh's Indochinese Communist Party founded two years later, but the organizational tradition which in fact was passed on also recognized that, in putting together a multi-class and group bloc, trade unions, peasant organizations and many other such bodies had to be built round the party. The Indochinese Communist Party is a good example here: claiming in May 1941 that a quarter of its members were workers, at the same time it launched an extensive programme of building up 'National Salvation' organizations for peasants, intellectuals, women, students, soldiers and other interests. In such circumstances vanguard parties become both putative leaders of the proletariat at the head of the revolution and the scaffolding which holds together an edifice of diverse bodies which they themselves often create.

The point is that the doctrine of the vanguard party, whatever the tactical shift of emphasis, has consistently appeared to meet a real need, namely that of taking an initiative and actively seeking to build the opposition bloc which would give a base and weight to the revolution. The real need arises from the breadth and heterogeneity of such a bloc in the typical situation of social struggle found on the periphery. Given this situation, leadership in building the necessary alliances has to come from somewhere, and given the difficulties which various subordinated classes and groups face in developing their own 'organic intellectuals' (a point to which we shall come), the chances are great that this leadership will come from outside them. The concept of the vanguard party serves as the crucial ideological instrument for the crystallization of the group of leaders, and the party itself as the necessary organizational vehicle for them to assert their dominance. As Gramsci put it:

A social group can, and indeed must, already exercise 'direction' before winning governmental power (this indeed is one of the principal conditions for the winning of such power); it subsequently becomes dominant when it exercises power, but even if it holds it firmly in its grasp, it must continue to 'direct' as well.[27]

Two further important points on leadership must be noted. First, the group does not always emerge as a fully-fledged vanguard party with the unity and 'iron discipline' beloved of the Stalinist Comintern. In the important case of Cuba, and more recently in Nicaragua, an organized but looser grouping has emerged to take the lead (the 26th July Movement and the Sandinist National Liberation Front). Some of the cases in which socialist ideology was heavily mixed with anti-colonial nationalism (Guinea-Bissau, Angola and Mozambique, South Yemen) were also characterized by somewhat less cohesive bodies. The main reason for this is probably the political, and therefore ideological, distance from the local Communist Party and its ideas which is determined by the history of previous class struggle (as in Cuba, where the party had compromised itself by siding at times with the regime), or even the absence of a separate Communist Party. In the first of these cases, the formation of the new leadership often seems to be associated also with the emergence of a new generation, sometimes literally in terms of age-group.

Second, there are some contemporary Marxist–Leninist regimes, namely the Congo, Benin, and Ethiopia, which are in fact the products of military coups and not directly of political movements at all. They do have crisis and popular unrest providing the opportunity for the seizure of power in common with the rest, but seem above all to show the utility of received ideas to revolutionary leaderships *after* they have taken control of the state, a point to which we shall return in Chapter 4.

Even in the case of these two variations, however, an important characteristic is usually shared with more formal vanguard parties. If the revolutionary leadership crystallizes in such forms, rather than emerging more directly from working-class, peasant, and other basic organizations, there can be little chance of control over it 'from below'. Rather, it imposes itself as the self-appointed vanguard, fully encouraged to do so, of course, by Stalinist received ideas. The party is then not merely directive before winning power, as Gramsci put it, but dominant in a much more direct way. The danger immediately arises that, once it has the state apparatus in its grasp, the leadership will in effect substitute itself for the workers, peasants and others and exercise that power for itself but in their name. This may prove to be a major obstacle to the socialist transformation.

This question has arisen in every case since Russia in 1917 and must be elaborated in Chapter 4. Here we would rather concentrate upon the struggle leading up to the moment when the revolutionaries occupy the strongpoints of state power. We have hypothesized that in the social conditions of the periphery this must mean that the leadership will be based upon a wide bloc of alienated class and other elements, and that this will be a strength, because it capitalizes upon the situation of multiple contradictions which the dominant class and power bloc find it increasingly difficult to handle. Once again, the mainstream ideas of Marxism–Leninism have a considerable utility here, in the sense that they direct the new leaders to seek to build a broad alliance. This follows from the conception of the revolution as proceeding in stages, with such broad objects in the first as were defined in the 1928 Comintern Programme – 'the struggle against feudalism, against pre-capitalist forms of exploitation, the consistent pursuit of the peasant agrarian revolution, and the struggle against foreign imperialism and for national independence'.[28] The result is that the vanguard party/movement is directed to do what is necessary: to take position upon the basis of the widest possible range of dissident elements.

The wider the range, however, the greater the difficulty of holding that bloc together. The vanguard party/movement, if it is to be successful, accomplishes this through three means. First of all, as we have already noted, it creates, or at least brings together, a range of organizations specific to the various interests grouped into its revolutionary bloc. (In order to do this, of course, it has to infiltrate and control them.) This is one of the essential moves in its war of position, as is the second way in which the vanguard holds the bloc together, namely by securing its overall hegemony (intellectual and moral authority) through infusing the whole bloc with common ideological themes.[29] Gramsci, from whom all recent discussions of hegemony derive, saw that ideological dominance as marking an advanced stage of the whole class struggle:

the phase in which previously germinated ideologies become 'party', come into confrontation and conflict, until one of them, or at least a single combination of them, tends to prevail, to gain the upper hand, to propagate itself throughout society – bringing about not only a union of political and economic aims, but also intellectual and moral unity, posing all the questions around which the struggle rages not only on a corporate but on a 'universal' plane, and thus creating the hegemony of a fundamental social group over a series of subordinate groups.[30]

Our point is that, in the conditions of underdeveloped capitalism, the propagation and creation of unity have to happen first in the revolutionary bloc, long before this can occur in terms of civil society as a whole, and that this is an essential part of the vanguard party/movement's taking of position. Indeed, it may well be that Gramsci's postulate of a society-wide hegemony may not in fact be a precondition of the revolutionaries' seizure of power in a peripheral country.

Given the heterogeneous composition of the bloc upon which the seizure of power must be based, preserving the purity of a 'proletarian' ideology might well also prove difficult. Ernesto Laclau has argued (though basically in the context of developed capitalisms) that the most appropriate counter to the power bloc is 'the people' and a 'popular-democratic' ideology.[31] Certainly in the countries of the capitalist periphery some sort of formulation of this kind – not directly related to class interests but rather cutting across them – has been common. This has been aided by the apparently universal acceptance of the concept of revolutionary stages, with the first not specifically directed towards socialist objectives. On the other hand, it is also worth remembering that at no time in history is one dealing with some pure, Marxist, proletarian ideology, certainly not in the Bolshevik paradigm, Russia in 1917. As our cases extend beyond that one the more muddy tend to become the ideological waters. Often we find instead a sort of petty bourgeois or peasant Jacobinism, a radicalism of small property when counterposed to large, democratic, and egalitarian rather than specifically socialist.

Most important of all has probably been the force of nationalism, at least in those cases where the socialist revolution has been intertwined with anti-colonial revolt or resistance to a foreign invader, as in Yugoslavia in the Second World War. What is perhaps most significant here is that Marxists have always treated nationalism as associated historically with the rise of the bourgeoisie. This has made it appear a suitable mobilizing force in the first stage of the revolution, that concerned with achieving national independence and the overthrow of feudalism (often, it should be noted, existing only by the most generous definition, i.e. any class situation marked by the presence of landowners and tenants). In order to make such a fusion of revolution and nationalist ideology, however, it has been necessary in fact to forget this class content and in effect to give the struggle for national sovereignty priority over the class struggle. The ten years between 1941 and 1951 in Viet Nam are a particularly marked case in point, where in order to win over 'patriotic' landlords, for example policies which would have benefited the peasantry were very much downplayed.

The main point here is the contradiction involved in this sort of ideological situation: nationalism or some sort of populist Jacobinism may permit the broadest possible rallying of strength to the revolution led by socialists, but conversely make the shift to an overt class struggle position that much more difficult at a later stage. Assuming that such a shift must occur, whether we postulate clearly separate stages or with Trotsky stress a 'permanent revolution' with a rapid escalation (and change in forms of struggle), the implication is that after state power has been seized there will be a struggle among the various class and other elements in the original bloc, since their interests as such will not necessarily be compatible with socialist policies.

This issue of ideology as an expression of class/social group interest or of that of some wider category ('nation', 'people') is closely bound up with the role in the revolutionary bloc of middle-strata elements. Ever since Lenin's formulation in *What Is To Be Done?* (1902) that Marxism must be brought to the proletariat from 'outside' by the vanguard party, debate has raged as to whether or not this represented in fact an imposition of non-proletarian leadership.[32] Certainly, whether we look at the Russian case or any of its successors, we see that predominantly middle-strata intellectuals have been the main 'bearers' of socialist doctrine on the periphery. The question is, to what extent, given the conditions there, must that necessarily be so? In order to begin to answer we may turn to certain propositions of Antonio Gramsci, himself the son of a minor Italian state official.

Gramsci's definition of intellectual is both broad and closely related to our class concept of the middle strata.

> By 'intellectuals' must be understood not those strata commonly described by this term, but in general the entire social stratum which exercises an organizational function in the wide sense – whether in the field of production, or in that of culture, or in that of political administration.[33]

Whether this goes all the way down to the humble clerk is unclear, but it obviously covers the great majority of those middle strata persons who sell their labour power and perform 'white collar' tasks. Though Gramsci himself was careful to point out that all work requires a combination of manual and mental capacities, it is clear that his intellectuals are distinguished by the emphasis in their occupations on the latter. In terms of their formation and historical existence he distinguished three different groups in his various essays, the 'organic', the 'traditional', and the 'rural', though the last in the special context of southern Italian history.[34]

Concentrating, therefore, upon the first two, we must first note that organic intellectuals are formed within capitalism as a necessary part on the one side of the capitalist and on the other of the working classes, necessary because in each case the intellectuals 'give it homogeneity and an awareness of its own function not only in the economic but also in the social and political fields'.[35] Thus the capitalist is not only himself an organizer with 'a certain technical capacity', he also 'creates alongside himself the industrial technician, the specialist in political economy, the organizers of a new culture, of a new legal system, etc.'. From this formulation it is evident that the intellectuals do not belong directly to the capitalist class but are created by capitalism in order to supply certain kinds of labour power necessary to it. This happened historically on the periphery as at the centre, though limited, among other things, by the smaller demand of underdeveloped capitalism and the colonial use of metropolitan personnel.

Traditional intellectuals, for Gramsci, are those whom capitalism may be said to inherit from preceding modes of production, above all priests, but also lawyers, philosophers, and others, 'categories of intellectuals already in existence and which seemed indeed to represent an historical continuity uninterrupted even by the most complicated and radical changes in political and social forms'.[36] These usually come to serve the new dominant class as they did the old. Obviously some, by becoming specialists in, say, business or administrative law, transform themselves into the organic category.

The dominant capitalist class thus creates for itself organically or annexes already existing intellectuals, whose role is to reproduce the necessary conditions for its perpetuation. The role of the organic intellectuals created by the working class is quite other, for their concern is organization and ideology expressing an antagonistic interest. Although it is possible to see the emergence of intellectuals from within the working class (which was also Lenin's concern, something frequently ignored by his critics), especially in the form of trade union organizers, this phenomenon does suffer a change as we move into the periphery. Gramsci noted that, 'In the modern world, technical education, closely bound to industrial labour even at the most primitive and unqualified level, must form the basis of the new type of intellectual'.[37] Despite his statement about levels, it may still be suggested that the way in which a working class forms in underdeveloped countries, mostly outside industry proper, with a low level of technology and division of labour, little education of any kind, and the tendency of many of its members to drift off into the peasantry or petty bourgeoisie (at least intermittently), places tremendous limits upon the capacity of that class for the organic creation of intellectuals. As for the peasantry, Gramsci denied categorically that they could create their own, seeing them only as a source of recruits for the traditional category.[38] We may well doubt this as a total statement; peasants do produce their own organizers and even ideologues, though often the latter are prophets of some millenarian or other cult. (These do express peasant class interests, even though the sort of practice which they recommend leads only to defeat.) Nevertheless, what holds good for the working class on the periphery is even more true for peasants.

It follows from the above that the main intellectuals who may undertake the organization and ideological formation of such workers and peasants (and all other alienated classes and groups) are dissident organic or traditional intellectuals who break ideologically from peripheral capitalism. In the case of the former, it would appear that most recruits in fact come from their cadets, the university students who have been exposed to new and exciting ideas – often including revolutionary ones – but have not yet been fully incorporated into the system. As for the traditional category, it may well be that their sons and daughters are the crucial group, and often coterminous with the new kind of students.

Seen more directly in class terms, it is possible that in peripheral formations there is some particular susceptibility of the middle strata to revolutionary ideas in general, including socialist ones. The explanation for this is complex and one about which we are only in a position to speculate. At risk of falling into some variant of 'marginality' theory, therefore, we would suggest that the material base for this susceptibility is the necessity of these elements to sell their labour power, in a situation where the low level of development of productive forces means that there is no guarantee of employment, at least not at the level expected. After an unusually long period of formation in secondary school and university, sometimes under conditions of hardship, often encouraged to develop their critical faculties, aspirant members of the middle strata (indeed, of its upper reaches) find entry closed. A generational factor enters here also, the capacity of the young to feel disgust at the hypocrisy and corruption of their elders. Cuba in the last ten or twelve years of the Batista regime provides a good example; Fidel Castro himself emerged precisely from this milieu, and the Student Directorate was one of the main organizational components of his revolutionary movement in the final phase.[39] Lastly, it may well be that the middle strata are more prone to be moved by ideology in general than other classes, since 'ideas' are the stock in trade of many of them, teachers, priests, journalists, lawyers, and so on. In that sense, since ideas are the source of their livelihood, ideology becomes a direct material force and source of contradictions.

Middle-strata intellectuals are a pivotal group in the revolutionary bloc. Particularly if it proves difficult for it to establish its ideological hegemony throughout the bloc, this leadership may well resort to a starker means of holding it together, namely the elimination, by expulsion or even by violence, of those whom it regards as untrustworthy, usually those who do not accept its direction completely. This is another direct heritage of the chill hand of Stalinism, and has thus often been accompanied by charges of 'Trotskyism' in the past, though perhaps the alternative of 'CIA agent' is now more common.

Two last points may be made about the revolutionary bloc. It is extremely important to note that, contrary to Gramsci's assumption, the hegemony which is achieved within the bloc is not that of the working class, but of the party/movement, which means of its leadership, and we have already noted that this is usually not itself working class in origin. Constant repetition of the assertion that the party is the vanguard of the working class is not sufficient to prove that it is truly the latter which is hegemonic. Even more deep a problem, it is not at all easy to see what the establishment of working-class hegemony in the bloc would mean, supposing it were to happen without the intervention of the party. What is supposed to be the content of that hegemony – the acceptance of workers' special interests as the interests of all, or a broader commitment to a socialist future? One reason why the leaders of the party/movement impose its hegemony within the revolutionary bloc is certainly because the working class is not able to do so.

WAR OF MANOEUVRE AND CRISIS OF THE REGIME

We have now opened up some of the issues involved in the war of position, seen as the necessity of a vanguard party/movement to root itself in a revolutionary bloc so strongly that, first, the power bloc, despite its control of the state apparatus, will never be able to destroy it, and, second, it will have a base from which to manoeuvre into power. Once the critical issues of the war of position are solved up to the point where the party/movement has rooted and based itself (which certainly does not imply any complete solution), the leadership can turn its attention to launching the war of manoeuvre. (Though such a neat division into stages does not, in fact, occur in real life.) In conceptualizing the latter we may begin with Gramsci again. Thus, in criticizing a too-great emphasis upon economic struggle, he spoke of the need at a certain moment for an 'appropriate political initiative' which 'is always necessary to liberate the economic thrust from the dead weight of traditional policies'.[40] What this means for us is that at a certain point in time (conjuncture), when the balance of class and other contradictions seems appropriate (conjunction), the revolutionary leadership takes a conscious political decision – not necessarily understood in all its implications immediately – which in effect launches the war of manoeuvre.[41] Such a break event occurred in Yugoslavia in April 1941, for example, when the leaders of the Communist Party decided to put it at the head of the resistance to the Axis invaders; or in Viet Nam a month later, when the Eighth Plenum of the Central Committee of the Indochinese Communist Party adopted a policy of political reorganization and preparation for military action. A later example is the landing from the *Granma* in Cuba in December 1956.

This kind of declaration of the war of manoeuvre implies a decision on the appropriate form it will take, and in almost every case we have seen so far, and in all foreseeable ones (El Salvador, South Africa, the Philippines, to name a few) this involves some sort of armed action. Here it is certainly difficult to distinguish any received idea which has come to dominate. Thus the Sixth Comintern Congress put forward a model which was essentially the Bolshevik seizure of power in October 1917. If the 'revolutionary tide' was rising, its Programme said, a 'frontal assault on the bourgeois state' would come onto the agenda, with 'transitional slogans on a rising scale' (such as demands for workers' councils and the arming of the workers), and mass actions such as strikes and demonstrations, leading up to a combination of strikes and armed demonstrations, a general strike, and armed insurrection.[42]

This model, however, was scarcely ever followed. Above all it was an urban strategy, dependent on a concentrated and militant working class, and the necessary conditions have not existed in most peripheral countries. More typical has been the Chinese pattern of base areas among the peasantry and guerrilla struggle gradually escalating into large-scale warfare and the destruction of the regime's armies in the field; this typified Viet Nam after 1945, Laos, Kampuchea, and the anti-colonial movements in Portuguese Africa (though the last did not reach the final phase). A third basic pattern is that of Cuba and South Yemen, with a combination of urban resistance through strikes and demonstrations with guerrilla warfare in the rural areas. A fourth pattern, of which Yugoslavia is the clearest example, is the combination of a war against foreign invaders with a civil war (which must be distinguished from the more common intervention by foreign forces in an internal struggle). There have been no clear examples of this since the Second World War, but it could well occur again in the context of a regional war.

Whatever the circumstances, there has been a crucial element in launching the war of manoeuvre in an armed form. Without a strong base in a revolutionary bloc, a vanguard party/movement which attempts this exposes itself to complete destruction, or at best limitation to a base in some remote area; this is typically the case with the Thai Communist Party, firmly enough rooted among minority peoples in the north-east to be effectively ineradicable, but lacking a broad enough bloc to be able to move out into the rest of the country.[43]

It is an interesting comment on the difficulties of finding an appropriate form for the armed struggle, as well as on the problem of correct timing in launching the war of manoeuvre, that in the 1960s in Latin America the doctrine emerged that revolutionaries must necessarily begin with a small armed nucleus, a *foco*, the actions of which would set in train mass movement. As the chief theorist of this line, Régis Debray, put it:

> it is necessary to proceed from the small to the large: to attempt to proceed by the opposite way is pointless. The smallest is the guerrilla *foco*, nucleus of the popular army. It is not a front which will create this nucleus, but rather the nucleus which, as it develops, will permit the creation of a national revolutionary front. One creates a front around something *extant*, not only around a program of liberation. It is the 'small motor' that sets the 'big motor' of the masses in motion and precipitates the formation of a front, as the victories won by the small motor increase.[44]

In a subsequent self-criticism the author himself listed the major weaknesses of such a strategy: a 'unilateral and grossly simplified image of the Cuban revolution ... resulted in dissociating the military struggle from the political, the underground struggle from the legal, the action of the vanguard from the mass movement, strategy from tactics, the hills from the towns, the advanced sectors of the populace from the more backward'.[45] The effect had been to turn the launching of the war of manoeuvre with no preceding war of position into the unorganized departure of small groups of urban elements, often students, for the mountains or jungle. As a result, they usually found themselves amid indifferent or even hostile local populations, and were quickly wiped out by the state apparatus.[46] The complex organizational and ideological tasks discussed above, therefore, are indispensable; what we would stress again here is that up to now they have always been performed by a self-appointed vanguard party/movement.[47]

Although the war of manoeuvre must necessarily find an appropriate combination of the political and the military, it may be noted that the launching of an armed conflict is usually necessary in the political conditions of the periphery, where the power bloc denies chances for peaceful access to control of the state apparatus. In addition, it stems ideologically from the concept of not merely seizing the apparatus, but smashing it in order to rebuild it in a socialist form. Smashing implies direct confrontation as part of the act of seizure, and a militarized form of the latter would be the starkest. Finding a suitable form of military struggle, once that becomes clearly necessary, is not an easy task for the vanguard. The essential organic form of workers' struggle is the strike, and this cannot easily be transformed into a guerrilla struggle (notably, most urban guerrilla groups draw heavily from the petty bourgeoisie and middle strata). Workers' armed defence units can become 'Red Guards' and take part in an urban seizure of power, but except in Russia in the conditions of the periphery that has not been enough. Similarly, the poor petty bourgeoisie and middle strata, the whole agglomeration of the urban shanty-towns which is particularly fluid in class terms, can typically riot and demonstrate but do not by themselves find a more directed form of revolutionary struggle. Organic to the peasantry are land seizure and the jacquerie, the localized striking out against oppression. From there to the rural guerrilla is not so great a step, if an outside force intervenes to guide it. It follows from the above that, as the war of manoeuvre takes on an increasingly militarized form in the face of the obduracy and repression of the regime, there is a shift to the rural areas, but also an increasing militarization of organization. The revolutionary bloc, but above all its leadership, is pushed out of the normal political system, as it were, but in fact is glad to go and may have chosen to do so. In these conditions, however, the war of manoeuvre becomes in fact a storming of the redoubt from outside, and in the end that often requires a still greater degree of militarization. Regular units are formed, with heavy weaponry requiring appropriate training, hierarchies of ranks are introduced, and unquestioning obedience demanded. The vanguard consolidates its control in yet another form.

We have now moved close to the final act of the seizure of power, the actual taking control of the state apparatus which has marked our cases since 1917. We must therefore turn our attention to the way in which peripheral regimes finally collapse in the face of socialist-led revolutionary blocs, which involves the conceptualization of their ultimate crisis.

Even though the pressure of class and other social contradictions upon them may be multiple and the appearance of strength of their state apparatuses deceptive, peripheral capitalist regimes do not fall to their knees and tremble in the mere presence of a vanguard party/movement. We have already noted that first comes the often long and arduous task of insertion into the complex of contradictions and building of a revolutionary bloc strong enough to raise the possibility of a successful confrontation. Then, with that support, the vanguard has to manoeuvre itself to the point where the seizure of state power is actually possible. Just as the manoeuvres of armies are directed towards finding favourable terrain, the manoeuvres of revolutionaries seek suitable conjunctions of contradictions; the great difference is that armies do not create the ground on which they move, whereas the revolutionary vanguard is actively involved in creating the political crisis which gives it the opportunity to attack.

The idea of political crisis invokes that of a related economic crisis. Nevertheless, on the periphery the situation is not simply one of economic crisis leading to political pressures on the power bloc. In one sense the social formations there appear to be constantly in crisis, above all because they are integrated in special ways into the world capitalist system. Thus accumulation based on realization of the surplus value generated from their raw materials and by their labour power is located in the advanced industrial countries, rather than locally; this leaves them constantly short of investment funds. The result is that they cannot produce what they need themselves and therefore have to import it. This in turn means that price inflation is passed back to them whenever they buy indispensable food, machinery, and oil (except for the fortunate few who produce the last themselves and they are not immune to the other price rises, only better cushioned). In order to buy imports and pay other rising costs the power bloc must find funds in the situation of low levels of local accumulation, and hence runs into a variant of the 'fiscal crisis of the state'. Resort is usually had to borrowing abroad, from governments, international agencies and, increasingly in the 1970s, private banks. Huge debts which cannot be paid in time and have to be covered by further borrowings (the 'debt trap') are the result. Lastly, what surplus can be realized locally is used to maintain the dominant class and its state apparatus, perpetuating the very unequal income distribution among different classes and groups.

All this would certainly seem to add up to a condition of permanent economic crisis, which may indeed grow worse, but then often because of political factors; thus, capital may be sent away in the face of mounting popular pressure. This implies a complex relationship between the economic and political aspects of regime crisis.

Basically, that complexity follows from the structure of peripheral capitalism as an articulation of a foreign-dominated capitalist mode of production with non-capitalist forms (advanced foreign-owned plants exist in combination with peasant agriculture and back street workshops). We have already emphasized that in terms of class struggle this situation creates multiple contradictions and potential pressures on the dominant class and power bloc. There is, however, an overall contradiction in this structure: it is basically unstable because of its class complexity, but at the same time that complexity serves to contain the emergence of an economic crisis which is both generalized and rapidly reaching a peak. Thus, all the while peasants have some control over land they at least have a chance to feed themselves, even if production for the market becomes minimal, and in fact they can go on sustaining relatives in towns. There the incredibly ingenious combinations of ways of subsisting which the poor put together often form a flexible means of dealing with unemployment. Women seek work to sustain workless men. Being in any case accustomed to a much lower level of living, the majority of the population can 'absorb' a gradual deterioration of the total economy along the lines just suggested up to a point which would be far beyond the capacity of the majority to endure in an advanced capitalist country. Economic deterioration much more rapidly becomes generalized economic crisis where the linkages between the economics of everyday life and broader structures and movements are above all an almost complete dependence upon wages earned and food purchased. On the periphery we are dealing with a more prolonged and fractured process.

Thus, paradoxically, economic crisis is almost endemic on the periphery but, just for that reason, is not necessarily rapidly generalizable in an acute form throughout the population. In some of the most important cases, like Russia, Yugoslavia and China, the decisive factor has been the role of war and foreign invasion in creating economic crisis in a general form. In our last chapter we shall consider the possible new significance of economic factors in cases of attempted transition to advanced integration. What we wish to emphasize (and this is true for all cases) is that the real crisis for the regime is political, that is when endemic economic crisis and its consequent social stresses are translated into confrontation with a rival force seeking to take power. In that very real sense it is the vanguard party/movement which creates the crisis by building its supporting bloc and by then being able to manoeuvre into a confrontation with the state apparatus. This, in its turn, is made the more easy by the prominence of the apparatus in protecting dominant class interests, especially by coercion, and in its interventions in the economy.[48]

Given the widely differing forms of the seizure of power (even including military coups) which have created Marxist–Leninist regimes up to now, it is difficult to see a common pattern to the political crises which have provided the opportunity, though the shifts over time are clearer. As to the future, a certain degree of speculation can be attempted in Chapter 5. Here it is sufficient to have established that, under certain conditions, intermediately integrated formations on the periphery are subject to seizures of power by avowed Marxist–Leninists. What may happen afterwards will be discussed in Chapters 3 and 4.

3

State socialist accumulation:
The resource-constrained economy

With this chapter we make a double shift in perspective. First of all, from now on our argument will assume that a Marxist–Leninist-led revolutionary movement has seized state power; the task will be to examine what in fact the leaders are likely to do with it. Second, while the emphasis in Chapter 2 was primarily on the condition of underdevelopment, from this Chapter onwards the received ideas and practices of state socialism will be brought much more centrally into the picture.

This chapter will differ from the last in another way. Up to now we have combined discussion of economic, social, and political factors, a method which reflects what actually happens. In the coming pages we shall isolate the economic level in order better to highlight the processes which are basic to all other developments under state socialism. On the basis of these we can continue in Chapter 4 to examine crucial aspects of the workings of politics and the distribution of power.

One last introductory point should be noted. The discussion in this chapter is based principally, though not exclusively, on the experience of the more mature state socialist economies. This partly reflects a bibliographical imbalance arising out of the much longer experience of the latter, but it also reflects our conviction that the experience of the more mature state socialist economies, with due allowance for geographical and historical differences, is highly relevant to post-revolutionary societies of more recent origin. This may be because the latter are either consciously or unconsciously attempting to emulate the more mature state socialist societies. Or it may be because they are reacting against the path taken by their forerunners, in which case our discussion embraces the major choices which they face, most of which have confronted the more mature state socialist societies at one time or another.

From the history of the more advanced state socialist societies thus far in this century the broad outlines of a law of tendency based upon three distinct stages of economic development can be posited. These are as follows.

First comes a stage of consolidation of power and reconstruction, which may involve the continuation of war against internal and/or external enemies. This stage is generally marked by a degree of pragmatism, underwritten by the doctrine that the revolution is in a first, pre-socialist phase, and the needs of the moment hold sway. Nationalization, however, is usually a key theme as part of the consolidation of power. Planning takes place in spheres over which control has been gained.

The second stage involves an attempt to implement the 'received ideas' of socialism, strongly to assert ideology (albeit perhaps for pragmatic reasons), and to set the new society on a footing for the ultimate attainment of socialist and, in theory at least, communist objectives. The received ideas may, as in the case of the Soviet Union, be a direct interpretation of the legacy of Marx and Lenin or, as in other cases, those of the Soviet interpretation. The key themes have been nationalization (usually formalizing or putting the finishing touches to programmes initiated during the first stage as part of the consolidation of power), industrialization, the collectivization of agriculture and the introduction of a more comprehensive and highly centralized planning system. The emphasis has been upon production rather than consumption, upon the role of the producer rather than the consumer.

The third stage involves moves towards deconcentration/ decentralization and in various guises. The key themes have been a considerable increase in the autonomy of enterprises (in certain instances extending to almost total freedom) and a concern to improve democracy by inviting much greater worker participation in the direction of enterprises, both with objectives of increasing efficiency and meeting the needs of consumers in a more satisfactory manner.

Before going any further, it should be made clear that the stages we discern are not the same as those projected by Marxist–Leninist received ideas, namely the national democratic, socialist, and communist. As was made clear in Chapter 2, we reject this perspective, or at least the first two parts of it. Our formulation is based on historical experience, not on an attempt to make history conform with theory.

The analysis in this chapter is focused on our stages one and two, but particularly on stage two. The reasons for this are twofold. First of all, and in spite of a recent spate of reforms, most state socialist societies have not yet really embarked upon stage three, remaining trapped in variants of stage two. Second, stage two has been the benchmark by which the world has tended to judge the socialist project. But this does not mean that we intend to ignore stage three. Indeed, the analysis in this chapter will show why progression to stage three should become necessary or desirable and then, further to this, the issues which it raises will be addressed directly in Chapter 5.

PLANNING AND POLITICAL ECONOMY

Once the seizure of power has taken place, many socialists have tended to assume that political economy becomes an inappropriate area of enquiry. After all, economics, the anarchy of the market, is now supposed to be subordinate to politics and the possibilities of planning. However, although such a sparkling intellect as Bukharin may have initially subscribed to this view, and even Lenin seemed to reduce economics to a question of efficient administration, it is obviously naive.[1] This is not simply because the planning process may not have reached a very high degree of sophistication, or because the information available to the planners is inevitably incomplete, or because the planned economy is only a segment of the whole (be that the national or the international economy), but because planning cannot eliminate contradiction, choice and dilemma. Although the future can be predicted and planned for, it can never be organized with absolute certainty. Just as under capitalism, in state socialist societies circumstances and conjunctures will arise which appear to be, and indeed are, independent of human will. Stalin recognized this just before his death when he wrote:

> Some comrades deny the objective character of laws of science, and of the laws of political economy particularly, under socialism. They deny that the laws of political economy reflect law-governed processes which operate independently of the will of man. They believe that in view of the specific role assigned to the Soviet state by history, the Soviet state and its leaders can abolish existing laws of political economy and can 'form', 'create', new laws. These comrades are profoundly mistaken.[2]

Admirable sentiments, if only a little ironic given that Stalin had outlawed all attempts at creative economic thought over the preceding quarter of a century, and indeed sent to his death perhaps the most forthright and creative advocate of this view, namely Evgeni Preobrazhensky. Moreover, and needless to say, Stalin did not develop these points much beyond the level of aphorism.

If these points establish the legitimacy of our quest to uncover the 'laws of motion' of state socialist societies, they also introduce what we believe to be a red-herring, but one which needs to be exposed as such before we can proceed any further. This concerns the relevance of the 'law of value' to the laws of motion of state socialist economies. As we have already seen in Chapter 1, the 'law of value' plays an important part in the analysis of at least one of the theorists of state capitalism (Cliff), something which we rejected then but only on the ground of the *a priori* assumption that it was relevant. Now we must extend our critique and address the question directly.

Orthodox Marxists generally view the law of value as the fundamental regulator of capitalist accumulation. Seen in terms of exchange (as Stalin and others have done), it states that the price ratios between different commodities will tend towards an (equilibrium) position which corresponds to the ratios of labour values embodied in the commodities. The capitalist mechanism is competition among autonomous units in a context where competitively formed price/profitability signals exclusively regulate the allocation of resources. With respect to its possible relevance to socialist economies, perhaps five different positions can be encountered in the literature:

- that the law of value does not operate in state socialist economies and should not (or cannot) operate: this position may be adopted by dogmatic Marxists and by those who reject the application to state socialist societies of categories appropriate to capitalism;
- that the law of value does not operate but should operate (or at least be simulated): this position may be attributed to pro-capitalist western critics, to certain of the decentralizing reformers within state socialist societies, and perhaps also to central planners who believe themselves capable of simulating the 'optimum' solutions of the perfectly competitive capitalist market;
- that a form of the law of value does operate and should operate (or at least be simulated): this was the position of certain east

European planners of the Stalinist era (e.g. Strumilin, a leading Soviet economist and planner);
* that the law of value does operate but should not: this position is common among western critics with their roots in the Trotskyist or the Maoist tradition and is implicit in both the concept of 'transition to socialism' and that of 'state capitalism';
* a cautious agnostic position.

These positions would seem to exhaust the possibilities and are illustrative of the confusion which reigns, as Brus confirms when he writes: 'In hardly any other theoretical problem has confusion reached dimensions similar to those reached in examining the law of value in a socialist economy.'[3] At the end of a lengthy enquiry he himself adopts the fifth, agnostic position.

Our own view is expressed in the first position (though not for reasons of dogmatism!), and is reflected by Bukharin when he wrote:

In the first serious attempt to really scientifically master that highly restless specific state which we call the economy of the transition period, we come up against the fact that the *old concepts of theoretical economy instantly refuse to be of any use* [our emphasis]. We come up against a curious contradiction. The old categories of political economy continue to take the form of *practical generalization* about a *continuously-changing*, living, economic reality. At the same time, these categories do not enable one to penetrate beneath the surface of phenomena, i.e. to shake off vulgar thinking and to understand the process and development of *economic life as a whole*. But this is understandable. By their very nature these elementary relations, which in ideological terms are represented by the categories of commodity, price, wages, etc. simultaneously exist and do not exist. It is as if they are non-existent. They drag out a strange kind of illusory real, and really illusory existence, like the old Slav notion of the souls of the dead or heathen gods in the pious Christian religion. Therefore, the old, tested tools of Marxist thought, coined by Marx on the basis of the very real existence of the appropriate relations of production, begin to misfire .... To make use of these categories for theoretical analysis now presupposes a complete understanding of their significance and an understanding of the limits of their significance and an understanding of the conditions, meaning and limits of their applicability to economic relations which are jumping over to fundamentally different rails.[4]

This is a lengthy quotation, and it might well have been longer, such are the further bold insights which Bukharin offers in the ensuing pages. It is perfectly in accord with our view that the law of value has an apparent but not real place in the analysis of state socialist economies. In stage one the continued existence of an extensive private sector and private trade, particularly in the agricultural sector, might seem, on the surface, to indicate the importance of the law of value. But usually credits, prices, wholesale trade, and employment are being controlled by the state, at least to some degree, thus preventing the law of value from operating freely. (This will be discussed further below.) In stage two the allocation of resources is only influenced to a more or less minor degree by market signals and to point to the limited operation of the price mechanism as evidence of the operation of the law of value, elevating this to the level of being the key analytical focus, is to ignore the main factors governing the economic behaviour of state socialist societies and to assume that the tail is wagging the dog.

Cliff's argument, though, is that the law of value makes itself felt through the international economy and this invites a different reply. First of all, it is true that small state socialist economies pursuing 'open' export-oriented strategies will be subject to the vicissitudes of the international market but, on the other hand, the law of value does not regulate the international economy.[5] Second, Cliff's argument is not actually about small economies and trade but about the Soviet Union and the arms race. The Soviet Union certainly does compete with the capitalist world in the arms race, but it is difficult to see what connection this has with the law of value.

Third, the claim that the 'law of value' provides an operational basis for planning, with the idea being that relative prices should reflect labour values or standardized labour time expended on a particular product, is just silly: it in effect arbitrarily counter-poses one (essentially impractical) method of evaluating the contribution of the worker as a producer to the interests of the same worker as a consumer.

Having cleared away some of the dead wood, we can now proceed to develop our analysis of state socialist economies, to elaborate the economic aspects of a new political economy (the political aspects will be examined in Chapter 4).

UNDERDEVELOPMENT, THE SEIZURE OF POWER, AND RECEIVED IDEAS

In Chapter 1 we identified three main elements in the problematic of socialism and underdevelopment: the material conditions of underdevelopment, the nature of the seizure of power, and the received ideas of socialism, which together would form the initial building blocks in our analysis. As far as the path of economic development is concerned, it is the material conditions of underdevelopment and the received ideas which are important. The nature of the seizure of power does have a bearing on the timing of the transition from stage one to stage two, and from stage two to stage three, but this will be discussed later.

The material conditions of underdevelopment and the received ideas of socialism are important in a fairly straightforward and perhaps self-evident way. First of all, the juxtaposition between underdevelopment and the received idea that socialism requires the rapid development of productive forces in order to eliminate scarcity generates a drive to *industrialize*. Not until the advent of Pol Pot in Kampuchea (and probably not entirely in that case) has the necessity to industrialize been seriously and practically questioned within the framework of socialist ideology. Second, another received idea, that socialism requires that economic activity must be planned, stands on its own and coupled with the above establishes the project of *planned industrialization* which then, in the context of comparisons with advanced capitalist countries, isolation in a hostile environment, and centrifugal tendencies usually becomes the project of *centrally planned, rapid industrialization*.

Nevertheless, although this has been the agenda, putting the industrialization part of it into practice has often been easier said than done. Outside eastern Europe, only China, North Viet Nam and North Korea have witnessed real industrial transformation, with partial success on the part of Cuba though much less than originally planned. However, with the full agenda having become central to Marxism–Leninism it has still affected the behaviour of leaderships, and even if the possibilities for industrialization have been limited, or attempts at it frustrated, they have still regarded the introduction of planning as axiomatic. Thus planning is often introduced well in advance of any real possibility of extensive industrialization and therefore most of what we have to say in this chapter is still relevant to these cases. If the project of centrally planned rapid industrialization establishes the basic direction of the economic development of the new society, then the contradictions which it generates and which form the core of our enquiry in this chapter are even more to the point.

THE RESOURCE-CONSTRAINED ECONOMY

With respect to central planning our basic postulate is that it does not provide economic *control*, a means to attain economic and social objectives along an undisturbed path, but rather establishes a *new set of parameters* within which economic activity takes place. Coupled with the dimension of industrialization, they establish what we shall refer to as a 'resource-constrained economy'.[6] *The principal characteristic of the resource-constrained economy is the continuous reproduction of shortages or, alternatively, continuous underproduction, in contrast to the overproduction of capitalism.* These shortages may be exacerbated by the unanticipated actions of individuals, but in general they can be revealed as a predictable function of the goals of economic activity, the way in which it is organized and the conflicts with which it is associated (although, of course, appropriate investigation may not be undertaken and thus what might have been predicted appears as unanticipated). In other words, from the outset we are not dealing with irrationality, un-trustworthiness, or deliberate sabotage. Moreover, while absolute scarcities associated with backwardness and a 'low level of development of the forces of production' may be an important cause of shortages, as we shall see they do not depend on this either.

This means that we are suggesting that the resource-constrained economy does have 'laws of motion' and that they are different from those of capitalism. They are to be found in the multidimensional conflicts over the distribution of resources with which the resource-constrained economy is associated. These conflicts are part of a reciprocal relationship: they are both function and cause of shortages. They arise over the distribution of physical rather than financial resources, over access to raw materials, investment goods, and consumption goods rather than over access to money because, as we shall see, access to money does not go hand-in-hand with access to physical resources. They will be examined first of all at a general level, and then in more detail, making a distinction between those which are essentially 'macro-economic', in the sense that they involve major strategic allocational decisions made centrally, and those which are 'micro-economic', occurring at a lower level and on a day-to-day basis. There is, however, extensive interaction between the two levels and a mutual reinforcement of the problem of shortage. Particularly because the macro-economic conflicts in general are not exclusive to either stage one or stage two, and the importance of particular conflicts varies between countries, our analysis will remain largely at an abstract level, in a sense constructing an 'ideal-typical' model or benchmark. Later, though, by way of illustration, a view of particular constellations and sequences of both macro- and micro-level conflicts will be brought to bear on the historical experiences of particular state socialist societies.

THE PRIMACY OF DISTRIBUTION

In claiming that the laws of motion of state socialist societies are to be found in conflicts over the distribution of resources, we are also suggesting that *distribution has primacy*. This raises two further sets of questions. First of all, what does this mean and why is it so? Second, what exactly is embraced by the term 'distribution of resources'?

Distribution has primacy in the sense that it is the sphere of activity in which are to be found the fundamental mechanisms which cause state socialist economies to behave in particular ways. This is, of course, in marked contrast to the conventional Marxist approach which would take relations of production as the starting point for analysing a mode of production (as in the orthodox Marxist analysis of capitalism). Indeed, what we are further suggesting is that *the relations of production in state socialist societies, and changes in those relations, are subordinate to distribution*. Thus, whatever the formal content of the relations of production, the actual experience of the individual, for better or for worse, will be a function of shifting distributional conflicts. Events with causes external to the workplace will generally be more important than the immediate experience of different degrees of democracy, hierarchy, or subordination within it: hierarchy, for example, will be more or less tolerable depending upon the tasks which society sets those at work and the resources which it provides to accomplish them. It also follows that pressure for changes in the relations of production will primarily emanate from distributional conflicts.

The reason why distribution has primacy is straightforward. Quite simply, through exercising its planning functions, the state inevitably assumes extended responsibilities for allocating resources and becomes a powerful distributor and arbiter of conflicting claims upon those resources. This, rather than exercising direct power over production, is the principal economic role of the state and it completely transforms a situation in which this distribution of resources was accomplished in an anonymous, decentralized way by the market as inputs and outputs changed hands for money at a micro-level. In taking the allocation of resources out of the hands of the market, access to resources is rendered more important than power over production and, simultaneously, access to the state, as all-powerful distributor, is rendered more important than access to money for gaining access to resources.

Moving on now to the question of what is embraced by the term 'distribution of resources', a useful distinction may be made between horizontal and vertical distribution. The former refers to the distribution of both investment and consumption resources between different sectors of economic activity, while the latter refers to the distribution of resources between investment and consumption, and to the distribution of consumption resources between individuals. In another vocabulary (used in referring to money distributions), the vertical distribution of resources embraces both the functional distribution of income and the interpersonal distribution of income.

However, the horizontal distribution of resources cannot be isolated from the vertical distribution of resources: they impinge on one another, as may be illustrated with the help of Figure 3.1.

The whole box in Figure 3.1 represents the total of available resources divided arbitrarily between the three principal sectors of economic activity, between consumption and investment and, within the allocation of consumption resources, between individuals grouped into quartiles. As an example of the dependency of the vertical distribution upon the horizontal distribution, and vice versa, it can be seen that the resources received by the top quartile in the distribution of consumption within the industrial sector (IC_1) is indeed dependent upon the vertical distribution within the industrial sector (between II and IC, and between IC_1, IC_2, IC_3, and IC_4), but it is also dependent on the horizontal distribution between the principal sectors. In other words the horizontal and vertical distributions interact to determine the allocation received by any particular sector, sub-category, or group.

More importantly, from this it can also be appreciated that there is a large number of potential choices, transfers, conflicts and trade-offs which might be associated with the pursuit of a particular policy. Two relatively straightforward examples are as follows. In order to boost industrial investment a direct decision of the planning authorities

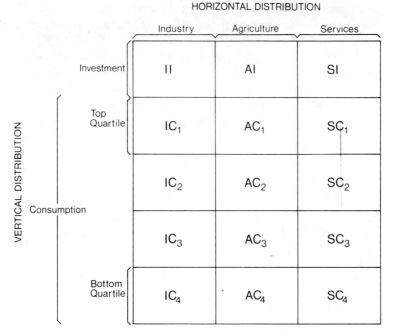

HORIZONTAL DISTRIBUTION

Figure 3.1 An illlustrative delineation of potential conflicts over the distribution of resources

Note: in the text IC without a subscript is used to refer to total consumption in the industrial sector.

might transfer resources away from agricultural investment – a transfer from AI to II. On the other hand, the same objective might be achieved via a movement in the internal terms of trade in favour of the industrial sector which transfers resources away from consumption in the agricultural sector – a transfer from AC_1, AC_2, AC_3 and AC_4 to II. Although the objective might be the same in both cases, the economic and political impact of these two ways of achieving it would obviously be quite different.

However, these illustrations only cover part of the ground. First of all, at a micro-level, individual enterprises and institutions will be jostling for resources within particular sectors and may well frustrate the initially envisaged distribution of resources between sectors. Second, there will be sectors with special claims which may exert a profound influence on the development of the whole economy; here the requirements of the military come most readily to mind. Third, there will be a regional dimension which will assume greater or lesser importance according to the importance which regional grievances played in the revolutionary process, and according to the degree of regional inequality.

To these aspects of distribution must be added three others which do not fall directly within the ambit of the state, namely, the distribution of resources between the state sector and the private sector (more important during stage one than stage two), between the economy in question and the international economy (influenced by external sector policy), and between individuals as they use their positions in a hierarchical division of labour to gain access to additional consumption goods, supplementing 'official' incomes prescribed by the vertical distribution of money income.

Thus it can be seen that the term 'distribution of resources' has many dimensions which permeate the whole fabric of state socialist societies, and the role of the state therefore extends beyond the more limited sphere of producing and distributing 'surplus' generated by the system.

The next step in our analysis will be to explore the main conflicts which arise from and shape the distribution of resources in state socialist societies, and here some anticipation would be useful. As we shall see, the causes of these conflicts are not exclusively those to which we have already alluded in general terms and which might be viewed as historically 'inevitable' (industrialization, central planning, absolute scarcity, and the dialectical relationship of conflict with shortage), but also extend to include 'avoidable' causes such as misconceptions and mistakes, plus non-recurrent events.

Moreover, two further important points need to be noted. First of all, it should be reiterated that although the state is a powerful allocator and arbiter of conflicting claims, this does not also imply that its directors exercise control, because the conflicting claims themselves will absorb much of its independent room for manoeuvre; *the degree of independent control exercised by the state will be inversely related to the degree of conflict over the distribution of resources*. If this were otherwise it would of course be impossible to suggest that state socialist economies are *subject* to laws of motion, rather, they would always be *masters* of them. Second, given the multifaceted character of conflict over the distribution of resources, there is no constant delineation of protagonists: these are always in flux as the requirements of accumulation, and the means of satisfying those requirements, change. Furthermore, given that the state is mediating conflicts, protagonists may not always be able to perceive each other's identity. Both the latter make an important contribution to the general cohesion and stability of the system and are in marked contrast to capitalism wherein, whatever the complexities of class relations, one can at least draw a line between owners and non-owners of the means of production.

MACRO-ECONOMIC DISTRIBUTIONAL CONFLICTS

The approach in this section might be likened to Mao Tse-tung's theses 'On the ten major relationships', but without the political and moral dimensions, and without resort to aphorism and tautology.[7] We focus on six major macro-economic distributional conflicts which cover the most important horizontal and vertical aspects of distribution (industry *v.* agriculture, investment *v.* consumption, and employment *v.* productivity), the most significant special claims on resources (military *v.* civilian expenditure and regional/nationality conflicts) and the two spheres of conflict where the state's influence can only be indirect (national economy *v.* international economy and state sector *v.* private sector).

Industry versus agriculture

We address this conflict first because it both epitomizes the imprint of underdevelopment on the socialist experiment, while at the same time presenting it with its most complex, and thereby difficult, political and economic problems in the context of a drive to industrialize. Much has been written about it. Perhaps the most important features of underdevelopment, and thus of the economies of countries intermediately integrated into the world capitalist system which have been visited by socialist revolutionary seizures of power in this century, are those of a relatively small and usually technologically backward urban industrial sector confronting a large and backward agricultural sector from which the vast majority of the population obtain their livelihoods. This means that the relationships between industry and agriculture, between town and country and between state and peasant assume critical importance for the evolution of state socialist societies.

It is possible to imagine a balanced or proportional expansion of industry, accompanied by a relative diminution in the importance of the agricultural sector, which occurs in a relatively smooth and conflict-free fashion as it generates rising living standards for both peasant and worker alike. However, actual historical experience has been different. Under capitalism the anarchy of the market, extremely unequal distributions of land and incomes, and violence and intimidation have prevented such an outcome. In state socialist societies conflict between industry and agriculture has been due to a quite different set of factors among which the following figure prominently:

- once and for all distributional disequilibria induced by the initial acts of revolutionary transformation;
- the elaboration of specific industrialization strategies with potentially adverse distributional consequences for agriculture;
- closely related to this, the application of received ideas specific to agriculture involving important misconceptions and guided by an inappropriate rationale;
- necessity.

All socialist revolutions inevitably create distributional disequilibria as various forms of exploitation are removed or at least alleviated. Typically, peasants may become owner-occupiers for the first time, lifting the burden of rents previously paid to landlords, while usury may be stamped out and taxation reduced. The latter may also apply to the working class. Furthermore, the corollary of this is that leakages to foreign demand are drastically curtailed as the upper classes no longer have the means to buy imported luxury consumption goods. These sorts of transformations imply a fundamental shift in the structure of demand which, according to Preobrazhensky, was mainly responsible for the 'goods famine' under NEP in the case of the Soviet Union.[8] There the change in the structure of demand involved was a relative increase in the demand for basic, domestically produced industrial goods which could not be met in the short term. Given also that the peasantry still retained the autonomy associated with the continued existence of the private sector in agriculture, they became reluctant to exchange grain for money which could not be spent and instead resorted to hoarding it and speculating, which in turn led to food shortages and spiralling prices. The latter then rebounded on the industrial working class, as the internal terms of trade moved against the industrial sector. More recently similar sorts of problems have emerged in Nicaragua, with a mismatch between the changed structure of demand and the structure of productive capacity inherited from the Somoza regime.[9]

The way in which the project of industrialization, once concretized into a specific strategy, might promote conflict between industry and agriculture is best illustrated in other, more celebrated contributions by Preobrazhensky who, like Bukharin, attached great importance to developing analytical categories appropriate to the specific social formation represented by the new Soviet economy. This led him to formulate his compelling 'law of original socialist accumulation' which was the first attempt to concretize the notion of a 'transition to socialism' by marrying it to an economic theory of industrialization.[10] He argued that, as an underdeveloped country, the Soviet Union was obliged to pass through a stage of 'original accumulation.' However, in contrast to the stage of original accumulation which preceded the development of capitalism, the Soviet Union was placed in entirely different circumstances: it did not have the advantages of access to colonial plunder or slowly accumulated surpluses from the gradual destruction of pre-capitalist modes of production (both at home and abroad) as sources of original accumulation. Nor could it engage in the barbarous capitalist forms of exploitation of the working class which had marked the beginning of the industrial revolution. Nevertheless, the Soviet Union still had to go through a stage of original accumulation and, according to Preobrazhensky, the most important source of surplus would inevitably be systematic transfers from pre-socialist forms of economy within the Soviet Union. This is the 'law of original accumulation'.[11] It embraced the transition to socialism because, as the law worked itself out, it would undermine pre-socialist, private forms of economy, and ultimately eliminate them altogether as the logic of the plan came to predominate over the logic of the market.[12] Whether the law was really a law in a deterministic sense is open to question because other strategies are conceivable: in fact Preobrazhensky himself was later to reformulate it as a 'condition of equilibrium'.[13]

In any event, although Preobrazhensky himself viewed this strategy as being of mutual benefit to peasant and worker alike, it did not bode well for relationships with the countryside because, of course, the bulk of the pre-socialist forms of economy in question consisted of peasant agriculture. Moreover, although achieving a net transfer of resources from peasant agriculture, as opposed to simply procuring a required supply of food for urban areas, is a difficult enterprise, particularly over a lengthy period, and although agriculture did not ultimately prove to be a source of 'original accumulation' in the Soviet Union, Preobrazhensky-style ideas have made their influence felt in other state socialist countries, even if the practitioners have not been directly inspired by his work, or shared his specific motives. Thus the peasantry in state socialist societies have had various forms of surplus extraction tried out upon them, such as outright requisition at prices below the cost of production, taxation, monetary emission (not backed by an availability of goods and services) and the establishment of 'non-equivalent exchange' via pricing policy, with respect to both the direct supply of domestically produced industrial goods and the foreign trade sector. Moreover, such efforts have not necessarily subsided after the socialization of agricultural production.

Closely related to this view of the role of the peasantry and the agricultural sector in socialist accumulation have been two important sets of misconceptions about how the agricultural sector should be socialized and the benefits which would ensue.

The first set had its origins in the pioneering work of Lenin on the development of capitalism in Russia, in which he mechanistically categorized the Russian peasantry into 'kulaks', 'middle peasants', and 'poor peasants'.[14] This analysis subsequently materialized as the underpinning for Bolshevik political strategy in the countryside, both before and after the revolution: the 'worker-peasant alliance' was really meant to be an alliance between the working class and poor peasants and perhaps middle peasants, with the attitude to kulaks definitely antagonistic because they were deemed to represent incipient capitalist development. Here the mistake or misconception was uncovered, and only fairly recently, in a detailed study of the social structure of Russian agriculture in the late nineteenth and early twentieth centuries.[15] It transpires that mobility between kulaks and poor peasants was very extensive, and occurred over relatively short periods, in particular as a result of land subdivision between male offspring: there was no primogeniture. It was, therefore, unlikely that any strong class antagonisms would develop between poor peasants and kulaks, thus rendering any political strategy based on an inflexible anticipation of such antagonisms largely impotent and definitely counterproductive; as in other Slav lands the antagonism of the village or *mir* as a whole towards the towns was always much stronger than any rifts within it, and any attempt to accentuate the latter was only likely to increase the former.[16] Variants of this problem have characterized all succeeding state socialist formations.

A further set of misconceptions surrounds the expected benefits from that symbol of socialist agriculture, collectivization. It has implicitly been assumed that industrial techniques of organization, such as large-scale production units and hierarchical methods of management, can be successfully transplanted to a kind of activity where these may well be counterproductive, and often are in fact.[17] In particular, agriculture embraces crops and husbandry activities requiring vastly different approaches in terms of techniques of production and organization, many of them, indeed, being best accomplished on a small scale with the extensive and painstaking application of individual labour. The blanket socialist vision of the future of agriculture based on collective property alongside that of the state is inimical to this.[18]

In addition, the image of collectivization has also suffered from actually having become a tool in sharp distributional conflicts between town and countryside, being born a child of necessity to ensure minimum food requirements for urban areas rather than as a progressive socialist policy measure with popular support. That this is a misguided and counterproductive rationale is illustrated in the case of the Soviet Union where, with the onset of the collectivization drive, while the rate of grain procurement increased substantially, grain output actually fell.[19] Moreover, as the possibility that agricultural surplus might contribute to industrial accumulation became non-existent, collectivization rebounded on the industrial working class as it had to shoulder the whole burden.[20] All in all, conflict between industry and agriculture, between town and countryside, results in shortages of food and raw materials as agricultural products diminish and/or less of them are marketed. In turn, and in various ways, this inhibits industrial development, thus provoking a vicious circle.

However, some of the conflicts which we have analysed are avoidable, but then perhaps only at the price of sustaining or provoking another set of conflicts. In so far as the latter are associated with the preservation of a substantial private sector in agriculture, they will be analysed in general terms in a subsequent section (state sector v. private sector).

Consumption versus investment

As Mao Tse-tung once remarked:

It is a complicated problem to settle a proper ratio between accumulation and consumption within that sector of socialist economy in which the means of production are owned by the whole people and that sector in which the means of production are collectively owned, as well as between those two sectors. It is not easy to work out a perfectly rational solution to this problem all at once.[21]

Moreover, it is a problem which is intertwined with the choice of technique (the degree of capital or labour intensity of production) and with the balance between capital goods industries and consumption goods industries, or Department 1 and Department 2 in Marxist terminology. The last is the material form which the problem assumes.

The reasons why the vertical distribution of resources between consumption and investment should generate conflict fall broadly into two categories:

• planning in general is conspicuous and is likely to place the planners in a position at odds with particular claims on available resources. This aspect of planning is especially important as far as the distribution of output between consumption and investment is concerned;

• state socialist societies have generally sustained very high rates of investment over lengthy periods and these have been accompanied by an emphasis on heavy industry, implying further sacrifices of current consumption.

With respect to the former the points are these. First, planning is conspicuous because it raises many economic decisions to the collective domain. Second, it involves the state in overseeing the general requirements of accumulation in pursuit of societal objectives, and this role may involve suppressing particular claims of consumers. On the one hand, determining the amount of investment is the most important decision affecting the growth of output (unlike under capitalism demand factors do not exercise an autonomous influence by stimulating changes in capacity or capacity utilization) and thus future living standards. On the other hand, the greater the amount of investment, the greater the sacrifice consumers have to make in foregoing improvement in current living standards. Unfortunately there is no objective way of resolving this dilemma, for the correct course of action depends upon the subjective value which society places upon future as compared to present consumption (or in other words, upon its discount rate).[22] Equally unfortunately, it is unlikely that there will be a societal consensus about the appropriate discount rate. Consumers are generally myopic and like to have their cake and eat it, and their view is therefore likely to come into conflict with the legitimate concern of planners with responsibility for future living standards to take a longer view.

However, such conflict has been exacerbated by the maintenance of very high rates of investment over lengthy periods, and by an attendant emphasis on 'heavy industry'. Three factors can be held to account for very high rates of investment:

- once-and-for-all conjunctural shifts in investment requirements;
- the exigencies of rapid industrialization;
- 'investment hunger' and 'investment tension' originating at a micro-level.

It is immediately clear why a programme of rapid industrialization will imply a heavy burden of investment, and because 'investment hunger' and 'investment tension' originate at a micro-level they will be discussed later in the more appropriate context of micro-economic distributional conflicts.

This leaves once-and-for-all shifts in investment requirements in need of further elaboration. These usually occur most dramatically not long after the seizure of power. Most socialist revolutions have come about during a protracted period of generalized war, often including, or followed by, civil war. Such circumstances, plus economic blockade, have generally resulted in a protracted period of capital consumption, or 'negative expanded reproduction' to use a term coined by Bukharin, as urgent requirements for current output are met at the expense of both new and replacement investment.[23] Ultimately, such urgent requirements for current output subside, in turn giving rise to an equally urgent requirement for a large-scale renewal of capital equipment. Total investment requirements will therefore be boosted by this heavy burden of replacement investment. The Soviet Union has, of course, had to bear this burden twice, after civil war and foreign intervention and then again after the Second World War. Viet Nam, too, had to bear a similar double burden, after the anti-French and anti-US struggles.

While these factors may account for very high rates of investment, they do not explain why the distribution of that investment should be concentrated on heavy industry (the capital goods sector), implying as it does further sacrifices of current consumption. Clearly this has often been related to the requirements of military production (which will be discussed separately in a subsequent section), as well as to other specific pragmatic requirements, but it has also been bolstered by

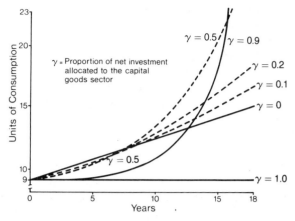

Figure 3.2 Variety of time-paths of consumption
Source: Domar, E. (1972) 'A Soviet Model of Growth', in A. Nove and D. Nuti (eds),
Socialist Economics, Harmondsworth: Penguin Books: 164 (English language rendition
of Fel'dman's ideas)

theory originally formulated by the Soviet economist, Fel'dman. Once
the decision has been taken to go for growth, Fel'dman suggested that
concentrating an appropriate amount of investment in the capital
goods sector would produce higher standards of living in the longer
term than pursuing this objective by investing as much as possible in
the consumption goods sector. Figure 3.2 illustrates this proposition.
It shows a variety of time-paths of consumption growth generated by
the allocation of different proportions of net investment to the capital
goods sector, under the assumption that the incremental capital–output
ratio in both capital and consumption goods sections is three (three
additional units of capital are required to produce one additional unit
of consumption).

The point of reference is the behaviour of consumption when all
available resources are allocated to the consumption goods sector
itself ($\gamma = 0$), since it can be seen that this strategy does not yield the
maximum level of consumption over the longer term compared with,
say, allocating one half of investment resources to the capital goods
sector and foregoing a relatively small amount of consumption for an
initial period ($\gamma = 0.5$). The reason for this is simply that if there is no
net investment in the capital goods sector, its output will remain
constant and thus place a constraint on the rate of expansion of the
consumption goods sector: it will only be able to grow at a *constant
absolute rate*.

Although in a less rigorous form, Preobrazhensky also espoused a similar line of argument in the course of his thinking about how to resolve the 'goods famine' of the mid-1920s in the Soviet Union. He availed himself of every opportunity to expound upon the need to develop the capital goods sector rapidly, if destabilizing shortages of consumer goods were not to arise again in the future.[24]

Sharp conflict between consumption and investment introduces new dimensions of shortage. While the growth potential of different national economic units may vary, as governed, say, by natural resource endowments, the skills of the labour force, and the level of development already attained, there is, as both Kornai and Horvat have suggested, a ceiling on the amount of investment which an economy can productively absorb.[25] Overinvestment beyond this ceiling is likely to prove counterproductive in various ways. Kornai sheds light on this problem by identifying, in general terms, three different sources of investment finance, or methods of 'intertemporal acceleration', as set out in Table 3.1.

Table 3.1 The intertemporal methods of acceleration

Sacrifice	Postponement	Neglect
Renunciation of present consumption (of flow)	Renunciation of present consumption capital formation (of stock)	Renunciation of present consumption and consumer capital formation
The non-satisfied need does not accumulate	The non-satisfied need accumulates	The non-satisfied need accumulates
It is not a burden on, or damaging to, the future	It is a burden on, but not damaging to, the future	It is both a burden on, and damaging to, the future

Source: Kornai, J., (1972) *Rush versus Harmonic Growth*, Amsterdam: Elsevier Science Publishers B.V., Information & Business Division (North Holland): 73.

It is generally assumed that an increase in the rate of investment occurs simply at the expense of an absolute or relative decline in consumption. This Kornai would describe as 'sacrifice', implying that some needs are not satisfied, but that these do not accumulate over time. However, in the context of an overriding drive for industrial growth, very high rates of investment may also involve 'postponement' and 'neglect' which are both more insidious and potentially more damaging in their effects. Postponement refers to giving low priority to particular tasks because they are marginal to the growth process in the short-term. However, these tasks will accumulate and in the longer term they will have to be carried out, imposing a disproportionate burden on future living standards. Typical examples of postponement might be a failure to maintain and/or improve existing roads, or a failure to renew ancient sewerage systems: consumption capital is usually the prime candidate.

Neglect is the most serious category. In common with postponement it will usually affect tasks which appear marginal to the growth process in the short term, and its effects accumulate. However, in contrast to postponement, practising neglect can do irretrievable damage in the long term. Absence of proper forest-management in North Viet Nam, the effects of which were becoming clear by the early 1970s, is a case in point.

That state socialist societies have generally suffered from postponement and neglect can be confirmed even from a cursory appreciation of their economic and social history in this century. In the case of the Soviet Union, these negative consequences of one-sided investment emphasis, or 'rush', as Kornai calls it, are vividly documented by Rakovsky in his commentary on the First Five-Year Plan.[26]

Employment versus productivity

Output may be increased by increasing employment (extensive growth) or by increasing labour productivity (intensive growth), or by a combination of the two. Our contention in this section is that typically in state socialist societies, and particularly in the earlier stages of their development, attempts have been made to increase output by both increasing employment and increasing labour productivity, and that the efforts in these two directions have come into conflict. Increasing employment absorption has tended to depress the rate of productivity growth, or even to negate it entirely: thus the various methods of increasing labour productivity in both the short and the longer run, such as improving the organization of production, learning-by-doing, increasing the speed of work, attempting to reap economies of scale by full capacity utilization and new investment, have not had the anticipated impact. Figure 3.3 provides a dramatic example of the depressing influence of rapid employment absorption on productivity in the Yugoslav metal products industry during the Yugoslav First Five-Year Plan.

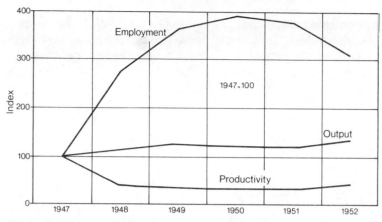

Figure 3.3 Output, employment, and productivity in the Yugoslav metal products industry, 1947–52

Source: *Indeks*, 3(1957) Belgrade: Savezni Zavod za Statistiku and *Privreda FNRJ u Perioda od 1947–1956 Godine*, Belgrade: Ekonomski Institut FNRJ, 1957, Table 341

If the engine behind this conflict has been rapid rates of employment absorption this has in turn been driven by the following macro-level and micro-level factors.

At a macro-level two factors may be at work. The first is that the availability of substantial labour reserves, particularly in the agricultural sector, means that the planners in a state socialist economy will initially perceive no constraints on the pursuit of industrialization based on a strategy of extensive growth. Second, and more positively, the position of the state in a state socialist economy with respect to employment policy is likely to be rather different from that of an individual capitalist entrepreneur because the state socialist state is both a universalistic employer and may also be the guarantor of a minimum standard of living for the unemployed. Whereas the individual capitalist does not assume direct responsibility for the standard of living of people without paid employment, this may not be the case for the state in a state socialist economy, and if so the cost of unemployment will appear directly as a deduction from the surplus available for accumulation. In turn this makes it rational for the state in a state socialist economy to promote employment, even if the consequence is that labour is employed at a loss by individual enterprises. For as long as that loss does not exceed the cost of the guaranteed minimum standard of living, plus the tax revenue lost by leaving idle somebody willing and able to work, the state will gain. In other words surplus will be being maximized by the state rather than by the enterprise - implying an employment policy under state socialism which is different from the capitalist outcome. This proposition is illustrated in Figure 3.4, assuming a fixed capital stock.

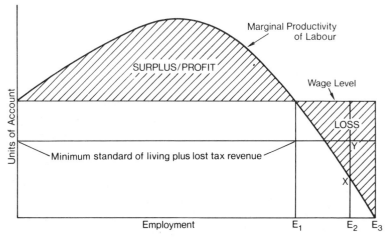

Figure 3.4 Employment absorption and surplus maximization

As employment increases the marginal productivity of labour at first rises (increasing returns to scale) and then falls towards the profit/surplus maximizing employment level for the enterprise (E_1). At this point it would be rational for a capitalist enterprise not to increase employment any further because it would mean employing labour at a loss and a consequent reduction in profit/surplus. However, if at this point there remained a substantial pool of unemployed labour it would be rational, in order to maximize surplus, for the state socialist state to expand employment further – if necessary up to a maximum defined by E_2 (where the loss is equal to the guaranteed minimum standard of living plus lost tax revenue). E_3 is the output maximising position where the marginal productivity of labour is zero.

This employment policy would still be rational even if the state was not guaranteeing any minimum standard of living, and if the problem was not one of open unemployment but of widespread under-employment, for example in the agricultural sector. In the first case, the state may not feel the direct costs of unemployment, but because the unemployed will become a burden on the resources of other individuals, families for example, it will feel them indirectly via upward pressure on the incomes of those in employment. In the second case, which has typically confronted state socialist societies in the early stages of industrialization, underemployment will appear as an opportunity cost to society. (Under capitalism, in contrast, underemployment would be seen as a useful flexible labour reserve and a tool for keeping wages down.) However, in confronting the problem of underemployment the surplus maximising position for the state will depend on the assumption made about the marginal productivity of labour in agriculture. If, as is common practice, it is assumed to be zero, then surplus maximization will still be compatible with a maximum employment level defined by E_2.

It would be wrong to suggest, though, that the above rationale is the only reason for rapid employment absorption in state socialist economies, or even that it is actually understood and acted upon. Other factors therefore come into play and at a micro-level. As will be discussed later in the chapter, the micro-level operation of a centrally planned economy creates powerful incentives to absorb and hoard labour, principally due to the phenomenon of 'suction'.

The result of rapid rates of employment absorption has not simply been a statistical impact on productivity. Conflict between employment and productivity has been actual in the sense that, as we have said, rapid employment absorption has been accompanied by positive attempts to increase labour productivity. In the context of shortages and difficulties in meeting plan targets, the state may typically pursue vigorous campaigns to raise labour productivity, using as vehicles trade unions and peasant and craft organizations to extract greater and greater efforts from workers by way of both moral and material incentives. If such campaigns are continually frustrated by rapid employment absorption they are a recipe for repression and this will be the case particularly if, as is likely, the two conflicting objectives are being pursued independently of each other at different levels in the system and by different institutions. Thus the conflict between the objectives may not be identified, and the resulting problem incorrectly diagnosed, such that workers are held responsible for the non-attainment of productivity objectives and consequently cajoled or coerced into even greater sacrifices.

Military versus civilian expenditure

It has been estimated that the Soviet Union devotes between 8 and 14 per cent of GNP and as much as 25 per cent of industrial production to the military.[27] Viet Nam has the largest armed force in the world after the three super powers, while Cuba's armed forces outnumber those of Venezuela by three to one, and it spends about twice as much on them, even though its population of around 10 million is about two-thirds that of Venezuela.[28] These are clearly large special claims on available resources, and whether or not they are justified by circumstances does not detract from the fact that they introduce, and have introduced in the past, another very important dimension into conflict over distribution. How does this manifest itself?

In the first place that clearly depends upon whether the country in question actually has indigenous military industries. If it has not then military expenditure will represent a significant burden on available foreign exchange resources and, as such, can be situated more appropriately in a subsequent section. This section is mainly concerned with state socialist countries which do have indigenous military industries. The approach will be to review briefly the economic role of military expenditure in the capitalist world, and then to point out some of the ways in which this will differ in state socialist economies.

Until fairly recently, and perhaps contrary to an intuitive view, it was suggested that military expenditure in the capitalist world had had a positive influence on economic performance. It was supposed to have maintained high levels of effective demand and employment, bolstered profit margins, and generated 'technological spin-off' for the civilian economy. Some even went as far as to claim that high levels of military expenditure were the main factor instigating and sustaining the prolonged post-war boom.[29]

In contrast, more careful, empirically based research stimulated by rising popular concern about nuclear weapons has recently been coming to quite opposite conclusions.[30] High levels of military expenditure and productivity appear to be correlated with slow productivity growth, slow rates of output growth, and higher levels of unemployment compared with economies which have not had to bear this burden. The reasons for this, it is argued, are particularly that military expenditure diverts resources away from civilian investment (rather than consumption), is expensive as a way of creating jobs (given that it is largely directed at capital-intensive, high technology industries), and absorbs a disproportionate amount of highly skilled personnel. Further, even though a country may not be dependent on imports of finished military products, military expenditure can still cause balance of payments difficulties, for example due to imports of inputs for military industries, the stationing of troops overseas, or military aid to client countries. Finally, military expenditure creates decadent industrial structures, dependent on and sheltered by military contracts, the sophisticated products of which have increasingly less application outside the military sphere. These problems have increased with time as military hardware has become more and more expensive, specialized, and 'baroque'.[31]

Turning now to state socialist economies, the first point to note is that because supply and demand are planned the possibility that military expenditure might have a positive impact on economic performance by eliciting autonomous demand-side multiplier effects is ruled out *a priori* – the extent to which supply can respond independently to increased effective demand is highly circumscribed by the planning process. On the other hand, in the case of the Soviet Union it has been suggested that there have been important 'spin-offs' from military programmes to civilian industry, although in the main these innovations could have been achieved independently by civilian industry.[32]

This leaves the negative implications of military expenditure and production, and although here too there are significant differences these have the effect of pushing the negative implications in different directions rather than cancelling them out. First of all, in state socialist economies military expenditure is more likely to be at the expense of civilian consumption than investment, although 'postponement' and 'neglect' may also be a consequence. In the capitalist world military expenditure has diverted resources away from civilian investment largely because military contractors have also been producers of civilian investment goods and have given priority to the more lucrative military market. In state socialist economies, in contrast, because this decision is not in the hands of individual enterprises and because investment in general has priority over consumption, military expenditure resulting in a larger number of competitors for investment resources will simply tend to reduce the residual left over for personal and collective consumption. The lack of any autonomous demand linkages between consumption and civilian investment means that this process can proceed unimpeded by any rebound effect on the demand for civilian investment. Moreover, the fact that a particular state socialist country may not possess indigenous military industries does not, of course, make it immune to this sacrifice of civilian consumption rather than investment induced by military expenditure.

Second, security considerations, both those internal to the state socialist country in question and those concerning potential adversaries (which may include other state socialist countries), are, in the context of a planned economy, likely to prevent domestic military procurement resulting in balance of payments problems. Nevertheless, military aid to client countries may have this effect, particularly for the largest state socialist economies. Third, the absence of competing private contractors coupled with the presence of centralized planning means that, while not immune, state socialist economies can avoid some of the excesses of 'baroque' military technology in the capitalist world and also eliminate wasteful duplication by standardization.

However, whatever slight advantages state socialist countries may have in mitigating some of the negative implications of military expenditure are overwhelmed by the burden which military expenditure generally represents for them. Despite the material progress made by the largest state socialist economies, they still lag behind their principal adversaries in the capitalist world while feeling compelled to compete for what they see as parity in the arms race. Moreover, competition within the socialist bloc, between the Soviet Union and China for example, is on the terrain established by competition with the capitalist world. In turn this means that the relative burden of military expenditure will tend to be greater for these economies than it is in the capitalist world, and this also implies the absorption of a larger proportion of available skilled labour. And, although consumption may suffer more than civilian investment, the devotion of resources to the military sector on this kind of scale has undoubtedly affected the quality, technological and otherwise, of civilian investment.

Region versus region, nationality versus nationality

Regional conflicts and conflicts between nationalities have been a particular aspect of the inheritance of some state socialist societies from peripheral capitalism. Economies which have been intermediately integrated into the international division of labour are likely to exhibit a heavy concentration of industry and commerce, in a very few urban centres, surrounded by extensive backward hinterlands with all the major arteries of communication designed to facilitate the export of primary commodities. This spatial distribution of economic activity may have spawned regional or nationality grievances which then played an important part in the political process leading to the seizure of power.

Understandably, after the seizure of power, this gives rise to special claims on resources from backward regions which imply a redistribution of resources away from more developed regions. Moreover, and quite apart from any political promises about greater equality which may have been made, it may be rational, for reasons analogous to those applying to employment policy, for the state policy-maker to support such claims.

Allowing more developed regions to retain their surpluses and invest them where there are existing concentrations of industry and commerce, and greater levels of skill among the workforce, while it might appear to offer the best return, may stimulate not only political conflict but also rapid migration to a few urban centres in the more developed regions. Unemployment and underemployment may build up there, exacerbating income inequalities and imposing a requirement for additional social capital, while wasting social capital in the deficit regions.

Thus the apparent benefits of investing in more developed regions may be outweighed by the more hidden costs, even if these are only defined in narrow economic terms. Redistributing resources away from more developed regions may mean slower productivity growth (further frustrating campaigns to raise it) and slower output growth, but the surplus available to the state for *net* investment may be larger.[33] However, in attempting to meet the special claims of backward regions, the state will encounter ideological objections of a more traditional capitalist sort in the more developed regions, which may not only object to having part of their surplus redistributed, but also be convinced that investing in their own regions would offer the best return to the economy and the country as a whole.

This incipient conflict can become acute, because attempting to create new comparative advantages in backward regions is fraught with difficulties, and the outcome for the backward regions themselves may also be frustrated by rogue factors such as population growth. In Yugoslavia, for example, particularly because of faster population growth in the poorer southern regions of the country than in the richer northern regions, *per capita* income differentials between these regions have actually widened since the Second World War in spite of above average investment in the poorer regions.[34] This kind of outcome is explosive because none of the parties are satisfied: the more developed regions resent what they feel to be the wasting of some of their investment opportunities to no avail, while the backward regions resent the non-materialization of greater equality and clamour for additional resources. Moreover, under these circumstances there still remains a considerable stimulus to migration, and although in the case of Yugoslavia much of it has been abroad, in other state socialist countries it has led to infringements of individual liberty in the form of internal passport systems designed to restrict internal migration.

Regional and nationality conflicts over the distribution of resources therefore continually threaten to dismember state socialist economies, paralyse central policy-making, foster individual grievances, and impair economic performance. Nevertheless, they cannot be avoided: to ignore the problems of backward regions would be to betray one of the justifications for revolutions and, in any event, would not eliminate the conflicts involved.

National economy versus international economy

Although the influence of the international economy on the internal behaviour of state socialist societies may be felt in a variety of ways, from the imitation of products, technologies, and labour practices to the impact of the arms race, it is most direct via the medium of trade in both goods and services (especially financial services). Moreover, this linkage with the international economy stands apart from the others because it is the terrain of distributional conflict between the national economy and the international economy.

Conventionally, in the literature, this issue has been overshadowed by the predominantly internal conflicts analysed thus far, principally because the largest and most mature state socialist societies have been able to opt for limited and tightly controlled interaction with the capitalist world. Their size, inheritance, and natural resource base made this possible, but it was also a question of conscious choice of strategy: although the initial period of revolutionary transformation may have been accompanied by blockade, businessmen have usually been prepared to do business again not long after even very bitter and extended bouts of political and military conflict. Nevertheless, even limited interaction with the international economy has had serious repercussions, as witnessed, for example, by the extremely adverse impact of falling grain prices on the Soviet First Five-Year Plan during the Great Depression.

More recently, though, new developments have raised the profile of the external sector and in some cases the handling of this sector has become the major strategic decision and source of conflict in the process of state socialist accumulation.

First of all, the extension of the Soviet sphere of influence in eastern Europe in the aftermath of the Second World War, while it did not immediately alter the stance regarding the capitalist world, did raise the new question of trading relationships between state socialist societies which, it was supposed, could be undertaken on a mutually advantageous co-operative basis. In fact it fairly rapidly provoked a sharp conflict of interest between Yugoslavia and the Soviet Union.[35] Second, during the 1960s, as the possibilities for 'extensive' growth began to be exhausted, with the absorption of the bulk of the potentially available labour force, the Soviet Union and its eastern European satellites began to display an increasing appetite for imported Western technology, often financed by loans, in an attempt to raise labour productivity and sustain growth rates. North Korea followed suit, as has China more recently. Third, the Soviet Union's agricultural problems have necessitated increased imports of food as has also been the case with other state socialist economies. Fourth, revolutionary transformations have occurred in smaller, more open economies, where the choice between autarchy and reintegration into the international economy has been much more starkly posed.

All of these changes, as we are currently witnessing, have made state socialist societies much more vulnerable to the anarchy of the capitalist world market, and nowhere has this had more serious implications than in the smaller economies. As we have said, for these economies the choices are more starkly posed and there is much more pressure upon them to remain open after the seizure of power. First of all, they may have a very limited resource base. Second, industrial development may be negligible and can only proceed at a very slow pace, if at all, unless there are substantial imports of industrial technology, particularly of capital goods.[36] Third, while revolutions since the Second World War involved economies which have been intermediately integrated into the world economy, the development of the dominant more advanced form of integration (see Chapter 1) has left such countries relatively even more 'backward' in a changing international division of labour. Fourth, these countries may need to import food in order to be able to provide their populations with an adequate diet. Fifth, having only a very limited capability to produce arms these countries have usually needed to import them in order to counter both external and internal security threats. Sixth, in so far as their pre-revolutionary economies have revolved around the export of a limited range of primary commodities, any attempt to disengage from the international economy may imply dramatic and potentially explosive changes in the structure of production. Finally, the strain on the state budget involved in embarking upon a programme of socialist transformation may lead to a need for foreign loans.

On the other hand, while these pressure points clearly represent powerful incentives for a continued integration in the world economy, there are no reasons for expecting that taking up this option in a socialist context will render such states immune to the problems encountered by peripheral capitalist economies, taking the same option. This is particularly because small state socialist economies have little bargaining power. Thus, even though the costs may be shared more equally, export earnings will be subject to the same vicissitudes of the world market, the 'debt trap' will beckon as it does for marginal capitalist economies and inevitably some control over economic activity will be surrendered to foreign enterprises and financial institutions. All of this will further exacerbate conflicts over the distribution of resources. Moreover, the need to accommodate possibly hostile foreign interests will give rise to difficult political decisions. This is exactly the situation faced by Nicaragua today. Like Nicaragua, but with a much longer experience, Cuba also initially set out to diversify through industrialization but the ensuing balance of payments crises led to greater specialization in agriculture and increased rather than decreased dependency on sugar exports.[37] This strategy has only been viable with Soviet assistance.[38]

Unfortunately, though, the alternatives to continued integration in the international economy are not very palatable either. Autarchy, at least from the capitalist world, has been an option taken at certain times by countries like Albania, North Korea, and Kampuchea. However, autarchy can have a price which ranges from not taking advantage of the cheapest, best-practice technology in the world to an actual reduction in living standards, accompanied by horrendous acts of barbarism. Mozambique went a little way along the autarchic road but recently decided that the price was too high and began a politically painful back-tracking.

Clearly the choices confronting state socialist accumulation in small, poor, open economies are painful. History seems to impose an unfortunate choice between autarchy in possibly worsening poverty or reintegration into the international economy in a bid to escape critical resource constraints, involving gravitation towards one of the superpowers in a bid to escape the consequent foreign exchange constraint. Gunder Frank goes as far as to contend that these economies are not in transition to socialism but rather on the road to neo-colonialism on the Kenyan or Ivory Coast models, though probably without the relative successes of these countries prior to their present crises.[39]

State sector versus private sector

The theorists of the 'transition to socialism' focus almost exclusively on this conflict in order to generate their idealist political economy. However, as a preliminary step the analytical terrain must be distinguished from other issues with which it might be confused, including the parameters used by the theorists of transition.

First of all, we are not concerned with this conflict in so far as it is tied up with the struggle for political power. This issue, it is assumed, has been resolved. Second, the questions posed are not the same as those posed by a decentralization of the whole economic system in which the market is allowed to play a greater role. Third, allowing a private sector to exist is not synonymous with allowing the 'law of value' to operate because, as we have already indicated, the activities of the private sector and the operation of the market will usually be tightly circumscribed by their relationship with the state sector. Moreover, in most cases the existence of the private sector does not harbour the threat of a restoration of fully fledged capitalism, for it usually only embraces the self-employed and very small-scale wage labour employers, with the latter being closely supervised by the state.[40] In fact, paradoxically, it may help to prevent the restoration of capitalism.

It should also be stressed that even if the question of conflict between the state sector and the private sector appears to be economically unimportant because most of the national private sector has been eliminated, it may still be a political issue because the reintroduction of the private sector in certain spheres of activity may be seen as a way of solving some of the problems encountered by collective forms of ownership. Moreover, learning from the experiences of some of the more mature state socialist societies, revolutionary regimes of more recent origin may, out of pragmatism, consciously opt not to accept the traditional objective of eliminating the bulk of the private sector and instead preserve it, particularly in the agricultural sector.

Strictly speaking, conflict between the state sector and the national private sector occupies a rather different terrain from the other macro-conflicts which we have been analysing. Distributional conflict arises out of the state ceding *control over production* to the private sector. The state thus mediates conflict indirectly rather than directly by such methods as pricing policy, credit policy, requisitioning requirements and specific circumscribing legislation. The lines of potential conflict in this situation can be sketched out as follows.

On the one hand, some kind of private sector may be seen as desirable because it is the most suitable form of ownership for certain kinds of economic activity, for example, personal services of various kinds and certain kinds of agricultural production which are not amenable to centralized planning, requiring the flexibility and speed of response associated with individual initiative and innovation. In addition, using the private sector may be seen as the only way of stimulating rapid increases in the production of certain goods in the short run.

On the other hand, having a private sector introduces a new dimension of anarchy into the system, but one with different consequences from those ensuing when private ownership is the predominant form. Because the private sector is operating in a resource-constrained environment, then, rather than exhibiting a tendency to overproduce, as under capitalism, it will be facing a sellers' market and will thus be tempted continually to raise prices. In turn this will redistribute income towards the private sector and if its expansion beyond a certain limit is legally prohibited these 'windfall' resource gains will go to swell consumption demand rather than investment demand, placing further pressure on the resources of the state sector, which may not be able to respond. If this is the case the private sector may react to the lack of goods upon which to spend its income by exercising its control over production in the direction of producing and/or selling less, with shortages as a consequence. This whole process also squeezes wages and/or profits in the state sector, making it that much more difficult for the state sector to respond. If these events occur as part of the relationship between industry and agriculture they correspond to the so-called 'scissors crisis' and the kind of scenario analysed by Preobrazhensky (see p.79).

If part of the private sector is in the export sector, in agriculture for example, then its relationship with the state sector has a further dimension. In contrast to the position of the private sector serving the domestic market, the private sector producing agricultural products for the export market faces the probability of sharp fluctuations, and possibly secular decline, in world market prices. If world market prices are rising sharply then the state faces the problems associated with private sector 'windfall' gains, as described above. If, however, world prices fall the state may have to step in to protect peasant incomes, giving rise to a drain on its resources which may be substantial. Moreover, this drain may be part of a vicious circle if there is also a state undertaking to maintain foreign exchange earnings in the face of falling prices by increasing output: this course of action may only serve to depress prices still further.

Those who control the state may react, or may have originally established the rules of the game, by fixing private sector prices and introducing steeply progressive taxation, perhaps by enforcing a policy of compulsory sales or even by establishing production quotas. But then, having circumscribed most of the private sector's sphere of autonomy, expropriation has occurred in all but name and the incentive to produce has been much reduced. In other words the reason for allowing a private sector to continue in existence has begun to disappear. In the case of small-scale agriculture, peasants may exercise their remaining option and revert to subsistence production, which is exactly what happened in Yugoslavia during the First Five-Year Plan.[41]

These, then, are the kinds of continuous conflicts and tensions which underlie the relationship between the state sector and the private sector. In essence they reflect the difficulties involved in managing the trade-off between output growth and equality in income distribution which, at its extremes, offers an equality of poverty or an inequality of riches.

Macro- and micro-levels

Despite the overall systemic importance of all six macro-level conflicts we have discussed, it is at the micro-level, emerging principally out of the framework for economic activity established by central planning systems, that the real engine of the resource-constrained economy is to be found. However, this does not mean that we propose now to examine the mechanics of central planning systems and the problems which they generate in detail; this task has been accomplished by others.[42] The objective in the next section is both much more limited and more general, namely, to provide an outline theoretical sketch of the principal characteristics of a centrally planned economy which lead to distributional conflict at a micro-level.

Our objective, to put it another way, is not to multiply examples like that of the nail producing enterprise which, facing an output target designated in kilograms, chooses to concentrate production on 10 cm nails and to neglect panel-pins, but, given that such examples can be multiplied, to focus on why enterprises should react in this way. In what follows we draw quite heavily upon the work of Janos Kornai, in particular upon his fascinating *Economics of Shortage*.

The principal feature of central planning as it sets the agenda for economic activity at a micro-level is that it transforms the competition for markets of capitalist enterprises into competition for inputs or resources. There is a transition from a buyer's to a seller's market and this implies the continuous reproduction of shortage at a micro-level.

Why this should be so can be explained in four steps describing the obligations placed upon enterprises by the planning authority (the resource constraint), the reactions of enterprises to these obligations ('forced substitution' and 'suction'), and the precondition which allows enterprises to react in the way that they do (the 'passivity' of money). Subsequently we take up specific aspects or consequences of the competition for inputs (investment 'hunger' and shortage and slack), and also consider the role of performance indicators in exacerbating the problem of shortage.

Enterprise versus enterprise

The resource constraint The underlying reason why competition for inputs occurs is the fact that procuring sufficient and appropriate supplies of inputs (including labour power) in order to produce enough to meet plan targets is the main uncertainty facing an enterprise in a centrally planned economy. In turn this goes back to the way in which plans are drawn up. First of all, they are inevitably designed to achieve maximum utilization of available resources, to make the economy operate at its resource limits. Second, imperfections are inevitable both in drawing up and implementing plans. Just as economic forecasters in capitalist economies rarely hit the mark with respect to what the future holds in store, so state socialist planners face analogous problems, although their chances are improved by not having to cope with domestic speculation and autonomous domestic demand factors. Thus available resources may be overestimated and unanticipated delays and bottlenecks may occur, with the latter capable of causing considerable damage because, with the economy operating at its resource limits, there is no slack available to relieve them.

Together with the fact that enterprises are obliged in various ways to meet plan targets, it is hardly surprising that this environment of constantly imminent shortage should cause enterprises to take a strong interest in securing adequate supplies of appropriate inputs. By the same token, this environment and the quite rational reactions of enterprises in their attempt to survive in it, mean that disposing of output, either to other firms or to private consumers (who we shall come to below), will not prove to be a problem: competition for inputs also means a seller's market.

Just to drive home the point that this system is quite different from capitalism, it is worth contrasting the situation faced by a state socialist enterprise with that of a capitalist enterprise. Table 3.2 is helpful in this respect.

Table 3.2 The two pure types of firm, and types of constraint

Type of constraint	Classical capitalist firm	Traditional socialist firm
Resource constraint	rarely effective	nearly always effective, more restrictive than demand constraints
Demand constraint	nearly always effective, more restrictive than resource constraint	rarely effective
Budget constraint	hard	soft
Production plan	autonomous: the firm lays it down at the level of demand constraints; within resource constraints	directive: prescribed by superior authority at the level of resource constraints; within demand constraints

Source: Kornai, J. (1980) *Economics of Shortage*, Amsterdam: Elsevier Science Publishers B.V., Information & Business Division (North Holland): 27.

Whereas, as we have said, the state socialist enterprise faces a resource constraint but no demand constraint, the exact opposite applies for a capitalist enterprise. Because the environment of the capitalist enterprise is not shaped by a plan it is therefore operating more or less in the dark about its competitors' intentions and about consumers' intentions and their ability to pay (goods being rationed by money). Consequently, its preoccupying uncertainty is not generally whether it can produce enough, but whether there will be a sufficient market for what it has produced at some point in the future. Even outside the context of recessions, capitalism is a demand-constrained system. In turn, it therefore also exhibits a permanent tendency to overproduce either because future demands have been incorrectly estimated or because it will be normal practice to hold stocks in order to be able to respond quickly to any market openings which may arise. Thus, just as the operation of a resource constraint and the imminence of shortage means that a state socialist enterprise does not generally face a demand constraint, the operations of a demand constraint and the attendant tendency to overproduce ensures that a capitalist enterprise does not generally face a resource constraint. Moreover, if some form of resource constraint does arise for a capitalist enterprise, the operation of the price mechanism may help to relieve it.

In fact, these differences between state socialism and capitalism were already appreciated by Soviet economists in the 1920s. Kritsman, for example, writing in 1924, asserted that 'in the commodity-capitalist economy there is a general slack, and in the proletarian-natural economy a general shortage', and at another point,' in the commodity-capitalist society the crisis appears in the form of an overproduction crisis, while in the natural proletarian society it appears in a contrary form: in the form of an underproduction crisis'. Similarly, in 1926, Novozhilov wrote: 'instead of a general over-production crisis a general commodity shortage develops.'[43]

Forced substitution and suction However, the resource constraint facing state socialist enterprises is not just a function of planning to produce at resource limits, for it is further tightened by the practice of what Kornai terms 'forced substitution'. If an enterprise is actually unable to secure adequate supplies of an input necessary to the production of a particular product but is still obliged to meet its plan target for that product, it may resort to what is a forced substitution by another, less appropriate input, but one which will allow the job to be completed. The immediate consequence of forced substitution is that it exacts a large toll in terms of generating waste and, by the same token, increases shortages. On the one hand, more costly inputs than necessary may be substituted in order to be able to produce a particular product. On the other hand, cheaper, lower quality inputs may be substituted such that the product does not satisfactorily fulfil the task for which it was designed, thus giving rise to consumer dissatisfaction or adversely affecting the quality of other products (if it is an investment good). At the extreme it may have to be scrapped altogether.

A secondary and extremely important consequence of forced substitution is that it directly increases shortages throughout the system because one enterprise may be finding unplanned suppliers and/or using inputs legitimately required by other enterprises. In other words, forced substitution causes a 'supply-side multiplier': forced substitution leads to further forced substitution throughout the system.

The overall consequence of the fierce competition for inputs by enterprises engendered by resource constraint and forced substitution is encapsulated by Kornai in the term 'suction'. Uncertainty about the future availability of adequate supplies of appropriate inputs leads enterprises to 'suck up' whatever inputs are available (including labour), even if they are neither strictly appropriate nor even necessary to the task in hand (the latter can always be used to barter with other enterprises in order to obtain inputs which are necessary). One aspect of this process is the overstatement of input requirements to planning authorities by enterprises, something which will be discussed below with respect to investment goods.

Suction, then, reproduces shortage, which in turn propels further suction and, it should be noted at this point, even though absolute scarcities associated with backwardness or a 'low level of development of the forces of production' may make a contribution, *their essential causes are to be found in the mechanisms of central planning and they can therefore be present even after a state socialist economy has attained a nominally high level of development.*

The passivity of money The ability of an enterprise to engage in 'suction' immediately reveals another important aspect of the operation of this system which provides the permissive precondition for suction to be able to occur, namely that of the 'passive' role played by money. Clearly, if enterprises are able to acquire inputs willy-nilly, they are not being subjected to any kind of financial discipline: using

Kornai's terminology (see Table 3.2) a state socialist enterprise only faces a 'soft' budget constraint, in contrast to a capitalist enterprise which may be forced into insolvency as the price for immoderate behaviour.[44] As Brus puts it, 'Money is not an active instrument affecting the movement of factors in the reproductive process, but on the contrary is its passive reflection'.[45] Because a state socialist enterprise is supposed to be fulfilling directives issued by a higher authority, if it can justify its actions as being in the line of that duty it is absolved of financial responsibility: means of exchange will be forthcoming as the servant rather than the master of the enterprise and the system.

The advantage of this state of affairs is that it recognizes that most of the factors affecting the financial performance of an enterprise are outside its control. Its disadvantage, of course, is that it provides a licence for the kind of arbitrariness associated with suction, and removes the incentive to improve efficiency.

Investment hunger An important specific manifestation of suction is investment 'hunger'. As Kornai comments, 'If there were no other factor making its influence felt in this direction, investment hunger and its result investment tension, would be enough to transform a system into a shortage economy.'[46] It is important both as cause and effect of shortage.

From preceding sections it can be appreciated that the endogenous causes of investment hunger are both reactive and permissive in character. On the one hand, investment is understandably perceived as a solution to the problem of shortage. On the other hand, it is not trammelled by financial considerations: in sharp contrast to capitalism, the passivity of money decouples investment from risk. However, investment hunger is further reinforced by the general prioritization of investment in the context of the society's drive to industrialize in order to break out of underdevelopment and 'catch up' (as discussed on p.83), and by the attractions of increased size for the status of an enterprise and its director. With respect to the latter, an enterprise director who did not present expansion plans would not be held in very high esteem.

Inevitably, though, investment does not serve to alleviate shortage because it simply adds suction associated with 'investment tension' to suction associated with the requirements of current production. Investment tension has three main aspects, described by Kornai as follows:

1. In the course of the official approval of investment projects the total of claims always surpasses prescribed investment quotas. There is tension between claim and quota.

2. Many investment projects approved cannot be carried out with the planned input–output combination and by the planned schedule. The investment plan is taut.

3. The initial demands of firms and non-profit institutions whose investment projects have been officially approved cannot be fully satisfied from the physical supplies from firms producing and selling investment goods and services. There is a tension between initial demand and actually available real resources.[47]

An important specific consequence of investment tension is that it makes it extremely difficult to meet urgent unplanned investment requirements, and these are thus likely to cause havoc should they arise. This incapacity is important because urgent unplanned investment requirements are indeed likely to arise continuously due to cost and time underestimation in investment applications. Given that partially complete projects are unlikely to be left to die for want of resources, enterprises know that the critical moment for their investment plans is in obtaining permission to make a start: they will thus tend to try and err on the side of underestimation in order to obtain that permission. In turn, the planning authorities continuously face overruns and suction in the form of unplanned claims on available resources.

Needless to say, investment hunger and investment tension also contribute powerfully to the general tendency to overinvest and thus to the problems with which this is associated, as discussed in the section on consumption versus investment.

Shortage and slack: a seeming paradox and another source of waste Without further reflection it would be understandable to conclude that planning to produce at resource limits, plus the impact of suction, would ensure an economy in which resources were being fully utilized. Paradoxically, however, this is not the case, for resources can only be utilized to the extent allowed by the availability to enterprises of all inputs in their appropriate proportions, and clearly suction may restrict the availability of some of them. If this is the case then the level of output from an enterprise will be governed by the availability of the input in shortest supply, giving rise to 'slack' as other complementary inputs, including labour power, are rendered idle. Evidently this is a further source of waste to be added to those arising out of forced substitution.

So, shortage is not incompatible with the existence of slack, with an economy in which, although resources are intended to be fully utilized, in fact they are not. Moreover, this kind of slack is quite different from the kind which typically appears in a capitalist, demand-constrained system. First, it is *non-mobilizable*, i.e. it is useless without the input or inputs which are in short supply. Figure 3.5 is helpful to illustrate this contrast.

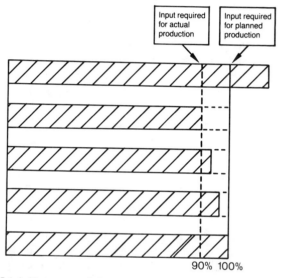

Figure 3.5 (a) Shortage and slack in resource-constrained production
Source: Kornai J., (1980) *Economics of Shortage*, Amsterdam: Elsevier Science Publishers B.V.: 34

Figure 3.5(a) represents the position likely to be faced by a state socialist enterprise with five complementary inputs depicted by shaded blocks. The unbroken vertical line depicts target output. The broken vertical line depicts actual output as constrained below target output by the availability of the input in shortest supply. The surplus of inputs extending beyond the broken vertical line is non-mobilizable slack. Only two inputs are available in sufficient quantity to meet the requirements of the plan.

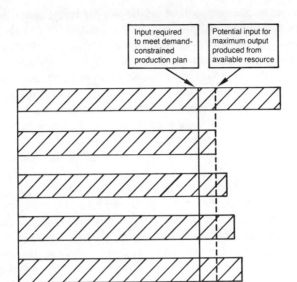

Figure 3.5 (b) Slack in demand-constrained production
Source Kornai J., (1980) *Economics of Shortage*, Amsterdam: Elsevier Science
Publishers B.V: 35

Figure 3.5(b) represents the position likely to be faced by a
capitalist enterprise. The unbroken vertical line depicts actual output
as constrained by market demand. Like the state socialist enterprise
the capitalist enterprise does have excess capacity or slack at this level
of output, but unlike the state socialist enterprise part of this slack is
mobilisable: sufficient amounts of all inputs are available to be able
to produce the level of output depicted by the broken line, should
demand increase.

Second, in a state socialist economy, suction means that all
available slack will be situated *within* the enterprise: it will be internal
slack. In contrast, the capitalist enterprise operating in a demand-
constrained economy will also usually draw on considerable external
slack, particularly of labour power in the form of the unemployed.

Performance indicators While our main concern has been with
different aspects of suction, an endogenous process which feeds upon
itself, it is also important to note that an independent source of
shortage and conflict may arise through the use of specific
performance indicators to target the operations of enterprises. Thus

while the example, cited earlier, of the nail enterprise producing only 10-cm nails and no panel-pins may be the result of forced substitution under circumstances in which there was a shortage of appropriate inputs for producing panel-pins, it may also be the result of an enterprise attempting to meet an output target designated in kilograms by the simplest route. While this kind of behaviour on the part of enterprises is given the label of sabotage more readily than is forced substitution, it is also indicative of real problems which absolve enterprises of at least some of the responsibility.

First of all, for enterprises to behave in this way dire consequences such as loss of income, dismissal from post, or even loss of personal liberty and threats to personal safety must have been looming for non-fulfilment of plan targets. A less severe regime might have elicited more rational responses from enterprises. Second, planning authorities do face real problems in laying down plans for enterprises. On the one hand, it is impossible to lay down a plan in sufficient detail to remove ambiguity and local discretion, even if this was thought to be desirable. On the other hand, all conceivable global measurements of success or failure suffer from drawbacks of one kind or another. We have already mentioned those pertaining to gross output in physical terms. If the yardstick was gross output expressed in terms of monetary value, then analogous problems would arise as enterprises sought to produce low-bulk, high-value products. If it was value-added or profit, achieved results might well be arbitrary if an enterprise could not exercise control over its wage fund, wage rates, investment funds, and prices – and allowing this kind of autonomy would mean the re-emergence of the problems associated with a demand-constrained economy, substituting macro-level problems for micro-level problems.[48] Nor, unfortunately, would the apparently attractive alternative of using a synthetic indicator resolve the problem, for it is highly likely that some of its components would be incompatible.

Consumer versus consumer It is the individual consumer who suffers most in a state socialist, resource-constrained economy: as the system's residual, he or she pays the price for its shortcomings. The prioritization of investment, investment hunger, and military expenditure suck goods out of the consumption sphere where, in addition, shortages are exacerbated as consumer is pitted against consumer in the bid to obtain desired provisions. Thus consumers, too, engage in suction and forced substitution, accumulating unnecessary and even unwanted stocks of goods as they become available. Moreover, if money cannot be spent on anything even remotely satisfactory, cash balances will increase as consumers are forced to save, and this endows consumers with greater suction power should desired goods become available. It is a logical consequence of such circumstances that privilege should become associated with direct access to goods and services, rather than with the possession of money.

However, the latter does not mean that money is unimportant for, unlike enterprises, consumers do face finite budget constraints in the form of money incomes and only limited access to credit. Rather, it would be incorrect to focus on money incomes and their distribution as the *major* source of conflict and dissatisfaction for consumers in state socialist societies. Whereas in a capitalist, demand-constrained economy, access to money automatically ensures access to desired private goods and services, in a resource-constrained state socialist economy, where most consumer goods and services are neither being rationed by price nor simply rationed, access to money is only the first hurdle. The real problem for consumers is the shortage, quality and variety of consumption goods and services; translating access to money into access to desired goods and services. By way of illustration, the peasantry may appear to have a reasonable standard of living as evidenced by the purchasing power of their marketed output in terms of industrial goods, but this will be meaningless if the industrial goods required by the peasantry are either not available at all or of low quality and/or in the wrong assortment.

THE DYNAMICS OF UNDERPRODUCTION

By now we have established that state socialist accumulation is characterized by continuous underproduction, the permanent reproduction of shortage reciprocally related to macro- and micro-level distributional conflicts. Furthermore, we have noted that in certain cases micro-level conflicts serve to reinforce tensions associated with macro-level conflicts. Thus suction in the labour market reinforces the promotion of rapid employment absorption, while investment hunger reinforces the subordination of consumption to investment. Now we must turn to the dynamics of the system and address more specifically the question of its 'laws of motion'.

Early on in the chapter we asserted that the laws of motion of a state socialist economy were expressed through various macro-level and micro-level distributional conflicts which were subsequently analysed. However, to be able to suggest that *laws* of motion are at work it would also seem necessary to ask whether the conflicts together manifest any *regularities* or predictable tendency towards a recurrent outcome, be it some kind of 'equilibrium' or some kind of 'disequilibrium'.

If an economic system is to exhibit regularities then it must also have inbuilt self-regulating mechanisms analogous to the stock signals and price/profitability signals of capitalism. In a mature state socialist economy of central allocation, Kornai suggests that such control mechanisms do exist at a micro-level, that enterprises do adjust their behaviour in the direction of restoring or preserving what is perceived as the 'normal' state of shortage.[49] One such feedback mechanism, he suggests, is 'queueing time', a measure of the intensity of shortage prevailing at a particular moment in time. When queueing time becomes longer than 'normal', enterprises may leave the queue to take up alternative courses of action (e.g. forced substitution), thus restoring 'normal' queueing time. However, Kornai is keen to stress that 'normality' is in no way analogous to the neo-classical, Walrasian concept of equilibrium for it does not involve a situation in which buyers and sellers are satisfied. Rather, *it is a steady state of chronic shortage*.

On the other hand, once macro-economic conflicts are also brought into the picture (something which Kornai does not consider), the power of these micro-economic laws of motion diminishes, particularly for smaller, less mature state socialist economies. The problem is that the macro-economic conflicts cannot be expected to exhibit regularities: they shift in intensity and importance over time. Thus the intensity of conflict between industry and agriculture is likely to diminish as industrialization proceeds; the intensity of conflict between employment and productivity is likely to diminish as available labour reserves are absorbed; the conflict between military expenditure and civilian expenditure will vary in intensity according to changes in perceived security requirements; and the conflict between the domestic economy and the international economy will increase as the former becomes more open. In other words, the macro-economic conflicts are constantly challenging perceptions of what is a 'normal' state of shortage, thereby undermining its validity as an operational concept at that level.

It may now seem that in questioning the concept of 'normal' shortage and thereby whether there can be any recurrent tendency towards such a macro 'steady state', we have also forfeited the possibility of identifying a recurrent tendency towards some kind of disequilibrium. If there are no regularities in the system taking it towards the equivalent of an equilibrium, if there is no constantly delineated and identifiable steady state, then regularities taking the system towards disequilibrium or crisis would also seem to be ruled out. In fact, though, this is only the case if disequilibrium is seen as necessarily juxtaposed with equilibrium, whereas *a resource-constrained economy is characterized by constant disequilibrium, by constant underproduction and shortage towards which there is clearly a recurrent tendency*, even if this disequilibrium can only be loosely defined in terms of greater or lesser shortage. However, this kind of disequilibrium associated with permanent underproduction does not easily wear the label of crisis in the more cataclysmic sense in which one might refer to a 'crisis' of capitalism. Rather, it is more analogous to creeping inflation; it is an insidious condition pervading the economic life of the society and to which people adapt.

Further to this, there is another sense in which distributional conflict creates a tendency towards disequilibrium, or rather towards a critical conjuncture, but this time on a longer-term basis and on a grander scale. We refer here to the role of distributional conflict in bringing about fundamental reorientation in the organization of the economic (and political) life of state socialist societies; to its role in driving these societies through the three stages identified right at the beginning of the chapter, consolidation, application of received ideas, and decentralization. We wish to dwell at greater length on this issue.

The transition from the first stage to the second stage initially appears to belie any attempt to detect economic laws at work. Viewed in a way different from ours, it is consonant with the Marxist–Leninist concept of revolutionary stages and as such is doctrinally bound to happen, given that the ultimate objective is to inaugurate a 'transition to socialism' and that stage two represents the initial understanding about how this should be accomplished. In addition, the length and character of stage one has been influenced by local peculiarities and by the timing of the revolution in question. Thus, being the first country of socialist revolution, this stage in the Soviet Union was relatively protracted, particularly because the failure of the revolution to spread beyond its borders created political uncertainty, an ideological vacuum, and political struggle. Subsequent revolutions, benefiting from Soviet advice and the example of the Soviet model, or effectively sponsored by the Soviet Union, could move much more quickly. Yugoslavia, for example, introduced its First Five-Year Plan as soon as 1947, China in 1953. Also, some revolutions, and most notably the more recent, have not been exclusively fashioned by socialist ideology or always happy with Soviet tutelage, and this too has had its effects upon this stage of development. Thus, in Cuba the revolution was only retrospectively theorized as following the orthodox stages after it had been formally designated 'socialist' in April 1961.

Nevertheless, macro-economic distributional conflicts have had some bearing on the precise timing of the transition from stage one to stage two. Thus, as in the case of the Soviet Union, the inauguration of comprehensive central planning, Five-Year Plans and collectivization can be related to conjunctural conflict between industry and agriculture, between investment and consumption, between military expenditure and civilian expenditure, and between state sector and domestic private sector, and can be seen as a way of shifting the balance of these conflicts to give priority to industry over agriculture, investment over consumption, military expenditure over civilian expenditure, and state sector over private sector, in other words as measures more pragmatic than socialist in intent but capable of finding legitimation through received ideas.

Once embarked upon stage two, though, distributional conflict becomes much more powerful as a motor of change, as the inauguration of a fully fledged resource-constrained economy, continuous underproduction, chronic shortage, and the resultant strain on the social fabric of state socialist societies drive these systems towards stage three. Making money 'active' rather than passive, tightening budget constraints by using money and prices to distribute resources, beckon as apparently the only way of breaking out of the vicious circle of suction and shortage. And, for this to be possible or meaningful, it must be accompanied by decentralization of decision-making and deconcentration of scale: financial discipline can only become an effective sanction if the ties between state and enterprise are loosened. Moreover, decentralization and deconcentration may appear to offer new possibilities for political democracy, to offer people better channels for exercising political control over their immediate environment.

However, the move towards decentralization/deconcentration has been slow and laboured such that, as we have said, most state socialist societies remain trapped in variants of stage two. Only Yugoslavia has really made a full transition to stage three. To explain these differential rates of progress the nature of the seizure of power in specific cases may be the key.

In the case of Yugoslavia, at least, the revolution was endowed with a massive popular base as manifested in the 800,000-strong National Liberation Army which finally freed the country from Germans, Italians, Hungarians, Bulgarians, and their quislings, and prevented either the royalist Chetniks or the Red Army from gaining a foothold.[50] Later this was to have two important consequences in the context of the initial adoption of an exaggerated version of the Soviet resource-constrained economy and the sharp distributional conflicts to which this rapidly gave rise. First of all, the Yugoslavs were sensitive to Soviet attempts to subvert their national independence, leading to the break with Stalin in 1948 and a subsequent willingness and need to subject to criticism their experiences with the Soviet resource-constrained economy. Second, given the popular base of the Yugoslav communist revolution it seems unlikely that the leadership of the party was either able or willing to engage in the kind of centralized coercion for which their exaggerated version of the Soviet resource-constrained economy called: dealing with the few recalcitrant 'Cominformists' (the name given to Stalin's Yugoslav supporters) was a less difficult option. In particular, almost half of the National Liberation Army had been made up of peasants and most of the remainder had close links with the countryside which a lengthy guerrilla war had only served to strengthen. Thus, the inauguration of the First Five-Year Plan in Yugoslavia was not the signal for rapid collectivization, and when the leadership was later spurred into this by concern about food supplies to urban areas and by Stalin's taunts about being 'soft on kulaks' it quickly drew back in the early 1950s in the context of its own lack of conviction and of widespread peasant discontent about other aspects of its agricultural policy.[51]

Thus it can be seen that the nature of the seizure of power was a crucial interventionary element in propelling the Yugoslav revolution towards stage three. Decentralization/deconcentration was also a political alternative to coercion.

In contrast, the foundations of power in the Soviet Union were fundamentally different. The Bolshevik revolution was an urban insurrection which, although it was accompanied by widespread peasant rebellion, had only marginal links with the countryside. It was largely consolidated there by the use of force and thereafter the peasant was generally considered to be politically suspect. The Soviet regime was therefore willing to use and capable of using coercion to implement its plans, particularly in the agricultural sector. Coercion was thus an option in the Soviet Union and later in its satellites to preserve the social fabric against the ravages of underproduction, something which has impeded moves towards stage three. Hungary, of course, had seen socialism basically imposed by the Soviet army, but the popular uprising in October 1956 set in train events which led eventually to the movement towards stage three. Only thus could the Soviet-backed regime increase consumption and become acceptable.

With an eye to the future, it is possible to speculate that transition through stages one, two, and three is not the only scenario for some state socialist societies which are presently still in the throes of stage one. Here the reference is to the more recent revolutions in small, previously open economies which have chosen to remain open and which may never in fact make the transition to stage two. This possibility arises not just because these revolutions may not have been exclusively fashioned by socialist ideology, but because of the much higher profile of the conflict between the domestic economy and the international economy, and a correspondingly greater degree of vulnerability to external influence. Coupled with a desire to be non-aligned and the benefits of hindsight with respect to the problems of the resource-constrained economy, this could result in a gradual transition straight from stage one to stage three as a way of appearing both less controversial to the capitalist world and still acceptable to the Soviet Union and/or China.

Finally, we would make the following short conclusion upon our attempt to outline economic 'laws of motion' for state socialist societies. Three main points can be made. First, we have identified a recurrent tendency to underproduction and shortage. Second, we have indicated how some or all of the distributional conflicts which are reciprocally linked with underproduction and shortage have played or are playing a role in driving state socialist economies through different stages of development. Third, in identifying these tendential laws we have shown them to be fundamentally different from those which drive capitalism. This may not seem much, but probably in the final resolve nothing more specific is known about the laws of motion of capitalism. Moreover, we have now laid the necessary foundations to be able to approach the question of politics and power in state socialist societies.

4

The politics of state socialist societies

In Chapter 3 we deliberately held the analysis quite rigidly at the economic level in order to expose the central dynamics of the transformation which takes place in underdeveloped societies which are able to follow the state socialist road. That permitted us to postulate the emergence of a resource-constrained economy which has its own distinctive characteristics. However, in doing this we in fact artificially separated the economic from the political sphere. In reality, of course, the policy decisions involved in the state socialist transformation and their execution, including – it might be said pre-eminently – those in the economic sphere, are governed by the demands of the reproduction of the system, that is, by the issue of political power and its uses.

In this, state socialist systems do not differ from any others. Thus politics in them is also the crucial sphere in which economic and most other social activities are generalized onto a society-wide basis and integrated in a way which sustains the various forms of unequal power relations which characterize them. Typically in their predecessors this meant the power of male over female, age over youth, landlord over peasant, capitalist over worker, and so on. The contradictions implicit in these relationships pose the question of inequalities of power. The interplay of contradictions and shifts in the balance of importance among them may lead to political change, sometimes of a radical, even revolutionary nature. State socialist systems do differ quite markedly from others, with respect to their typical contradictions, we would argue, and this is because the specific nature of their politics is something quite different from other systems.

The single most important factor which was left implicit in the whole discussion in Chapter 3 was the meaning for the role of the state of a situation in which nationalization, central planning, and at least some industrialization are laying the foundations for a resource-constrained economy. In all societies the state apparatus (seen, it should be remembered, as involving an institutional complex, concentrated power and authority) is by far the most important single element in generalizing and integrating power relations in a way which sustains patterns of dominance. The point about the politics of state socialist systems, as we have already noted, is that there is a law of constant tendency for that apparatus to extend its direct control over all aspects of civil society.

At this point in the discussion we are introducing more directly into it than before the concept of a dichotomy between state and civil society. Again, this is an artificial separation, since the state apparatus in fact plays an active role in maintaining the conditions for the existence of civil society and in shaping its relations. But it is central to our argument that *in all previously existing societies the bases for the existence of classes and other social groups have lain outside the state apparatus*, even though their relations may only have been completely realized through it.[1] Thus, for us, civil society is a complex of social relations among men and women, landlords and peasants, capitalists and workers, and so on, which express their nature as social beings engaged in practice (activity). It is out of this complex that the material and cognitive bases of class and other social identities emerge, expressed in economic roles, gender stereotypes, patterns of consciousness, organizational affiliations, and many other ways.

The essential feature of state socialist systems, as the phrase suggests, is that their basic dynamics, above all economic ones, impel an increasing encroachment by the state apparatus upon civil society. This may be seen as a process of 'colonization', akin to that which historically created most of the countries on the capitalist periphery (though with the very important difference that the original capitalist colonization came from outside). Thus, under state socialism:

- state representatives are placed at all strategic points in order to ensure control of power by the centre;
- everyone is reduced to a common status of 'subject', with no autonomous power bases;
- all real possibilities of social advancement are channelled through the state apparatus;
- a new ideology/value system, assumed to be superior to all others, is imposed through it.

These points will be taken up in detail below. In general we stress that the final effect of the process of colonization is that if its dynamics work themselves out completely the socialist state in effect swallows up civil society. *It does not just continue to be the chief agent of the necessary process of the political generalization and integration of relations in civil society: it tends to become identified with it.* In the original frontispiece of Thomas Hobbes's famous treatise, *Leviathan* is portrayed as a crowned giant whose body is composed of those of many ordinary human beings. A similar image might be used for the socialist Leviathan state, for one of its main tendencies is to swallow up all the elements of civil society, at the same time digesting them in a sort of homogenization process. It is the details and results of that process which will concern us in this chapter.

THE CONCENTRATION OF POWER

The basic process whereby the socialist state 'colonizes' civil society is by concentrating all significant sources of political power, previously distributed (though unevenly) throughout society, into itself. Basically the causes of this and the forms in which it occurs are conjunctural in nature, stemming from the circumstances of the seizure of power in conditions of underdevelopment and the demands of the situation in the next few years. Above all, socio-economic conditions on the periphery produce small 'vanguard' revolutionary leaderships with complex multiclass and group followings, while politically their struggle is usually illegal and violent.

In Chapter 2 we attempted an analysis of the vitally important period during which the revolutionary movement takes position amidst the range of contradictions which implicitly at least challenge the continuation of the existing regime and then manoeuvres itself towards actually taking state power. As suggested there, many of the characteristics of that struggle have a determining effect upon what occurs after that seizure.

Most important of all is the nature and role of the 'vanguard' which has led the struggle. Its existence, of course, is one of the central tenets of Marxism–Leninism, the most important of the received ideas on politics which have been passed on from the experience of the Soviet Union. It seems self-evident that the organization of illegal and hence clandestine political activity, or even legal forms of activity but with revolutionary intent, demand great dedication and tight discipline. This is more the case when the seizure of power takes a military form, as usually happens. Guerrilla comradeship must go hand in hand with the strict carrying out of orders, and if necessary yield to it. Hierarchy must prevail over democracy, the balance of practices implied in the doctrine of democratic centralism swings always towards the attenuation of the democratic element and the continual increase of centralism. Here let us turn to the problems which seem to follow from vanguard party leadership.

It has already been pointed out in Chapter 2 that not all revolutions in underdeveloped countries, not even all those which in the name of socialism take a 'statist' direction, are led by something which claims to be a vanguard party and organized completely on Lenin's Bolshevik model. Sometimes, as in the case of Ethiopia, where the building of socialism came onto the agenda after a military coup, there was no leadership by a party at all, or even by some looser political organization. In Chapter 2 we indicated that cases like Ethiopia are for us extreme ones, but that of Zimbabwe is closer to the point. There it was not until mid-1984, more than four years after it actually took state power, that ZANU-PC declared itself to be a Marxist–Leninist vanguard. However, *in the conditions of winning power on the capitalist periphery all political configurations which are in some degree inspired by the received ideas of socialism contain an element of vanguardism.* (In any case, military leadership is 'vanguardist' virtually by definition.) Moreover, whatever may be their intent, the kind of objective conditions outlined in the previous paragraph will always tend to propel revolutionary groups on the periphery in these directions.

That being the case, a number of situations may arise. Even where the party is relatively open and seeks to recruit widely, it develops an inner core which increasingly monopolizes decision-making and expects obedience. Where the party is part of a wider movement, in alliance with other parties and with organizations of special interests (women, students, ethnic minorities) grouped round it, it attempts to infiltrate and control these, and may even create them as its direct instruments. Where a party as such does not formally exist and leadership is in the hands of a broader, looser movement or front (26th July in Cuba or the Sandinistas in Nicaragua), the central leadership core in fact behaves as a vanguard and has its expectations, at least once differences among themselves have been resolved.

It is obvious that, given these alternative patterns, a very important factor is the solidarity of the central group of leaders. This may, of course, be affected by such factors as class background, regional and ethnic origin, variations of ideological orientation, and role in the struggle. Part of the war of manoeuvre in particular is thus usually a contest among leaders and the elimination of some of them; the result is to make the remainder an even more cohesive body. On the other hand, where organization is through a looser movement or front, autonomous power bases for some leadership elements may continue to exist, such as trade unions, with consequences which we shall examine later.

At this point the discussion needs to broaden from the leadership to the rank and file. A major part of the war of position, as we have argued, consists of building a broad base of support, at least in the sense of making people willing to defy authority and deny themselves in order to supply guerrilla fighters, which greatly extends the problem of discipline. Beyond that, of course, the demand may be for work, recruits, demonstrators (perhaps in the face of armed troops or police), and other actions and roles implying sacrifice. In order to achieve this support much emphasis is, of course, laid on ideological and moral persuasion, the by-now notorious issue of 'winning the hearts and minds of the people'. On the other hand, it must not be forgotten that discipline is also imposed by revolutionary movements on both members and the broader spectrum of supporters by coercive means, often including execution.

Where the revolutionaries have control of whole 'liberated areas', a tradition going back to Kiangsi, Yenan, and other localities in the Chinese case, they will be able to reinforce nocturnal proselytizing or armed swoops with daily administration. This constitutes, in appearance at least, an embryo state apparatus, an alternative to the one they are trying to seize. Liberated areas are also usually the scenes of attempts to apply economic and social reform measures which are held to prefigure what will happen in rural areas after final victory.[2] The point is that great care must be paid to examining what actually happens in terms of democracy and popular control. Such 'democratic' claims are almost always an important part of the rhetoric used, and there may be institutional changes which suggest a practical reality, an apparatus of 'people's councils' and committees. Moreover, the heavy emphasis often placed on mass mobilization to compensate for material and technological shortages gives a democratic impression. However, behind rhetoric, institutions, and mass mobilization there may well be manipulation and even coercion. The democratic acid test must surely be whether policies suggested by the leaders are ever rejected by the majority (if indeed they are even put up for consideration) or reversed after popular debate on their effects.

In practice, for reasons to which we shall come, institutional arrangements and methods pioneered in liberated areas – which do not in any case always form part of the revolutionary struggle – tend not to be taken over effectively into politics and administration once state power is seized. Rather, two other aspects of mass involvement seem to have more lasting long-term effects. First, at least where there has been a protracted armed struggle, and above all where this has led to large-scale battles involving regular forces, a considerable degree of militarization of the broad support of the revolutionary party or front may have occurred. Hierarchies and tables of ranks, distinctive dress and insignia, demands for immediate and unquestioning obedience, rewards graded according to rank, all applied to tens or hundreds of thousands of people, are not good preparations for democratic socialist relations under the new order. A countervailing tendency may be intensive politicization of the ranks and a fostered spirit of comradeship irrespective of rank, but a contradiction is bound to exist, with pressures towards a spirit of 'commandism', at least among cadres. A combination of vanguard party and widespread militarization is particularly problematic.

Politicization of the rank and file is the second important issue affecting the base of the movement. The problem is that usually this is likely to be broad but shallow, or where it avoids the latter the explanation is that the leadership has tapped some very deep, even pre-colonial, roots. Perhaps the most prominent example is the ability over the years of Vietnamese communists to secure a virtual monopoly of the theme of patriotism and resistance to foreign invasion. In some cases the timespan of the struggle may be comparatively short (Cuba, Nicaragua), giving insufficient time for thorough political work. Again, effective contact with large numbers of people may be made only at a very late stage; in Nicaragua even rudimentary liberated areas only came into being in late 1978, little more than half a year before final victory. There are, however, usually much deeper obstacles to the full politicization of the mass base (by which we mean not merely their mobilization but the development of some capacity to evaluate what is happening and participate in decision-making). These obstacles stem from the nature of the base itself and its organizational expression. As we argued in Chapter 2, the very nature of the underdeveloped social formations on the periphery means that the revolutionary blocs which may be constituted will contain a wide range of class and other social elements. That being so, as we also pointed out, the ideological cement which is used must necessarily be capable of binding all of these, hence the prevalence of national and populist themes rather than explicitly socialist ones. Indeed, if questions of class interests, or feminist concerns, for example, were to come to the fore, they would at this stage probably cause division rather than foster the unity upon which the leadership places a premium.

It is to the leaders that we must return for a last point on the question of ideology and consciousness. Obviously they are by definition much more educated and aware than their followers, particularly since they are drawn for the most part from the urban, better-schooled levels of the old society. Not only this, however, but in the course of struggle ideas work their way very deep within them. It must be recognized that the leadership pays a price, as does the rank and file, perhaps not so often death or torture (though frequently these as well) but the sacrifice in many cases of career, relative wealth, and family life. The reward is often a self-image of dedication to principles and programmes, absolute and unyielding political and ideological honesty. Inevitably this phases into a sense of moral rectitude. Not only open enemies but in the end all who disagree with central decisions, especially those who do not abandon their position in the name of democratic centralism, become not merely wrong but morally tainted, fit to be loaded with epithets – 'petty bourgeois' and 'individualist' are favourites – and subjected to disciplinary measures.

Much of the above may appear to be a calumny upon a whole series of revolutionary leaders on the capitalist periphery – on, say, the Ho Chi Minh of 1954, the Fidel Castro of 1959, or the Samora Machel of 1975. The intention is not to suggest that some secret longing for power was their 'real' motivation, and the movements they led undoubtedly liberated the vast majority of their peoples. The point is, rather, that from the moment they seized control of the state apparatus they were involved, like others of their kind, in a process which is foreordained by any attempt to build socialism on the periphery through giving Marxist-Leninist received ideas material form. The intensely contradictory nature of the experience before coming to power lies in the fact, as we shall show, that much of the liberation struggle prepares the ground for features which hardly seem to be socialist.

Turning to the situation once power is won, in case after case we see *the continued use of the existing state apparatus rather than an attempt to smash it and build a radically different one.* This issue was, of course, classically raised by Lenin in his *State and Revolution*, on the immediate eve of the Bolshevik revolution of 1917, and what in fact happened in Russia again set the classical pattern. Once in the seats of power, Lenin and his comrades ignored almost all the fine talk about elections for all offices, non-professional bureaucrats, and no special salary scales, and in effect retained and expanded the old centralized ministerial and departmental structure, along with much of the existing personnel. This pattern has been basically repeated in every subsequent case, representing in fact a sort of grafting of some new political elements onto the old administrative structure. Why, then, is this pattern so common? Is it to be ascribed to an absence of real revolutionary zeal on the part of leaders, to a secret desire for power? In most cases not: motives are in any case more complex than that. The proximate cause at least is the existence of immediate intense demands upon the new rulers.

Taking control of a country which has just fought a guerrilla struggle or civil war, or at least been disrupted by intense political crisis, while at the same time promising massive improvements in the lives of most people, is a situation of immense pressure. Vitally important decisions have to be taken at once. Should bank transactions be immediately frozen and prices controlled? Which bureaucrats should be retained from the old regime (if they have not fled)? Which supporters of the previous government should be arrested and which left free? In matters of government, decisions can only be taken in the context of established structures and procedures which permit the use of stored information, the systematic relation of new decisions to old ones and of ends to means. (Can a decision be carried out anyway?) What must be at hand, therefore, from the beginning, is the necessary apparatus to provide these things and other essentials. There is no time to build from scratch, so the overriding tendency – despite ideological notions to the contrary – is to see these apparatuses as neutral, just as usable for socialist construction as for administering capitalism. The pressure to use what is directly at hand proves overwhelming.

Another element of the immediate post-seizure situation in past cases and in almost any foreseeable future case, is the threat from outside the country, or even within it. Unless victory has been absolutely complete there may still be armed forces of the old regime in outlying areas, regrouping to launch a counter-attack. Otherwise they may be just across the border, commanded by the newly exiled and supported by the USA, Britain, France or one of their surrogates like Israel or South Africa. Grenada in October 1983 (after a coup by the Marxist–Leninist faction) showed that direct foreign intervention remains a possibility if the international conjunction permits it. (In other words, the USSR is prepared to keep effectively silent.) In such a situation, attempting to restructure the state radically may seem at best quixotic, at worst lunatic.

Beyond these immediate issues lies another which goes deeper. Even where there have been liberated areas of some long duration, the sort of Marxist–Leninist influenced movements which have come into being up to now have in practice not made concerted efforts to have new blueprints ready and new doctrines of administration developed *before* coming to power. Thus, even assuming for the moment will and possibility, there are no concrete measures which can be taken. In fact, the reverse happens. There usually are initiatives from below at the moment of seizure, on the local level of districts, wards, even whole towns, and of factories and plantations, in which supporters of the revolution take control of administration. Part of the first phase after the seizure of power then becomes the reassertion of central control.

Assuming that the new rulers are able to extend their hold fully over the national territory, avert foreign-backed counter-blows, and begin to take enforceable decisions on policy matters, certain further tendencies begin to take shape. (In fact, there is no neat sequence, and Mozambique is a case in point. Although by 1986, a decade after independence, the FRELIMO leaders could not in fact assure any of the basics just mentioned, they were also well into the process about to be outlined.) This is the consolidation of political power, which has three main features.

First, the leadership completes the process which, as we saw above, already probably began before the seizure of state power, namely the elimination of dissident elements within itself. This is particularly the case where the struggle has been waged through a broad movement or front embracing a variety of organizations and class elements, since the revolutionary hard core is impelled in the difficult post-seizure circumstances to extend its previous dominant influence into complete control. Above all, in such circumstances, this involves effectively eliminating members of the old capitalist and petty bourgeois classes, along with middle-strata elements most closely aligned with these, or at least subordinating them and ensuring that they no longer have autonomous power bases as part of the general colonization of civil society. This is, of course, related to the establishment of control over private enterprise leading up to its nationalization. A ready pretext may be found in the previous associations of their classes in general with the old system, and in the cry that they are in league with foreign enemies and exiles. On this basis the elimination and subordination usually prove quite easy.

With the effective elimination of capitalist-aligned elements from the revolutionary front (in situations where they entered in the first place on a 'national democratic' basis), the threat of a possible restoration of capitalism, though with little material foundation as we shall note below, still remains a powerful ideological weapon for the leaders who survive. It can be used, for example, as part of the second main aspect of the consolidation of their power. Civil society is further colonized by the destruction or complete subordination of all remaining independent parties, trade unions, peasant organizations, and the like. Thus even bodies representing class forces in contradiction with capitalism can be said to be acting 'objectively' in favour of it, for example by demanding better supplies of consumer goods or the ability to sell produce on an uncontrolled market. Alternatively, especially with regard to some unions, the allegation may be made of 'ultra-leftism', of failing to understand the real needs of the moment, say by demanding immediate wage raises in face of promises of future amelioration of conditions of underdevelopment. It is possible that the new government may have good arguments for resisting all these demands; our doubt must begin to be expressed when the result is removal, even imprisonment of leaders and banning of organizations, usually involving the establishment of a monopoly over membership on the part of state- and party-sponsored unions and others. In the case of political parties, though, it may be found useful to retain some carefully controlled ones separate from the dominant party, in order to give orchestrated expression to the social role of, say, 'patriotic' businessmen. This technique has been used for long periods, for example, in China and Viet Nam.

The question of parties brings us to a third, enormously important aspect of the consolidation of their power by state socialist leaders. The most significant single feature of the political life of their systems is that at the centre lies the vanguard party with an avowed allegiance to Marxism–Leninism. In the older cases the party led, or at least took part in, the struggle leading up to the seizure of power. In the more recent examples, particularly where they stemmed from an anti-colonial struggle fought on national and democratic lines, the party or front has often only announced its transformation shortly before or even after coming to power, in the People's Democratic Republic of Yemen, for example, or Mozambique. In Cuba also a wholly new party was created, absorbing the old communist one. Whatever the pattern, however, an inevitable process, already predicted by Trotsky in response to Lenin's 1902 views on leadership, seems to set in sooner or later. This we may term substitutionism. By a sort of double movement at the ideological level, *the party in effect substitutes itself for the working class (and by extension peasantry and other labouring people) which it claims to represent and the leadership substitutes itself for the rank and file.* That is to say, the party identifies itself so closely with those classes that it in effect assumes that anything it chooses to do *must* be in their best interests, and even that merely by joining it a person assumes a working-class identity. In this sense, such are the powers of received ideas that its leaders, who assume an absolute monopoly over decision-making, *become* the working class and the rest as far as policy is concerned. Moreover, on the same basis, they assume a total moral authority.

In the name of the dictatorship of the proletariat the party then goes on to permeate every level and activity of the state apparatus, though it would be a mistake to assume complete identity of state and party and the impossibility of a clash of interests between their different personnels. Nevertheless, for a full combination of political control and policy execution, both are necessary. The case of Ethiopia, noted in Chapter 2, emphasizes this point; there the military leadership came round to setting up a Commission for Organizing the Party of the Workers of Ethiopia after the state had already taken on many 'state socialist' characteristics. A government stemming from a coup carried out by dissident officers and NCOs, admittedly with mass urban support but no party or even front organization, felt impelled once it had decided to term itself Marxist–Leninist to have such a vanguard.[3] Once again, the power of the received ideas (and also in this case the direct influence of the Soviet Union) is clear, but even more so the logic of development of the system for which the leadership had opted.

Undoubtedly the most important single function which the party performs in state socialist systems is to support the various arms of the state apparatus in their mobilization efforts. However, the maintenance of public order and security are also key activities. Starting from the immediate post-seizure uncertainties, control of the population indeed becomes one of the major occupations of the state apparatus. Moreover, this is a centralized control, despite the existence of militias, local committees, or whatever, since these are under the direction of both state and party, which also operates from the centre outwards. Indeed, part of the assertion of control by the central state over civil society may even be the use of legalized terror on a large scale. State socialist systems are always marked by structures of popular participation which may be quite elaborate in nature, and may even include, directly on the Soviet model, a special apparatus of 'people's control committees', the function of which is to check bureaucratic activities and protect citizens from abuse. However, in situations where – to mention only the main factors – party and state enforce a monopoly of political organization and supervise any other kind, monopolize ideology and ideas in general, claim to represent the only legitimate authority, control if not most employment then the most prestigious jobs, and decide who can stand for election, political control from below must be a highly qualified concept.[4] It follows from this characteristic of the political system that the spheres of law, education and culture, and the media are also brought under the control of party and state.

Expansion in such latter spheres is, in fact, characteristic. First, there is normally a massive extension of the educational and cultural spheres, and also of health facilities. Provision of these is, of course, laudable and counts among the real successes of state socialism (leaving aside for the moment the very important qualification that the former sphere provides opportunities for ideological manipulation). The point is that they represent a major growth point of the new state apparatus. A similar point must be made with regard to the expansion of the armed forces, also a feature of these systems. Under the constant threat of attempted counter-revolution or foreign intervention this is entirely understandable, but again has an impact on the state. Given that the regular forces are usually backed by the training of popular militias on a large scale, which also have to be incorporated into state planning systems and supply networks, this feature represents a significant militarization of the state, and also of society at large, which of course reinforces emphases on discipline and hierarchy. Such a tendency is further strongly supported by the related expansion of the security apparatus, which also involves a not insignificant number of people and, like the military, is often extended on a part-time basis into society through some variant of 'committees for the defence of the revolution'.

A final point must be made concerning the international role which the state in these systems immediately takes on once power has been seized and consolidated. In all cases so far, and in all foreseeable future situations, power will be seized at the 'national' level, since that is the territorial basis upon which the state exists. (Even in the colonial cases which are now behind us, territory and a colonial extension of a metropolitan state coincided.) Socialist revolutionaries thus take control of a specific state apparatus committed to certain frontiers and with long-standing interests in such things as migration, transport networks, access to the sea, and water supplies, which transcend those boundaries. Ideologically they also cannot avoid historical concepts of regional influence, 'lost' territories, and the like. This identification of the new socialist state with territory and interest may well make the new ruling elite an uncomfortable neighbour, and just as nationalistic as, if not more so than its pre-revolutionary predecessors. This is particularly so if the pre-revolutionary appeal of that elite has been as much nationalist as socialist. As we have seen in terms of the China–Kampuchea–Viet Nam triangle, war may even result between 'fraternal socialist' states.

THE SOCIALIST LEVIATHAN

The discussion so far is intended to serve as an elaboration of our basic proposition that the currently existing form of socialist state has a built-in tendency to swallow up society, to subordinate all else in the most direct way to the exigencies of the new system of power. The reasons which we have so far given for this have been basically conjunctural in nature, related to the forms and circumstances of seizure of power and the immediate demands of consolidation after it. The explanation, however, needs to be deepened.

We have seen that these regimes are the products of the materialization of 'socialist' received ideas through particular kinds of leaderships in circumstances where revolutionary blocs can be built and manoeuvred to victory. Once in power the revolutionary leaders are impelled by doctrine, conviction, and the conditions of underdevelopment to launch a process of transformation of social relations, to which we shall turn next, and to begin to build a new kind of mode of production which, as it develops, provides the parameters for a resource-constrained economy. At this stage of the argument let us emphasize the importance of the latter as an underlying cause of the emergence of the socialist party–state political system. In analysing the emergence of the resource-constrained economy we presented it as the product of the demands associated with a combination of central planning, state ownership, and industrialization. This, as we tried to show, produces entirely unintended results. The point is that all aspects of the process imply centralized political control. That is obvious in the case of central planning and, in so far as the basic economic units are an extension of the centre in the planning system, applies to them. Since various parts of the Leviathan state may also be seen as being in contradiction with one another (the heart of the dialectic which creates the tensions in the resource-constrained economy), it is evident that a premium will be placed on attempting to assert the power of the centre to counteract the distortions caused by 'suction' and other unplanned phenomena.

From this characteristic of the economic system a constant effort follows to find political and administrative means to compensate for inadequate economic control. This, along with the great increase in the role of the state apparatus, as most of what was organized in civil society comes to be relocated there, means a massive expansion of the institutional network and therefore of state personnel. New bodies proliferate and old ones are extended. New ministries, boards, departments, and so on are fitted in or tacked on until the organizational chart is likely to resemble the wildest efforts of a home electronics hobbyist designing his or her own system.

Nor is the simile misplaced, because one of the basic weaknesses that results is precisely that as information systems, and hence as decision-making and executing vehicles, the new apparatuses are likely to be unwieldy if not almost unworkable. After all, most of the decisions taken in the whole of civil society previously are being assumed by the state. The characteristics of economic enterprises, it may be argued, are taken over by the administrative system generally. 'Suction' occurs because each department attempts to ensure that it has enough resources, above all personnel, to meet any new demand from above. Demands produce the phenomenon of 'forced substitution' to meet them, especially in so far as this carries over from economic activities. (Administrative personnel may even be diverted to directly economic tasks, such as bringing in a harvest.) 'Shortage' of resources and 'slack' in performance can also be found quite readily in bureaucratic structures. One common result is what has been referred to as a 'simultaneous surfeit and dearth of information at all levels'.[5] Duplication of authority and inadequately defined administrative procedures are only two of the other main problems which beset socialist state apparatuses.

Moreover, a gap tends to open between those at the centre who give orders and the executants further out in the system, the result of these cumulative problems, but also of another, even more deep-rooted characteristic of the system. As Konrad and Szelenyi point out, the concentration of so many functions in the state apparatus involves 'an enormous number of concrete, hierarchically ordered decisions, unsurveyable as a whole'.[6] As a result, those at the centre tend to view problems ideologically rather than technically. Doctrine begins to conflict with administrative reality, in the sense that what it is deemed 'must' be done intervenes between the would-be controllers of the system and perception of the real nature of the problem.[7]

It is important to notice that this increased emphasis on central control and monopoly of power is caused by developments *within* the state apparatus, once its post-revolutionary consolidation is complete, and takes place there. Conversely, what we have described as more conjunctural causes for the extension of state power immediately after the seizure of power are determined by relationships extending outside the apparatus and even outside the country. The point is that, irrespective of these conjunctural factors, *the deeper-seated causes, expressed in the sort of centripetal tendencies of power within the apparatus itself, are an expression of the innermost logic of state socialist systems as such.*

They are not short term, conjunctural, or external but trends of long duration and the most basic character. Through them the Leviathan state, by tending increasingly to swallow up all else, takes its most significant form.

Indeed, it is because the concentration and monopolization of power are inherent in the very nature and logic of these systems that none of them can remain immune from such phenomena. On the other hand, their different historical backgrounds and concrete circumstances after the revolution will ensure that the *speed* at which the process unfolds and the *degree* of its development will vary. Nevertheless, Leviathan will always try to emerge and grow, and he will not be a deformation of a previously healthy body. On the contrary, the conditions of peripheral capitalism, which we looked at in Chapter 2, are often those of endemic crisis and the new state socialist regime will have come into being because of this. A marked feature will have been the weakness and/or incompetence of the state apparatus, another the poverty of 'modern' organization within civil society, a third chronic rivalries among classes and their parts, regions, and religious and ethnic groups. It is these which the ruling party and its state are impelled to overcome by monopolizing organization and enforcing unity.

Conversely, it is evident that in a number of state socialist systems such phenomena are strong enough to block a full development of Leviathan, particularly when fostered by outside forces. Thus, as already mentioned, the state apparatus and bureaucracy may be largely inherited by the new regime. Lack of organizational experience on the part of fairly large numbers of people means educating them in participation from scratch. This is not to suggest, however, that there is no organization at all. The problem is rather that much of it may be religious or 'tribal' in nature and often inimical to the secular message of socialism. This links with the third factor mentioned above, the strength of special interests which often represent a tradition predating even colonialism, while on the other hand they may have been actively fostered by it, as with 'tribalism' in Africa. It is on that continent, indeed, that the capacity of a Marxist–Leninist Leviathan to carry out its own kind of colonialism seems most inhibited.

As this new kind of state begins to swallow up civil society, then, all sorts of social groups are involved. The most important of these are whole social classes, and it is to what happens to them that we first turn.

SOCIAL TRANSFORMATION IN STATE SOCIALIST SOCIETIES

It was shown in Chapter 2 how Marxist–Leninist revolutions are born out of the complex social structures and relations which characterize the intermediately-integrated countries of the capitalist periphery. With the seizure of state power begins a process of transformation of class and other social relations. This is like no other which has gone before and implies that we must begin to think of what, in other societies, are termed classes in a very different way. As a further general remark, it should be stressed that, while making all due allowance for historical, cultural, and other variations, the tendencies to be outlined below have occurred in every 'Marxist–Leninist' case so far and it can confidently be predicted that they will appear in future ones.

A twofold enterprise is launched after the seizure of power. First we find the destruction of old classes. The process is now not the sort of evolution of new class relationships, often over long periods of time, that we have seen in the past. Individuals do not gradually fall into place until whole structures appear, like sediment slowly forming sandbars, with occasional revolutionary flash floods to sweep them (partly at least) away. There is now a conscious direction, based on an explicit concept of existing classes (whether accurate or not), with a conscious intent of rapid but controlled change.

The second undertaking tends to become prominent somewhat later than the first – indeed, is partially dependent upon it. As previously existing classes are broken up and transformed, groups and individuals are allocated a place in society less now by conscious intention of the new ruling elite than by the effects of the emergence of a resource-constrained economy and the Leviathan state. As all previously existing class positions are redefined in terms of their members finding a place as one or another variant of 'working people', *individuals derive social position not from a relation to property in civil society but to their location in the system of distribution of resources, both means of consumption and means of production, by the state apparatus.* Moreover, this is secured by a diversity of participations, as employee of one or another sector of the economy, by residence in a particular location, as employee of a specific enterprise, as member of a consuming household, and so on. These are no longer necessarily held together by a cross-cutting homogeneity of class membership and depend directly or indirectly on the state apparatus, not on corporate or individual decisions outside it. In that way, social fragmentation is a result of the swallowing of civil society by the state, but it also facilitates the process.

The implications of these last points will be brought out later. Here let us concentrate upon the phase of transformation of the old classes. Basically, the leadership, informed by its received ideas, designates some classes as enemies and others as friends of socialism. This in itself is not invalid. It is indeed scarcely likely that landlords, if such a class exists in the pre-capitalist sense, and/or capitalists will look with favour upon a doctrine which speaks of revolutionary change on behalf of workers and peasants. Though some of them may, for particular reasons, have joined the revolutionary bloc, it was not in order to lose property and position but rather in face of the competition and violence of one of their own number turned dictator, like Batista or Somoza, or in the name of nationalism, or both. Other classes after the revolution may be regarded as being in the balance, capable of favouring the new socialism or of supporting a capitalist counter-blow. This particularly involves what Marxist–Leninists commonly call the old and new petty bourgeoisie, what in Chapter 2 we separated as a petty bourgeoisie which is pre-capitalist in origins and middle strata which are more closely bound historically to capital. The leadership's distrust, informed by received ideas, usually also extends to rich and upper-middle peasants.

In all cases, the will of the leadership is directed towards the transformation of the old classes, in the case of landlords and capitalists to the extent of abolishing them as such. It is land reform which deals the former their mightiest single blow, expropriating their basic means of production completely or reducing them to an average level. The blow is doubtless genuine and radical; it is difficult to conceive of establishing a socialist system without land reform, and it does destroy the old social relations which determined the existence of the peasantry. (Again, it must be said that a landlord class in the sense used here is not to be found in most African or some Asian countries, and has largely been transformed into a rural sector of capitalism in Latin America.) As for capitalists, they are tackled by nationalization, whether they be urban or rural in location. However, this usually takes place over a somewhat longer period than land reform, and the old employers of wage labour find themselves in turn employed if not in retirement, perhaps as managers in their own former enterprises, or somewhere else in the bureaucracy. Again, as with the ex-landlords, their further transformation has to be on an individual basis, learning, along with their families, to be the 'new socialist person' beloved of official ideologists.

The reverse side of these two transformations is, of course, that of peasants and workers. Above all, they will no longer be confronted by the exploiting classes which previously defined their existence. Their basic social relations will no longer be with other classes at all but with the state apparatus and moreover, as we have seen, at an economic level these relations are fragmented, particularly for the working class, and no longer involve surplus extraction in the old sense, as we shall see later. All this means that class relations are essentially reduced to political relations, to ideological constructs in the hands of those who control the state apparatus. As a preliminary generalization it is clear, therefore, that *the use of the term classes is taking on a new meaning when we define the nature of some as being determined by the interposition of the state without the old 'classical' dominant classes behind it and with the absence of any homogenizing economic relationship.*

Transformation of the peasantry in state socialist systems is radical, and not only because of the removal of landlords and capitalists. It has internal aspects for one thing, involving a change in the internal stratification of the class. Accepting for the moment the terminology which is customarily employed by the leadership, rich and upper-middle peasants tend to be reduced during land reform to the level of middle-middle or even lower-middle peasants from the point of view of control of the means of production. Poor peasants and landless labourers usually gain and thus move up to lower-middle or middle-middle status, in other words with sufficient means at their disposal to make a living under normal conditions using only family labour. In this way a sort of 'compression' of the peasantry takes place, making the old categories, in themselves fairly imprecise, no longer of any real analytical use. This can be a problem when they continue to be used as the basis for the 'class line' if collectivization is attempted. The period of land reform may be marked by struggle and the resistance of rich and upper-middle peasants, but in many past cases has been surprisingly quick and without open conflict; what later became the Democratic People's Republic of Korea seems to hold the record for speed, a claimed three weeks in March 1946.

Land reform does not, of course, abolish private property; indeed, it extends the control of the majority of peasants over the means of production through legal ownership (or through direct use if land is nationalized). In this way a sort of 'independent' peasantry is formed, which has to be tied to the state apparatus by means of its purchase of produce and sales of producer and consumer goods, either through its own direct agents or co-operatives, and by taxation. Similarly, the provision of credit helps tie the new peasant producers into state policy and planning. The situation can be left at this, but with two implications from the point of view of the leadership. First, in practice, political and economic control over what in fact constitutes a majority of the population will never be complete. This is above all the case when it becomes necessary to leave an important part of trade in agricultural produce to the free market. Second, at least as the leadership sees it, partly because of the working of market forces, a new process of differentiation among the peasants will begin, creating a new rich (*kulak*) stratum and making others once more short of land, animals, and tools.

The answer suggested by doctrine is, of course, collectivization, which would complete the transformation of the peasants into something quite new. By no means all state socialist systems take this second step, however, and some have even reversed it temporarily (Mongolia) or permanently (Yugoslavia which, of course, went on to break altogether with the model). Cuba, by nationalizing sugar and cattle enterprises, has created state farms rather than production co-operatives, so that the bulk of those employed in agriculture are wage labourers.[8] This has probably helped to restrict the free market because, conversely, it has to be remembered that even full collectivization, that is, with all significant means of production owned by the collective, does not imply the abandonment of all crop- and livestock-raising on private plots with family labour. Significant resources may be left in private peasant hands. In class terms, the phenomenon means that the transformation of the peasantry is not fully carried out. Developments in both China and Viet Nam in recent years, with important parts of production formally contracted out by the collective to individual households, seem to indicate that in certain circumstances the tendency may even be partially in the opposite direction, as part of the third phase of economic development predicated in Chapter 3.

The petty bourgeoisie of small producers and traders experiences a process of class transformation closely allied to that of the peasantry. Again, the basic point is that their determining relationship is now with the state apparatus, not the capitalist class. It must be stressed that, usually in conditions of the capitalist periphery, the petty bourgeoisie is a very numerous class and of considerable economic and social significance, producing the bulk of consumer goods and many means of production and controlling much of the direct retailing of goods to workers and peasants. It is also at the heart of the so-called 'informal economy' which, as noted in Chapter 2, provides the crucial if minimal income which keeps many urban migrants going.

In doctrinal terms this class is destined for transformation and, indeed, ultimate disappearance, with its members absorbed into the new working class or collective peasantry. Again, the means chosen for this are producer or trading co-operatives. In practice the class may diminish little if at all, substantial numbers of traders remain independent and totally within the free market, and even though formally incorporated into collectives artisan producers go on 'moonlighting' and doing private work, often using the collective's raw materials and machinery. An alternative, and more catastrophic pattern, as evinced for example in Mozambique, is that cumulative shortages of necessary inputs, on the one hand, and hesitancies on the part of policy-makers concerning the petty bourgeoisie, on the other, together virtually ruin this class and thus contribute to a decline in the standard of living of its members and many other consumers.[9] Leaving aside this second possibility, it must be stressed that the retention of an only partially transformed petty bourgeoisie may long remain a necessity for state socialist systems, given the incapacity of state agencies and collectives to do what is expected of them and a growing appreciation of the value of this class in providing some goods and services.

The working class is now also basically defined by its relationship to the state apparatus. The supposed transformation of that class, as envisaged by doctrine, into a socialist ruling class given expression through the dictatorship of the proletariat does not, of course, occur. Rather, there are three somewhat more mundane ways in which it is actually transformed, at least in cases where the system has a chance to develop its own dynamic without major distortions. First, it tends to grow considerably in size, mostly on the basis of rural recruits unused to factory work and usually illiterate (at least until the extension of basic education catches up with this recruitment). The immediate effect of this is an increased emphasis on discipline and productivity. The latter usually also finds expression in a second phenomenon, an attempt to raise the general technical level of workers. Linked to the overall emphasis on education, which we have already noted as one of the more successful sides of such systems, this may have quite widespread effects, assuming that industry is actually growing rapidly enough to give new expertise a material base. Third, a process of differentiation usually sets in among workers, based on skills and, related to this, earning capacity.

However, although a national structure of wage rates based on skill differentials may be established, an important determinant of differentials in earnings, or at least of differential ability to turn earnings into real goods and services, will be factors associated with the behaviour of a resource-constrained economy. In particular, once material incentives have overtaken moral incentives as the principal mechanism for squeezing out short-run increases in labour productivity (as they tend to do), earnings, as well as 'drifting' away from basic wage rates, will reflect the nature of the enterprise, its location, and the success of a particular manager in procuring supplies of inputs to meet and exceed plan targets.[10] This, of course, has a fragmenting effect on the class.

Before taking up at greater length the matter of the transformation of the workers into a 'ruling class', special attention must first of all be drawn to what happens to other social categories which exist alongside and in close relation to classes and are also subject to transformation under the aegis of state and party. Most significant here are women, youth, and ethnic (and religious) minorities, themselves overlapping.

Women constitute at least half the population of the countries on the capitalist periphery, and they experience both class exploitation and their own special forms through patriarchy and household labour. As we noted in Chapter 1, a basic received idea of socialism has been that this condition must be brought to an end, and can be by instituting legal equality and protection, opening work outside the household to women, providing childcare facilities, and raising their political consciousness. Some achievements along these lines on the part of state socialist systems cannot be denied, and this is another feature which marks them off from capitalism on the periphery. However, there is now plenty of evidence to show that such liberation is highly qualified.[11] Changes in the law do not automatically mean differences in practice; working outside the household often only adds a double burden, since unpaid domestic labour continues without sufficient relief through collective forms such as nurseries and dining halls; male patriarchalism continues even at the highest levels and is still reproduced in women's perceptions. Like capitalism, and indeed all the preceding modes of production, the state socialist one continues to depend upon the relegation of women as a whole to a position of subordination and particular forms of oppression.

As for youth, whether male or female, their fortunes under these systems seem more auspicious. Especially given their demographic preponderance, great emphasis is customarily laid upon the new generations as those who will truly become socialist people, freed from old hesitancies and misconceptions. Real opportunities are opened by the spread of education. However, at least two prices are paid. First, young people are expected to behave much better and make far higher sacrifices than others; the present deprivation for the sake of future enjoyment, which is central to official ideology, is expected to find fullest expression in them. Hence the puritanism which is also a distressing feature of Marxism–Leninism is most strongly imposed upon those for whom the senses still represent an important adventure. Second, through their enclosure within the educational system above all, but also in general, young people are kept in line intellectually and ideologically to an extent which probably surpasses that of their elders, who still remember something from a more pluralist intellectual tradition.

Both women and youth in state socialist systems normally have their own special organizations, and this provides a contrast with our other special groups. Ethnic minorities usually do not (though religious ones often retain their old churches and temples in the formal name of freedom of belief). It is extremely important that most underdeveloped countries are multi-ethnic agglomerations, either in the direct sense of racial divisions or the qualified situation more typical of Africa of racial uniformity (by and large) but with 'tribal' varieties of culture and language. The real historical divisions (though possibly only as old as colonial 'divide and rule') which result necessarily cause the leaders of party and state to distrust separate ethnic organization, though this is but an extension of their general desire for monopoly. On the other hand, there is no doubt that some of the most serious challenges which state socialist regimes have faced have come from dissident ethnic minorities, and this has included armed resistance. A prominent example is the People's Republic of Angola, which since attaining independence in 1975 has never enjoyed full sway over its entire territory, much of the south and east being held by Jonas Savimbi's tribally based, pro-capitalist, and South Africa and US-backed UNITA. The approved Marxist–Leninist answer, though by no means universally applied, is to grant varying degrees of local powers formally to minority regions. The best general measure of this technique is probably to remind readers that the USSR is itself constitutionally a federation.

ACCUMULATION, EXPLOITATION, AND CLASS

So far we have argued that, as state socialist systems develop and begin more and more to follow the law of motion of a resource-constrained economy, their state apparatuses acquire increasing political dominance and themselves define social roles and statuses, and bestow or withhold power. This is in marked contrast to previous class systems, in which role, status, and power are determined basically outside the state apparatus, in civil society, though the state is of course necessary for their expression and reproduction. This line must now be pushed further, into other realms of classical class analysis.

It would no doubt be agreed that class societies are characterized by social relations of exploitation which permit accumulation by one group at the expense of another. Once more, it can be argued that parallel processes in state socialist societies work in very different ways from those determined by class relations.

It follows from the whole argument in Chapter 3 that *concepts of surplus expropriation and exploitation, central to class analysis, lose meaning in the movement from capitalism to state socialism.* Under the latter regime, surplus use values are produced but not put into circuits of exchange in order to create capital. Instead, because for planning purposes it remains in a direct material form, surplus is in fact indistinguishable from the rest of current output. Although it may be given a monetary value for book-keeping purposes, it is never concentrated in some central pot in either a monetary or physical form, to be dished out to different competing claimants. Rather, it is directed, along with other current outputs, to meeting particular plan targets and *the preceding bids cover the whole of current output.* Accumulation in such a society thus involves not a concentration of surplus at a number of poles (enterprises), or at one particular pole (the state), but the total process of organizing economic activity to produce growth. Bearing this in mind we must now examine the concept of exploitation, as a means of coming to grips with the position of workers, peasants, other labouring people, and their rulers under state socialism.

In capitalist systems, exploitation implies class relations in which some classes have little control over the use of their labour power and in one way or another have surplus extracted from them because their members work for longer than is necessary for their reproduction and that of their families (socially necessary labour time). Under state socialism workers, peasants, and other labouring people have little say concerning the work situation in which their labour power is put to use or the allocations of what they produce. Moreover, there clearly exist ruling groups which enjoy significantly greater material privileges than the mass of the population.

Nevertheless, the concept of exploitation has little explicatory value in these systems. We have already noted that any surplus generated by state socialist economies remains somewhat intangible and is dispersed as soon as it is produced rather than being concentrated in a monetary form. This, of course, seems to preclude the existence of a group of exploiters, a question to which we shall return below. The other side of the coin is our immediate concern, for it exposes the position of the potential recruits for exploitation.

First of all, and mirroring the lack of a sharp, unchanging delineation of protagonists in the conflict over the distribution of resources identified in Chapter 3, there are, in effect, no regularities of relationships among large and stable social groups which could be illuminated by the term exploitation. Not only are classes transformed, but the economic terrain of conflict cuts across and fragments them as it follows the contours of conflicts over the allocation of resources, which in turn change as industrialization progresses and the requirements of accumulation change. Moreover, and in spite of appearances, this view is not contradicted by the existence of stable monetary values for commodities and labour power: prices are generally administered and therefore monetary profit rates provide no illumination about the source of economic surplus. Second, suppose for one moment that the state, or rather key personnel in the state apparatus, were to be identified as the 'exploiters': then the power of the state to appropriate surplus would be found in exchange relationships, as it exercised its function of allocating resources, something inadmissible as evidence of exploitation in the orthodox Marxist sense.

Third, and more fundamentally, behind the veil of the relationship between the different and changing protagonists in the conflict over the distribution of resources is not in fact an economic relationship with the state as such but with other, perhaps unknown or unperceived protagonists. The state is simply a *mediator* in a process which will result in some protagonists appropriating surplus produced by others, not in the state appropriating surplus produced by all of them.

This point returns us to the position of the potential 'exploiters', the ruling group, bureaucrats, and others exercising power from a base in the state apparatus. If we have already dispelled the imagery of a corrupt oligarchy using power derived from the planning functions of the state to garner a pot of 'surplus' and then allocating a disproportionate share to itself, there still remain important observations to be made which clarify the ruling group's position in crucial respects and distance it still further from the classical Marxist notions of class and exploitation.

First, it will be recalled from Chapter 3 that various aspects of the workings of the resource-constrained economy, from the prioritization of rapid industrialization and the concentration on heavy industry to specific manifestations of suction such as 'investment hunger' and 'investment tension', mean that consumption is subordinate to investment: consumption is a residual after all other claims on available resources have been met. In other words, this is not a system which gives priority in advance to the consumption requirements of its ruling group. The only power of the ruling group resides in its capacity to carve out privileged, non-monetary access channels to whatever consumption goods and services are available: in the struggle between consumers for access to consumption resources the ruling group places itself at the front of the queue. Moreover, even these privileges, though greatly superior to those of the vast majority, in no way rival what is open to their capitalist counterparts. Comparing like with like by remaining on the periphery, top Nigerian capitalists would sniff at the life of leaders in Angola; Indonesian magnates never wish to swap with North Koreans. Lower down in the bureaucracy, access to the occasional bottle of scotch or use of state vehicles may represent a dreamed-of privilege.[12] Furthermore, the latter illustrates the restricted nature of many privileges, given that they are often not accompanied by the power and prestige which goes with ownership in the capitalist world.

Second, these points beg a more general question – simply, why is this so? Why are the material privileges of the ruling group in fact rather paltry compared with overall subordination of consumption to investment? The answer is not to be found in ideology or the personal, perhaps puritanical, attitudes of the rulers, but in the fact that in reality their economic power is limited: as we have repeatedly stressed they do not *control* the economy, they are as much its subjects, if more comfortably placed, as the rest of the population. As we sought to demonstrate in Chapter 3, a resource-constrained economy has its own tendential law of motion which embraces the whole social organism and which both underwrites and defies the political power of the rulers. The fact that even when there is a consensus among the ruling group about the need for change, considerable political upheaval is necessary to enact even minor adjustments to the parameters of the system bears ample enough witness to this point. Moreover, it also illustrates the continuing importance of political economy as opposed to political sociology: 'dictatorship over needs' is a system and not the whim of a ruling group.

All of these points make for a society which is opaque, based on a shifting hierarchy of material rewards associated with success or failure in the conflict over the distribution of resources, and unamenable to established historical categories. Attempts to apply the latter can therefore only have a 'sociologistic' or non-material content. Subordinate classes are both transformed and then pulled apart at the economic level, leaving them with a purely political existence (in the sense of relations with the state apparatus – Leviathan) which serves as a tool for ideological manipulation in the hands of the ruling group. State socialist societies accumulate and are therefore clearly capable of generating a surplus. However, who pays and who benefits most, and how, is inevitably obscure and probably beside the point. The issue of control over means of production, 'class' consciousness, and action lose most of their real meaning.

Nevertheless, even though it may not be based on economic power, as the state swallows civil society the ruling group appropriates a degree of political power almost unprecedented in human history. It is therefore time to examine more closely the social nature of the actual people who control decision-making. With this point we return to the very basic question, who rules? Now, however, we can recognize that in state socialist societies this is no longer a *class* question.[13]

POWER, POLITICAL ELITES, AND THE LEVIATHAN STATE

Following Trotsky, it has been common to describe these systems as being 'bureaucratically deformed'. The problem is that this suggests a deviation from a norm. Undoubtedly, as we have already noted, from very early after the revolution state socialist systems experience a rapid growth of the bureaucracy. This even begins in a preliminary way during the period of seizure of power, at least if it is protracted and involves the administration of liberated areas. When victory brings control over the state apparatus, administrative and political cadres and fighters immediately move into it. There they join those servants of the old regime who are willing to change sides and are acceptable. This greatly reinforces the already strong links with the old middle strata, from whom the bulk of the revolutionary leaders were in any case drawn. (On the role of these 'organic intellectuals', see Chapter 2.) This core is usually soon joined by former capitalists whose enterprises have been nationalized and who have entered the bureaucracy, along with former managers from private business and formerly independent professionals. The greater part of those who occupy the top- and middle-level positions may thus be incompletely transformed elements from the old capitalist class and middle strata who were at best passive supporters of the revolution. Given that their interests, outlook, and tastes will scarcely have been changed, their effect on the original revolutionaries may well be very deleterious.

It is, on the other hand, undoubtedly true that large numbers of workers, petty bourgeois individuals, and even peasants very quickly begin to be recruited into the bureaucracy. First of all those with some degree of education above basics are skimmed off, then special courses are usually instituted to bring others up to scratch, quite large numbers of future specialists are sent off to fraternal countries for training, then the first products of the newly expanded school and university system start to come through. In the last way many sons and even daughters of the previously suppressed classes do get the chance to become upwardly mobile. But education, new forms of work and new lifestyles change them; they do not bring new egalitarian values from below (always assuming such existed there in the first place), but rather the ineffable trend is for them to subscribe happily to the elitism of party and state bureaucracies.

At least on the surface, the bureaucracy gives an impression of being a new ruling class – indeed, more directly 'ruling' than the old capitalist class – since, unlike their predecessors, their position is determined by direct incorporation into the state apparatus, not by control of bases outside it. However, it is obvious that the political control which prevails throughout society is tightly enforced within the ranks of the bureaucracy itself, denying real power to the great majority. The ranks of actual decision-makers are in practice very small. It is thus more meaningful to see most bureaucrats as forming various 'constituencies' which exert influence in a passive way, in the sense that military, industrial, educational, and other interests are represented in the top leadership and have to be satisfied by allocations of investment and consumption resources. (In some state socialist systems constituencies may also exist on other bases, for example, region or ethnicity.)

These points tend to take us further away from seeing the bureaucracy as a new ruling class, and are intended to do so. The crucial point, in fact, is that *in these societies there is no ruling class or other directly comparable group. The wielding of political power there is a phenomenon of a new kind.* Moreover, the new elite does not emerge as a deformation of a normal situation, but as a logical result of the development of a resource-constrained economy, directly linked with the swallowing of civil society by the state. Unlike any dominant class which has ever existed before in history, the office-holders who actually make the key policy decisions have no economic and social base outside it. They represent no one else (whatever their claims to speak for the 'working people'), except perhaps the bureaucracy, and have relations with other social groups only by virtue of belonging to the state apparatus, without which they are nothing. It seems useful to regard such a group as a power bloc, recognizing that, as in capitalist systems, there is a constellation of those who have particular significance because they control key decisions, but that, unlike under capitalism, the bloc is not defined by its relations to classes in civil society. Though somewhat fluid, because different policy spheres may involve different personnel, it would be possible by analysis to establish membership of the bloc in any particular system; to a large extent it would be coterminous with the party central committee (or comparable body where a party as such was still lacking), reinforced by a few other senior figures. Usually, indeed, a smaller circle of perhaps ten or fifteen people forms the heart of the power bloc.

Members of the power bloc usually owe their position initially to their role in the leadership of the revolution, with further recruits added by dint of service within the apparatus. All of them, however, derive power, income and, after the original revolutionary generation, prestige from belonging to it and from nothing else. If their colleagues turn against them they can be cast out and are then left with nothing, perhaps not even their lives, unless favoured with a state pension. They cannot pass on their positions to their children, since office is not hereditary.

That does not mean, of course, that to be the son or daughter of at any rate a middle- or upper-level state employee is not an advantage, especially in terms of access to the educational system. Not all school-age children can perhaps yet gain admission, but it is virtually certain that they will. Moreover, it is a very reasonable assumption that they, impelled by ambitious and relatively privileged parents, will pass disproportionately through to middle and higher levels. This is crucial. Of course, social position in their case is not maintained by inheriting wealth; it is secured by access to education, the higher the better, which often then ensures a similar job to that of their parents, or an even better one. Admittedly many fall back, usually into the new working class, but the trend is there. Evidence from the older state socialist systems, albeit very patchy, seems to indicate that between 45 and 70 per cent of children of state personnel hold similar jobs and it seems very likely that the higher proportions come from the higher levels.[14] (It must also be remembered that the children do not have to become bureaucrats in a narrow sense to remain part of the state apparatus. All educational and cultural personnel, for example, are now formed within it.)

In no sense, however, does this represent the inheritance of wealth, office, and power in the way in which that may occur in class systems. The cases of Kim Il Sung and his son and the Ceauşescu clan aside, membership of the power bloc cannot be inherited. The problem of succession is, of course, a notoriously difficult one in such systems. In the absence of set rules and procedures for this, with everything depending on co-option by incumbents on the basis of past service and factional adherence, mutual jealousies and all sorts of rivalries make for reluctance to admit new faces. The need to hang on to office again reflects the fact that the only basis for relative wealth and prestige is finding and retaining a place within the state apparatus. Once again, *it is the system of institutionalized power in its own right which makes or breaks individuals. In logic and in actual workings it is prior to those who take decisions, not their instrument.* As was the common statement amid the horrors of the Pol Pot regime in Kampuchea, everything done was the will of Angka – the disembodied 'Organization'.

This further manifestation of the dominance of the state apparatus and consequent personal insecurity (which is felt more keenly the lower down the bureaucratic hierarchy) also explains two other political features of state socialist leaderships. At first sight these appear to be opposites, but they are in fact manifestations of the same phenomenon. Thus, on the one hand, it is common for such leaders to insist on collective responsibility for decisions; with all dependent upon office none of them can afford to stand above the rest. On the other hand, in some of them at least, a veritable cult of the leader develops. This is in part due to the fact that some do enjoy personal prestige, and it can also be a useful ideological weapon to project a leader in a way readily understood in terms of mass culture – Ho Chi Minh as the venerated teacher, Fidel Castro as 'the Stallion'. A deeper systemic reason, however, lies in the need of the leadership as a group – and by extension the whole bureaucracy as it stands against the general population – to evade responsibility for collective decisions and acts by shifting them from the many shoulders to two. Every revered leader is a potential scapegoat; the cult of Stalin was not only a projection of his ego, it was also a necessity for his colleagues.

A need for solidarity among the leaders when facing the general population implies the possibility of dissent at the base. Since this is potentially the most likely cause of radical change in these systems – as it was in a very different way in their predecessors' – it is to this issue which we must turn in concluding this chapter.

SOCIAL STRUGGLE IN STATE SOCIALIST SYSTEMS

Marx and Engels stressed the prevalence of class struggle in pre-socialist history, and, in those post-revolutionary systems which claim to be based upon their ideas, it is true that such is difficult to find. However, this is not because inimical relations between social groups no longer exist except in a residual sense of combatting remnants of capitalism and feudalism, as the leadership insists. Rather, it is for the more general reason insisted upon above, namely that, with peasants, workers, petty bourgeoisie, and middle strata all now defined politically by their relations with the state apparatus and fragmented economically, class struggle in its normal sense loses meaning. Nevertheless, very important social struggles still continue in state socialist systems and can bring them into situations of political crisis to match their precarious economic conditions.

As just noted, official doctrine denies that class struggle can exist under socialism, except in the limited sense of a fight against remaining capitalist elements and against the possibility of a restoration of capitalism. ('Limited' here must not be taken necessarily to imply scale; the Cultural Revolution in China convulsed the whole country and included even armed clashes between rival factions.) However, the chances for the officially stressed danger of a capitalist restoration to become reality (except through foreign or foreign-backed invasion) are in our view nil. Though small capitalists can survive, and even expand somewhat if permitted within the sphere of trade on the free market, state control of all wholesale trade, credit facilities, and bank accounts and the lack of investment opportunities in production must necessarily rule out the resurgence of a capitalist class. (China is important here, since openings for such possibilities have recently been created.) For similar reasons, it is absurd to see the decentralization of some decisions to enterprise managers through a so-called introduction of market principles as giving them the chance to become capitalists. In practice official warnings about the dangers of capitalism become reduced to attacks upon the survival not of material bases and relations but of ideas, which may in various ways corrupt people. For that matter, a similar view is taken of 'feudal' survivals, especially among the peasantry. That such influences continue is undoubted; people's minds do indeed change more slowly than their material circumstances. But that cannot be the basis for a revival of the old classes as such.

The limited application of the concept of class struggle in official doctrine could be seen in another way. It is, in fact, supposed to become increasingly irrelevant the more old classes are transformed and old relations of production disappear; the struggle focuses then, it is said, upon the raising of the forces of production, which is seen as a struggle by classes but not between them. At most it is conceded that certain 'non-antagonistic' contradictions remain, for example between workers and peasants because of the issue of the relative prices of food and industrial goods. It should be clear that we regard this as a quite misplaced view, which serves in fact as the basis for an attempted ideological diffusion of social struggle.

For it is clear that social struggle continues to exist in state socialist societies. What happens is that the basic nature of that struggle changes. The more or less speedy destruction of the old dominant and exploiting classes by the state apparatus after the seizure of power serves to dissolve the old forms of struggle. In the early stages a process of mass demobilization tends to occur. At first, of course, this is because the masses believe that their aims have been achieved. Workers, peasants, and others who rallied to the revolutionary bloc now await a speedy improvement of their lot, and often, as we have noted in several places above, it occurs in material or non-material ways. However, at the same time the forms of political control also noted above are being introduced, as new social relations and contradictions take shape. This means that the only mobilization which can henceforth occur – unless control by the party and state is lost, as in Poland in 1980-1 – is that which is needed for the purposes of the new system.

This tendency is strongly reinforced by another. The more successful of these systems are indeed able to bring both psychic and material benefits to large numbers of people; Cuba and North Korea are cases in point. The leaderships of these may thus continue to enjoy widespread support, particularly if socialist themes can be backed by patriotic ones in face of foreign menaces. In any case, however, the great proliferation of state employment creates a wide vested interest in the system, and this is extended into the working class and peasantry by the existence of enterprises and co-operatives which are doing relatively well because of access to inputs, efficiency, or some other reason. Moreover, 'advanced' elements are admitted to the relatively privileged ranks of the party. Further, mass base must not be confused with majority of the population. All that is required is a sufficient 'critical mass' to respond to emulation campaigns and other mobilizations and carry more people along with it.

Though previously mobilized classes may subside again after the revolution, and Leviathan do his best to keep them divided, the development of the resource-constrained economy in an underdeveloped country on the capitalist periphery inevitably produces myriad disappointed expectations and pressures to survive. New material bases for social struggle emerge, though, with interests above all focused on distribution and consumption, struggle becomes diffused and in a sense atomized. It is not only managers or cadres in collectives who are seen as opponents but fellow workers or members, because of the differentials in income introduced by piece-work, different skills, emulation campaigns, and similar devices. On the other hand, solidarity is not entirely absent: workers in factories may agree to resist piece-rates by trying to keep earnings more or less equal, what in Viet Nam has been denounced as 'averageism'. Partly in concert, but mainly in an individualist way, every conceivable form of resistance is adopted against the imposition of discipline necessitated by the working of the resource-constrained economy. Agricultural collectives can be shaped even as a form of defence for their members if state and party apparatuses have an insufficient grip and cadres draw a blind eye or actively connive, for example at disguising the true level of the harvest and keeping some back from delivery. Trade co-operatives can sell secretly on the free market, craft co-operative members divert materials to their own use, even employ cheap labour to fulfil state quotas while working for the free market themselves. Wage workers produce only enough to meet their quotas, concentrate on quantity rather than quality if piece-work is brought in, are frequently absent, and so on. It must be emphasized that *without opportunities for more dramatic manifestations, all of these practices and others represent resistance to the pressures caused by suction and shortage.*

Part of the population may indeed take much more visible armed action against the new states; such has been the case in recent years in Angola, Mozambique, Laos, Kampuchea, Viet Nam, and Ethiopia. In all but the Kampuchean case this has been the action of ethnic minorities, and in that sense not a form peculiar to state socialist societies. Women may also find that their liberation under state socialism is not all they expected; Marxism–Leninism perhaps bears a patriarchal mark of Cain (who like its founders, was a man...). Intellectuals and their cadets among students are just as prone to the discontents caused by their structural location in society (discussed in Chapter 2), if subjected to disillusionment. (This may well be related to failure to gain as privileged a status as hoped for under the new regime.)

Obviously, it cannot be expected that any real change can result from these kinds of struggle, though some shifts in policy may well occur as the decision-makers try to curb discontent. Disagreements among the leaders over what must be done can bite deep if various 'constituencies' are brought into play and a real struggle for power breaks out; the most dramatic example of this so far is the Chinese Cultural Revolution period. In China a very prestigious leader made a special appeal to a key constituency, youth, and also used a powerful part of the state apparatus, the army. However, there is no real indication that any side wanted to effect a major transformation of the system; 'Maoist' strategies still depended on industrialization, collective agriculture, and party monopoly. Czechoslovakia in 1968 provides another example of splits in the leadership leading to attempts at more radical change.

Further discussion along these lines could only be speculative and at this point in our analysis misplaced. One thing alone seems almost certain. No path would be taken towards any radically different form of socialism unless leadership, doctrine, followers, and the relations among them were quite different from anything we have seen up to now, except that is in some very incomplete forms. We shall return to this in attempting to conclude our analysis in Chapter 5. There we may also most conveniently pick up again the theme briefly raised by the conceptualization in Chapter 3 of a third stage of economic development which marks a conscious attempt by the elite itself to break out of the problems of the resource-constrained economy.

5

Towards a balance sheet

In one of the less publicized passages of his May 1986 'winds of freedom' speech to the US Chamber of Commerce, President Reagan claimed: 'The world, especially the developing world, is leaving behind the dismal failure of statism and redistribution.'[1] This self-confidence about the failure of socialism and about a 'new and wondrous horizon' opening up for world capitalism, nurtured by the so-called 'New Right' and expressed as we were drafting this chapter, served to confirm our concern about the fate of socialism, voiced in the opening chapter.

Our initial concern in setting up our project had been to unravel the tendential 'laws of motion' of state socialist societies and this drew us inexorably into what we have called the problematic of 'socialism and underdevelopment' because, of course, the essential feature of the Marxist–Leninist version of socialism is that it has been applied on the capitalist periphery and not at its centre. Out of this emerged the building-blocks of our analysis, involving the interplay between what we have called the 'received ideas' of socialism, the problems of underdevelopment, and the different forms of seizure of power. Underdevelopment was also seen as significant in another sense, for it provided us with a central question to answer, namely, to what extent has it been socialist ideology, expressed through particular seizures of power and particular post-revolutionary strategies, or the array of problems associated with underdevelopment, which have been responsible for the current world image of socialism which President Reagan finds it so easy to lambast? It seemed to us that the enterprise of extricating the 'received ideas' of socialism from the quagmire of the circumstances in which they have been deployed and identifying their weak spots or contradictory implications might facilitate new and more fruitful debates. In turn, and although we shall inevitably deviate to consider other issues along the way, this question would seem to provide the most productive focus for our conclusions. Clearly President Reagan is convinced that the problems of socialism, or 'statism' as he prefers to call it, have little to do with the legacies of peripheral capitalism and everything to do with socialist ideology. But what can *we* now conclude?

Our approach will be to draw up a 'balance sheet' for each chapter, highlighting the issues which seem to harbour serious implications for the 'received ideas' of socialism. Subsequently, and rather than indulging in wishful thinking or ending on a Utopian note, we shall attempt to identify a series of policy 'trade-offs' which, in our view, should inform debate about socialist strategy, both in the centre, on the periphery, and in state socialist countries. From there we can end with some tentative prognoses for future developments.

SOCIALISM AND UNDERDEVELOPMENT

A balance sheet based upon Chapter 1 is in essence an expression of issues underlying our whole project. As just stated, we may see these as two, that of the 'received ideas' of socialism, and the fact that their application has been virtually without exception in the context of seizures of power in underdeveloped countries.

What seems clear is that the shift of the historical problematic of socialism to the capitalist periphery was not accidental. Given that at least some of what has been written in this book may have seemed to suggest that truly socialist systems cannot be built under conditions of underdevelopment, it is necessary to face that issue squarely, and most of this chapter represents, in fact, an attempt to recapitulate our arguments in those terms. First of all, then, we find the Marxist-Leninist argument concerning the projection of capitalism onto a world scale and the appearance of weak links, though still somewhat primitive, basically acceptable. Indeed, it follows from our own analysis in Chapters 1 and 2, and especially the postulation there of a stage of 'intermediate integration', that there are plenty of such soft spots in the international capitalist system, which is marked by its own great contradiction, namely that its financial and trade flows cut across formal boundaries but issues of policy and political power have largely to be expressed within them, through a plethora of separate states.

The question is, once again, can breaks in these links lead to *socialist* seizures of power? (There is also the problem of what constitutes a *break*; obviously, various authoritarian regimes of the right or radical populist left can emerge from *crisis* on the periphery.) The answer may be based on a rereading of one of the most enigmatic and tantalizing passages ever written by Karl Marx. In his 'Preface' to "A Contribution to the Critique of Political Economy",' he wrote that

> A social order never perishes before all the productive forces for which it is broadly sufficient have been developed and new superior relations of production never replace older ones before the material conditions for their existence have matured within the womb of the old society.[2]

This was originally taken in the sense referred to earlier, namely that capitalism would not be replaced by socialism until it had exhausted all its potential, and that this therefore meant that places like Britain or Germany would see the revolution first. In the conditions of the late twentieth century (and indeed earlier) it seems to us to be essential to grasp the idea that capitalism and its potentialities are not everywhere uniform. To put it more directly, these work themselves out to completion (exhaustion) more rapidly on the periphery than at the centre. As we tried to argue in this book, there are significant variations between these two broad divisions of the same world phenomenon (as well as within them), which make the different patterns axiomatic.

Let us reformulate the point in terms of social struggle. *The working out of capitalism in parts of the periphery prepares not only the minority working class but peasants and other working people, women, youth and minorities for a socialist solution, even though the political manifestation of this may not initially take the form of a socialist movement.* In the case of those who are *not* wage labourers (the classical class associated with that new order), capitalism has still so permeated the social relations which determine their existences, even though it may not have followed the western European pattern of 'freeing' their labour power, that to be liberated from it is their only salvation. Thus, for example, peasants, artisans, and petty traders are now so linked to the market that much of their labour is devoted to producing a surplus drained from them and turned into value for capital – not, of course, in the wage form but through the anarchy of the market. Women have to reproduce the current labour power of their men so that capital may use it, produce new generations of labourers, and themselves work outside or inside the household to meet increased demands by the market. Youth are able to make careers or even a livelihood only if capital needs them. Minorities are pushed to the wall if they occupy land or control water resources upon which capital's acquisitive eye falls. The objective need for socialism of these elements can thus be no less than that of the worker imprisoned in the factory and disciplined by the whip of unemployment. These prices are paid in even the most 'successful' of the underdeveloped countries, and others additionally experience mass destitution.

Finding another path has thus become a desperate necessity if the alternative of continuing, if not increasing, barbarism is to be escaped. We have seen, above all in Chapter 2, that Marxist–Leninist intellectuals on the periphery are sometimes able to combine disparate forces and lead them to a successful seizure of power in the name of socialism. In Chapters 3 and 4 we have detailed how, in the name of the traditionally revolutionary working class for which they substitute a vanguard party, they go on to build a new society based on classes and other social groups which are transformed but do not control the state. The point is that experience seems to reveal that Marxist–Leninist received ideas are a doctrine of liberation which is inherently undemocratic, a contradiction which has played all too readily into the hands of the enemies of socialism. Indeed, its friends must conversely face quite directly the fact that the contradiction has now too often worked itself out to gloomy or even barbarous conclusions for these to be taken as occasional aberrations.

We have posited that conditions on the periphery make revolutionary attempts (as well as military coups and other manifestations of political instability) particularly likely there. Our postulate is not that such, where they express real mass discontents, can *only* take a path into an authoritarian dead end. There is, of course, a very real danger that they will move in such a direction; this has been borne out historically to one degree or another by every case so far, with the exception of Yugoslavia. Such a danger is inherent in the combination of received ideas, the conditions of underdevelopment, and the circumstances of the seizure of power in those which we have characterized as marked by 'intermediate integration' into the world capitalist system.

THE SEIZURE OF POWER

In Chapter 2 we advanced a wide range of theoretical and analytical propositions, with concrete references broadly spread in both space and time. In looking more to the future we shall have to narrow our points of reference, since four of the five groups of cases distinguished there will not be expanded. Thus, the effects of the two World Wars are unrepeatable events (and a third would have very different consequences), and socialist-inclined national liberation wars will become less common with the end of colonialism (though Eritrea shows that this form may sometimes occur again). This leaves us with cases like that of Cuba, in which a regime was overthrown in a country which had been formally independent for some time. Nicaragua is another case which may have a socialist outcome. Possible candidates within the next decade are South Africa and the Philippines. Before going on to examine the implications of this apparent narrowing of focus, we shall summarize the general analysis we have offered regarding seizures of power in intermediately integrated formations on the periphery.

These, then, are marked by a complex social structure with multiple forms of exploitation and oppression and hence contradictions. This situation provides the crucial basic potentiality for multiple pressure upon the power bloc and its state apparatus. The idea that socialist revolutions on the periphery are in any real sense the expression above all of the working class is not sustainable. As argued above, many more social elements have an interest in a possible socialist future. The Marxist–Leninist formula of a worker–peasant alliance which in turn leads a broader grouping of 'labouring people' is in practice only a way by which the leading nucleus of intellectuals (whatever their social origin) preserve control over strategy in the wars of position and manoeuvre.

In turn, the power bloc, especially in terms of its uneven relationship with the dominant class, is prone to internal divisions and also to confrontations with parts of that class. Moreover, the uncertainties of its position incline it towards coercion rather than ideological manipulation, while the state apparatus, the parts of which are of uneven strength and efficiency, lends itself to such usage. In this situation foreign support, economic, technical, and if necessary armed, is very important for preserving the regime.

The fundamental determinants of the existence of the whole formation are, in fact, its structural linkages with the world system controlled by the advanced capitalist industrial countries. These create a situation of almost perpetual economic crisis, which in many cases on the periphery constantly challenges the capacity of the dominant class(es) and power bloc to reproduce their position. A combination of coercion, ideology, and social inertia (with some elements of the subordinate classes supporting the system) serves, however, to preserve the regime as a pattern of very unevenly distributed power. This is backed up at the economic level by the contradictions of the social structure, which both express the miseries of underdevelopment and provide ways in which they may be dispersed into forms of bare subsistence.

The crisis which really challenges the regime and puts on the agenda a socialist seizure of power, then, is more directly political than economic in form. However, the preconditions for this are very difficult to achieve. A solid vanguard party/movement has to crystallize, led by socialists and acting as the bearer of their ideas. In the conditions of peripheral capitalism this leadership comes most often from outside the ranks of the poor, while its socialist ideas have historically been much influenced by the received ideas of the Stalinist tradition. Only very recently have we begun to see some 'loosening' in this situation, both organizationally, with less cohesive movements rather than parties of the Vietnamese or (original) Yugoslav types, and rather more flexibility in ideas. On the other hand, the broader range ideologically is not new, for it has been implicit in the 'front' strategy since 1920. This implies the putting together by the vanguard of a revolutionary bloc of as wide a range of dissident elements as possible, including from among the more affluent, which will bring into play the widest range of contradictions; in this sense the role of the vanguard is to 'orchestrate' the contradictions. On the other hand, at the organizational and ideological levels the price paid is to submerge socialist doctrine in much broader ideas, some of which (commitment to a bourgeois formulation of a concept of democracy, for example) may later prove political handicaps to the socialist trans-formation.

To put the issue in another way, a full development of capitalism in the sense of the metropolitan centre is not something which needs to be passed over by applying a socialist strategy with a preliminary 'national democratic stage' to accomplish some of its unfinished tasks (like land reform). It was never on the cards anyway. The coming of the revolution is a sign that, in that particular peripheral link in the totality, capitalism *had* gone as far as it could. There are no 'historical tasks' of capitalism which socialists have to accomplish; socialist land reform, say, or democratic liberties, are fundamentally different from capitalist ones.

Beneath the above there lies, in fact, an assumption, namely that the old regime will be overthrown by a mass movement. That will undoubtedly not always be the case. Military coups are likely to be a continually recurring form of seizure of state power. Given certain necessary preconditions of leadership, ideology, and organization, it is possible quite readily to see a popular uprising as having a socialist content. Coups are a different matter, since they will acquire a socialist orientation only if led by a group of radicalized officers and it is open to considerable doubt whether they can then effectively mobilize the masses of labouring people from above. (Ethiopia is a test case here.)

There seem to be no particular reasons why future cases should be marked by coups as opposed to mass movements, or vice versa. We would, however, offer a speculation as to the sort of formation which may be most often marked by such phenomena, namely that it is likely to be an intermediately integrated one which has attempted to make the step to advanced status and failed. Beginning with the 'modernization' (capitalization) of agriculture, import-substitution and export-oriented industrialization, and going on to increased penetration by the transnationals, such a strategy involves forcing more peasants off the land, expanding the ranks of the working class and middle strata, and strengthening links between local capital, the state, and foreign capital. All this will exacerbate existing contradictions and create new ones (the Shah's Iran was a classic case, and also shows that even a mass movement may not be driven by a socialist ideology). Should such a situation give rise to popular unrest which appears threatening, a military coup may then follow and the new regime may attempt to push the process of international integration further; this may be done from a radical populist position (Peru 1968) or a conservative one (Brazil 1964). However, an increasingly successful war of position may entrench a new socialist vanguard deeply enough to begin its war of manoeuvre towards the seizure of state power, as may now be happening in the Philippines. Further failures in the attempt to attain advanced status and consequently deepening economic and social crisis may provide new opportunities for revolutionary positioning and manoeuvring.

It may be questioned whether such an escalation will necessarily involve the 'Maoist' strategy of a long drawn-out guerrilla civil war. The technology and organization of 'counter-insurgency' are now so highly developed that guerrilla movements, though troublesome and even debilitating, may be containable out in the bush away from crucial central regions. A particularly weak link in this kind of manoeuvring may be the movement into the last, large-unit, open battle stage. The revolutionary forces in the future may well reach the capital not solely through armed columns but because the urban population has risen in mass strikes and demonstrations to open the way for them. Indeed, the latter might provide the way to power without the armed columns as such at all.

A probable political scenario, therefore, might well run something like this. Under pressure from military action in the provinces the regime begins to tighten security and become more repressive. Added to the fact that many students and others likely to be killed or arrested are from the capitalist class and upper-middle stratum, efforts by the power bloc to ensure that it retains economic control alienate some of the wealthy supporters of the regime. This schism spreads into the power bloc itself, facilitated by the broad political appeals of the revolutionary bloc. Seeing this, and as the scale of repression spreads, substantial elements of the middle strata and petty bourgeoisie, which had previously given some sort of base to the power bloc, begin to drop away and become neutral or even swing to the revolution. Political work by the revolutionary bloc encourages this, as well as continuing to build a mass base among peasants, workers, and other poor, with significant gains in urban areas made possible by the middle-strata and petty bourgeois defections. This is probably the last chance for the (now-reduced) power bloc, which might just succeed in buying its way out of the political crisis by concessions. However, a mixture of limited resources, greed, and panic will probably prevent this policy being adopted, and if it is then it may well fail or enjoy only short- run success. This is made more likely by the impact of political developments upon the economy, with a flight of capital abroad, drying up of foreign investment, and so on. The resultant tightening of the screw on the mass of the population and increasing repression will drive growing numbers into the revolutionary armed forces and, even more significantly, will swell the ranks of those ready to rise up in the capital and other towns. Then, provided the revolutionary bloc has enough of an organization in place, and with further military thrusts to draw off the power bloc's armed forces, the mass urban struggle in the heart of the enemy's stronghold can be launched. If this is sustained, even the security forces will begin to crumble and victory will be imminent.

Since we are already working on a highly speculative level, there seems no reason why we should not push the argument a little further. As noted above, it seems very likely that socialist-inspired seizures of power will continue to be attempted, mainly in countries which remain intermediately integrated into the world capitalist system. However, we should not rule out all possibilities of such occurrences in cases of advanced integration, or even at the centre itself, should recession and unemployment go together with mass radicalization. Obviously there the seizure will take a distinct shape, though not one qualitatively different from that postulated above. The distinct variations are likely to be caused by the fact that such systems tend to be characterized by a multi-class 'constituency' for reformist parliamentary democracy. Given this, in conditions of crisis we might expect: a complete absence of any armed struggle (though 'terrorist' actions by extreme groups may exist); focus upon electoral struggle, though with accompanying mass pressure through strikes and demonstrations; and a particularly broad opposition front within which socialists might occupy a key place but with demands tending to be more democratic and reformist in nature than overtly revolutionary. This would obviously leave a major political struggle to be fought out *after* the new forces gained access to state power. That would make them, among other things, more exposed to a rightist military coup, though such might well be in fact preventive, timed just before the key election. This would have to be expected in countries of advanced integration, like South Korea or Brazil.

Speculation should certainly not be permitted to go further, if only because countries like Brazil are not our main focus. Rather, we should now turn to the post-seizure of power situation and to the first of the 'laws' which we have discerned as coming into play then, the emergence of the resource-constrained economy.

THE RESOURCE-CONSTRAINED ECONOMY

Chapter 3 postulated a law of economic tendency pushing a resource-constrained economy through three stages of development following upon the seizure of power. The focus, however, was on stage two wherein the principal received ideas of socialism are really put on trial. The ideas which were on trial were nationalization (of which collectivization can be considered a special sub-category), planning and the requirement to achieve a rapid development of the forces of production.

Taking the last idea first, it is really impossible to disentangle the impact of this from that of the problems of underdevelopment and isolation in a hostile environment. The socialist project of developing the forces of production to eliminate scarcity and prepare the way for full communism is closely intertwined with the straightforward pragmatic imperatives which would have informed the priorities of any regime: here socialism clearly wears the overriding imprint of underdevelopment, with ideology being essentially secondary, a convenient peg upon which to hang the dictates of circumstance.

Moreover, socialism's manifestation in rapid industrialization was also inevitable. Industrialization was, and still is, the only method known to the human race for achieving substantial increases in labour productivity and rising living standards (measured in material terms). That it fuels sharp distributional conflicts between industry and agriculture, between consumption and investment, between employment and productivity, which in turn contribute to the make-up of the resource-constrained economy, still does not detract from the fact that underdevelopment rather than faulty socialist ideology has been the essential cause.

Likewise, although socialism has become associated with the all-pervasive militarization of society, this aspect of the resource-constrained economy, as manifest in the distributional conflict between military and civilian expenditure, cannot be traced back to a socialist idea. It has certainly drawn succour from Stalin's concept of 'socialism in one country', but it is more the product of the unanticipated failure of instantaneous international revolution which brought with it a bitter harvest of experience both during and after the seizure of power, and which has since become embedded in a world order characterized by super-power rivalry and conflict within the state socialist bloc.

This takes us on then to consider the methods used to achieve a rapid development of the forces of production, i.e. to consider the impacts of nationalization and planning, ideas more amenable to drawing up a balance sheet. Moreover, although they are clearly closely interrelated, their impacts can be distinguished and discussed separately.

Nationalization (taken as a generic term referring to the expropriation of private property in general, rather than to a specific form of expropriation) is, of course, the bedrock of the socialist project; take it away and socialism loses meaning, a seizure of power becomes without purpose. If there is to be a revolutionary transformation of society then the transferral of the ownership of the means of production from private hands to the hands of the people is an absolute prerequisite: it cannot be baulked at. From Chapter 3, therefore, the question marks initially hang over its extent, the form which it takes (e.g. state ownership or 'socialization'?) and the confusion which arises through it being a policy which is automatically associated with socialist advance, whatever form it takes. At the contemporary stage of development of world capitalism a further question arises, relevant also to socialist prospects in advanced capitalist countries, namely, to what extent is it actually a practical policy option?

There is a question mark over the desirable extent of nationalization because of the adverse implications which wholesale nationalization has had for both consumer and producer power (here considered more from an economic angle; the next section will dwell on the political angles), both generally and in the agricultural sector in particular. The relationships concerned are principally those between industry and agriculture, and between the state and the private sector, although the relationship between the national economy and the international economy would also seem to be affected. The issue at the heart of the matter is not whether the large capitalist or the large landlord should be expropriated but rather the role which should be played by the petty commodity producer, the self-employed person, in a socialist economy. Should his or her means of production be subject to nationalization?

As far as agriculture is concerned, this question centres on collectivization which, although not strictly nationalization, essentially amounts to the same thing. Clearly, the logic of socialist ideas makes it rather untidy to omit an important sector of the economy from the collective domain but, on the other hand, it has rarely been the logic of socialist ideas or the evolution of socialist consciousness in the countryside which has propelled collectivization in state socialist countries. More usually, as we have seen, it has been an economic logic which has propelled collectivization.

Given this pragmatism it would seem best to be honest about it and in turn make a judgement based on economic logic rather than adherence to a preconceived socialist programme. On this score the balance sheet does not come out particularly favourably. In terms of enhancing consumer power collectivization has generally not secured a reliable supply and good variety of agricultural products nor, even in the case of the Soviet Union, has it provided a source of investible surplus for the industrial sector. In terms of enhancing producer power, in essence the traditional objective of a socialist programme, the peasant has been removed from a situation in which the possession of limited means of production brought with it some producer power, however subject to the vicissitudes of market anarchy, and reduced to a situation of powerlessness ruled by a vicious circle of necessity. The result has been considerable frustration which has put back indefinitely the possibility of an evolving socialist consciousness in the countryside and made a mockery of the received idea that socialism would dissolve the dichotomy between town and countryside.

At the same time these judgements do not mean that there cannot be advantages in the partial collectivization of agriculture, but this should be embarked upon on a pragmatic basis, selecting the activities most suited to this form of utilizing labour. For example, it is evident from experience in both advanced capitalist and state socialist countries that cereals production is more amenable to large-scale cultivation than is the production of vegetables. Agricultural production collectives are not a universal solution to problems of productivity, whether for supplying non-agricultural populations or raising peasant living standards. Mixtures of productive forms, bound together by co-operatives supplying credit, inputs and marketing facilities and by various types of contract, may be much more flexible. In addition, such a diversity lends itself more readily to self-management and democratic controls.

Crucial to any decision is the state of storage facilities and the transport system. In certain lines of cultivation the peasant may be a relatively inefficient producer but in fact more efficient at getting fresh produce to market on an individual basis than the available alternatives.

Moreover, there are now other important factors to be weighed in the balance when considering agricultural strategy, namely the impact on the environment and health. Capital-intensive agriculture in advanced capitalist countries is now causing unease, expressed most forcefully by the various 'green' movements, as it completes the dismantling of the rural social structure, uproots the last remaining copses and hedges, alienates the admittedly contradictory and confused relationship between human and animal, and introduces increasing numbers of preservatives and flavourings into our diet in order to satisfy the insatiable demand for an increasing variety of exotic products which have to reach the market in 'perfect' condition. Many state socialist countries can still avoid these problems by also considering the role of the peasant as guardian of the countryside and custodian of the health of their populations. Needless to say, such a role would also have wider ramifications in terms of helping to stem migration and thus preventing urban environments from getting out of control. All of these reflections perhaps indicate that the Hungarian attempt to incorporate consideration of the mistakes made by others into their policy-making machinery is a wise course to chart.[3]

The relationship between the state and the private sector takes the question of nationalization beyond agriculture and into the context of the whole economy, bringing a wide range of small-scale purveyors of goods and services into the picture. Here again a degree of pragmatism would seem to be in order, if only because the frustration of consumer power associated with bringing inappropriate activities into the nationalized sector will merely give rise to rampant black markets and moonlighting. Nevertheless, selectivity should still be practised: allowing self-employed mechanics, plumbers, and electricians to operate freely (Gorbachev's USSR) is one thing, allowing private empires to grow in rented accommodation (Deng Shaoping's China) is quite another.

Moreover, there are, of course, macro-economic implications following from any particular stance towards the private sector in both non-agriculture and agriculture. Allowing certain activities to remain in the private domain is, in fact, a partial restoration of a 'demand-constrained economy' which, in the context of a resource-constrained environment, poses particularly tricky dilemmas as we noted in Chapter 3. It also implies a diminution of self-reliance with respect to the international economy (this is how the question of nationalization impinges on the relationship between the national economy and the international economy – the more 'nationalized' state socialist economies appear to be the most self-reliant) with all the potentially disastrous pitfalls which this can harbour, again as we saw in Chapter 3. In turn this means that a policy stance towards the private sector must be taken in the context of that towards planning, something which we shall come to in a moment.

The question of the form of nationalization revolves around the desirability of the kind of centralized state ownership which has been the hallmark of stage two in the development of state socialist societies. However, this is also a question about which it is difficult to engage in abstract or rather disembodied speculation. Surely, on the basis of the analysis in Chapters 3 and 4, a number of negative observations can be proferred, for example, that centralized state ownership appears to be inimical to the development of producer and consumer power. Nevertheless, because such traits are intimately bound up with methods of planning, to consider alternatives such as decentralized ownership or 'social ownership' in the abstract, without considering the changes in planning methods which they necessitate in order to be meaningful, to change the deployment of power, would *a priori* be fruitless. All that can be firmly stated at this stage, before becoming involved in a discussion of planning, is that centralized state ownership and planning by administrative allocation are preconditions of each other: one cannot be meaningfully tinkered with or addressed independently of the other. Moreover, this is also why socialism cannot be dogmatically associated with any particular form of nationalization, for this only embraces a property relationship: the planning system and deployment of power which accompany it are equally important and involve 'trade-offs' because one approach will never be universally superior to another, a theme which we shall take much further in a later section.

The final point about nationalization concerns its practicality in a world in which the internationalization of capital has taken vast strides since the word nationalization entered socialist vocabulary. Thus private property may indeed be 'nationalized', but this is no longer synonymous with control if what has been nationalized is simply a cog in a large organization practising a division of labour on a world scale. It may, indeed, be an entirely worthless acquisition. This may indicate that such companies are better dealt with less directly – certainly most state socialist countries which have never had the opportunity to nationalize them have no qualms about inviting them in, and some even boast their own transnationals – but it does indicate that it is more satisfactory to identify candidates for nationalization which actually can be nationalized. Here a broad criterion might be whether the good or service has to be produced at or near the end-user point, i.e. on the territory over which the government considering nationalization has sovereignty and can therefore hope to exercise control. Fortunately, a number of areas of basic needs provision, such as construction, have this characteristic.

Turning now to the received idea of planning, again we are dealing with an idea which is absolutely axiomatic to the socialist project: the abstract notion of replacing market anarchy with organization may not have been a slogan on the lips of the supporters of revolutionary seizures of power, but it has certainly been a central component of the ideological baggage of revolutionary leaderships. How else to confront capitalism? Moreover, although the Soviet model which has dominated stage two in the development of state socialist societies may not have corresponded to the rather vague notions of planning inherited from Marx, it has to be recognized that it was a sincere attempt to put planning into practice in a non-utopian context and in the only way that was probably conceivable at the time.

From Chapter 3 the balance sheet for this form of planning is not particularly favourable. Although it has been demonstrated to be entirely different from capitalism, indeed its mirror image, and although the problems of underdevelopment, expressed particularly through macro-economic distributional conflicts, have contributed to its malaise, the system of centralized administrative allocation has been the mainstay of the resource-constrained economy, replacing competition for markets with competition for inputs and continually reproducing shortage. Clearly this system has had recognizable advantages in terms of forcing major structural changes under conditions of extensive growth in the economies concerned, and in maintaining full employment, but, as well as being associated with anti-democratic political regimes, it has frustrated both producer and consumer power and floundered as consumers have become more sophisticated, economies more complex.

The first question is this: can such a system of centralized administrative allocation be reformed, be made more democratic, to establish 'real' planning, as some would advocate?[4] The answer is quite simply no, and for several reasons. First of all, such a proposition is simply impractical and could only result in a proliferation of pseudo-democracy. The thousands of output and price decisions involved in planning inevitably generate centrifugal tendencies which tip the balance in favour of administrative power and away from democratic participation. The prospect of information technology coming to the rescue here, as some would hope, is also misconceived; if every household were to be equipped with a terminal with which to participate in planning, inconsistencies would still have to be sorted out, and anyway it would in effect restore a kind of market anarchy ruled by push-button votes rather than by money and prices. Nor would making people's sphere of participation more limited, and therefore more manageable, resolve these difficulties. As Nove remarks caustically in the course of a polemic against Bettelheim:

A factory making sulphuric acid or machine tools is a segment of a closely inter-related whole, as Bettelheim knows, indeed insists. In the absence of market-type links with the rest of the economy, the workers can no more be allowed to decide on their own what they should do than the railwaymen at Crewe can decide what trains should run through Crewe.[5]

Second, a greater degree of democratic participation in the planning process, even if it were feasible, would in no sense change the way in which planning instructions, once democratically conceived, are implemented. In other words the parameters of the system which are the mainstay of the resource-constrained economy would remain intact. (How could it be otherwise without a complete transformation of the system?) There would therefore be no disincentive to 'suction' and shortage would continue to be reproduced. Again, better management based on information technology cannot offer solace. There would still be no particular incentive to provide the correct information, upon which the success of technology in this task would depend, and in any event information technology is not a formula for controlling the future. Again, the decentralization of allocative implementation makes little difference if the same methods of allocation continue to be employed: the sub-system will simply reproduce the shortage of the whole on a smaller scale.

Third, such a project for enhanced democracy in a system of administrative allocation would, in the absence of a change in property relations, have no material basis and therefore would not signal a real change in the deployment of power. A change in property relations, implying as it does a move away from centralized state ownership, would of course be a transformation of the system rather than a reform, throwing the traditional conceptions of planning and socialism into the melting pot. To this we now turn.

In considering the dynamics of underproduction in Chapter 3 we noted that the problems of suction and shortage did beckon state societies towards stage three, which appears to offer solutions in terms of making money 'active' rather than 'passive', and then using money and prices rather than administrative methods to distribute resources. Nevertheless, most state socialist countries have only taken pseudo-steps along this path, using money and prices *within the context of the resource-constrained economy*, not therefore in order to transform it but rather in a vain attempt to make it work better, e.g. establishing material incentives for managers and workers; using the market in consumer goods to correct anomalies in administrative pricing. China is currently witnessing the biggest shifts along these lines, but the USSR under Gorbachev's leadership is now following suit. Only in Yugoslavia, however, and only then after major and prolonged upheaval, has this path been worked through to its logical conclusion and then in a quite distinctive way. This is because the effective use of money and prices requires a change in property relations: money and prices can only be meaningful control mechanisms if enterprises are able to set their own prices, control their own costs, obtain their own inputs, and establish their own investment programmes, and this implies that the state will have to relinquish the power over property associated with state ownership of the means of production. In Yugoslavia self-management and 'social ownership' were the result. As stated above, planning and forms of property are inextricably intertwined.

Whatever the role played by political atrophy and vested interest in forestalling a move into stage three by the majority of state socialist countries, it is also clear that there are real risks involved as well as some advantages. Most fundamentally, in replacing centralized state decision-making and co-ordination with a multiplicity of decentralized decision-making bodies with effective power to act in an unco-ordinated manner, there is bound to be an increase in the anarchy of the system. More concretely, the system would be transformed from a resource-constrained system to a demand-constrained system, bringing in its wake problems analogous to those of capitalism. In particular, there would be a strong incentive to 'externalize' slack in the system, giving rise to the possibility of unemployment. In the absence of market demand for a commodity and with the enterprise as a recognized cost centre, laying off labour would be one method of reducing costs to meet reduced circumstances.

For the consumer the advantage would come in the form of an increase in the responsiveness of enterprises to their requirements and an increase in the dynamism and micro-economic efficiency of the system. On the other hand, goods and services would be rationed by income rather than by administrative methods. A further potential problem would be the unequal capacity of regions to function as consumers and growing disparities uncompensated by central allocations. For the producer the advantage would come in the form of the possibility of exercising greater democratic control over a decentralized micro-economic environment. On the other hand, whereas in a resource-constrained economy producer power is frustrated by the centralized administrative apparatus, in a demand-constrained economy producer power is tempered by the market.

Finally, what are the implications for planning itself of the transition from a resource-constrained to a demand-constrained economy? The implication is that of abdication, that planning can no longer play a serious role in the absence of centralized interventionary powers which would prevent the advantages of demand-constrained production from materializing. Clearly it has to be admitted that to a large extent this is the case: to effect a transition to a demand-constrained economy, using the market to distribute resources and mediate conflicting claims, is to sacrifice the possibility of attempting to control the future.

Nevertheless, there are some senses in which a democratically based planning system can retain a presence. First of all, and although tempered by the market, a decentralized system does offer the possibility of participation in planning the future of an enterprise by its own workers. Second, this can be broadened out to involve representation from the local and regional community. Third, central government can still monitor developments and pinpoint decisions which lack macro-economic rationality. Fourth, central government could still retain an important indirect influence if it did not decentralize the banking system which, with the advent of active money and in the absence of a capital market, would become a potentially powerful interventionary tool. All of these channels for discussing rather than instrumentally planning the future, both from the bottom upwards and the top downwards, will not pre-empt the market but they can establish a coherent set of 'checks and balances' in the system.

These are the choices which are available and the risks which have to be taken on board. All of them involve 'trade-offs', something which we shall dwell on at greater length in the next but one section. Unfortunately there is no perfect economic system, nor will any radically new system evolve in the future, for all the possible ways of organizing economic activity are already known.

STATE, CLASS, AND POLITICS

We have stated the second 'law' governing the development of state socialist systems to be the extension of control by the state apparatus over civil society through a sort of 'colonization.' This occurs for immediate conjunctural reasons related to the process of seizure of state power, but more importantly because of the whole nature of politics under the new regime. Seen in terms of the distribution of power and ways of reproducing this, the new ruling elite in part consciously, in part impelled by the dialectic between their received ideas and reality, move always to concentrate power in the state apparatus.

The factors which intervene already during the wars of position and manoeuvre which bring socialist revolutionaries to power relate first to their clandestine and often military nature. The demand for loyalty and discipline above all else creates a contradiction with any impulse towards control at the base, which is then shaped by the doctrine of democratic centralism. Moreover, second, it is a limited group of leaders which is applying the doctrine, in all aspects, including received ideas concerning the class basis of the struggle. We have seen that the dialectics of the political struggle itself in fact shape the balance of classes, rather than the other way round. That tends to put leadership in the hands of a small intellectual elite, even before state power is finally captured. The administration of liberated areas and mass political education become their instruments, implicitly contradicting the upsurge of exploited and oppressed people which is what carries them to power. In summary, then, the ultimately decisive dialectic of that struggle can be stated as: the vanguard party plus Marxist–Leninist received ideas (of which it is in any case one) equals substitution of the leadership for the revolutionary classes and groups.

Once state power has been captured, the process of consolidation of the leadership group itself continues, but now – and this is the crucial transition – within the framework of a state apparatus. What is more, immediate pressures enforce the use of the old apparatus as an information-supplying and decision-making system. Moreover, it also serves as a base from which to eliminate dissidents and suppress all independent organizations. Control and mobilization of the population become priorities. Masked ideologically by the claim that their party/movement is the vanguard of the toiling masses, the leadership in effect substitutes itself for both as the only legitimate decision-maker.

As the received ideas on nationalization and central planning begin to be applied, the whole logic of previous class rule is turned on its head, with the bases in civil society being consciously destroyed. The distribution of power and its reproduction become centred only in the state apparatus, controlled by an elite recruited in part from the old revolutionaries, in part from new converts. The latter are generated by the deliberate break-up of old classes which is set in train (though with varying degrees of radicality) and the allocation of their previous members to new social locations. Basically, landlords and capitalists disappear as classes; middle-strata, petty bourgeois, peasant, and worker elements re-form but now in relation to the state alone, not to other dominant classes. The point is that this does not constitute a process of class formation in the established sense, but rather the creation of new hierarchies of consumption powers. The last is in principle determined by central control over distribution, but as the resource-constrained economy develops its own dialectic strong countervailing tendencies emerge at the base, as we have seen in Chapter 3.

Under state socialism reward according to labour performed, which is of course treated as the appropriate practice at that stage, becomes in fact a means by which those who control the labour process through the state apparatus ensure inequalities of distribution and the hierarchy of access to consumption resources which is the social basis for their power. The deconcentration of resources which is the real result of central planning reinforces this tendency because of its uneven effects. Unequal distribution and hierarchies of consumption are also sustained by the division of labour and different levels of development of rural and urban areas. Already in the *Communist Manifesto* Marx and Engels posited the disappearance of these, but later orthodoxy pushed them into the final stage of withering away of classes and the state.

On the other hand, even under a putative classless communism, and certainly under another form of socialism, the demands of complex economic and other organization seem to suggest that division of labour will have to exist. Here we begin to move into more speculative realms. As we tried to establish in Chapter 4, the actual experience of state socialism shows that the theoretical concepts of class, accumulation, and exploitation originally developed by Marx for the analysis of capitalism are not adequate when applied to these new formations. Viewed from that perspective, what we see forming within the state apparatus as Leviathan begins to grow (and not as a deformation of something else but in his own right) is thus not a new ruling *class* but something new. What it is exactly requires further theorizing and research.

Similarly, how to counter its development is a problem for further work. Clearly, access to education and democratic control of information systems would have to exist from the very beginning of socialist construction, along with the ability to change jobs, to prevent classes being replaced by status and power hierarchies of occupation. Similarly, equality of access to services would be used to prevent disparities among localities. All this implies a more decentralized and deconcentrated state structure, without a totally dominant party.

Before we leave this section, which has attempted to sum up and develop upon Chapter 4, two other points looking to the future need to be made. First, in the conditions of the periphery, and now that the anti-colonial phase is basically past, the issue of national self-determination will take the form of the place of nationalities within existing state frontiers. Leninist principles, including the right to secession, need a re-examination but above all reassertion here. No truly socialist state can bind an unwilling nationality (or group of them, if they desire another association) to itself.

Second, internationalism is a necessary principle for all socialists. Support for the struggle of others seeking to liberate themselves on a national or social basis is axiomatic. However, such support can never bestow the right to dictate policy. Moreover, however difficult it may be, the situation of countries on the periphery will continue to force socialists to combine fraternal support with dealing with capitalist interests from which indispensable technology, capital, and other supplies can be obtained. Much as it may stick in socialist throats, but absolute principles are luxury commodities and not basic needs.

The foregoing are basic qualifications upon Marxist–Leninist political ideas as we summarized them in Chapter 1 which seem to follow from our subsequent analysis. It now seems useful to bring our review of these and the arguments of Chapters 2, 3, and 4 together.

THE ANTINOMIES OF SOCIALISM AND UNDERDEVELOPMENT

Having reviewed the apparent weaknesses in a number of the received ideas of socialism, establishing those negative features of state socialist societies which can be traced back to applying faulty or misconceived socialist ideology in conditions of underdevelopment, we can now synthesize our arguments by pointing more systematically to the implications of particular policy stances, identifying the 'trade-off' which they involve. Our use of the word 'trade-off' underwrites a strongly held view, namely that there is no perfect economic and political system *nor is it possible to conceive one or to believe that the future will offer some radically new blueprint.* Unilinear views of the future which presage some new and unforetold mode of production must be rejected. As already noted, the principles of all conceivable methods of organizing an economic and political system are already known and they all have advantages and disadvantages which differ both qualitatively and over time. The essential task is therefore to weigh up, as precisely as possible, the risks inherent in the possible alternatives in order both to facilitate a well-informed debate and to relegate the quasi-religious dogma which often pervades this subject matter to the dustbin of history.

Before proceeding to discuss the detail of particular policy options and the trade-offs which they imply, we have to confront what is perhaps the greatest trade-off of all and which we have not yet touched upon, namely that between capitalism and socialism, or more particularly in the context of our main theme, that between peripheral capitalism and socialism in conditions of underdevelopment. Do the advantages of socialism on the periphery outweigh those of capitalism, or perhaps more pertinently, are the disadvantages of socialism on the periphery outweighed by those of capitalism? Were the Mensheviks in Russia in fact right to insist on the Marxist orthodoxy that the success of socialism depended upon a mature capitalism having exhausted its potential for developing the forces of production?

By emphasizing underdevelopment it might appear that we have taken the answer to this question for granted, but in fact what we have taken for granted is that revolutionary seizures of power in the name of socialism have necessarily taken place on the periphery, while counterpoising the *possibilities* of socialism with an ever-more sophisticated and dangerous barbarism at work in the world. A comprehensive answer would have to be empirically based in a way which is beyond the scope of this study, and even then it would still be speculative because both capitalism and socialism have had different implications at different historical moments of time and space and will do so in the future. We shall therefore only offer some general observations on this score, always bearing in mind that it is much more of an academic question than the other trade-offs. While the answer may have some minor influence on very slowly evolving general perceptions and consciousness, revolutions are not made in a spirit of cold, rational calculation about the costs and benefits of particular socio-economic systems, but in the face of oppression and in the hope of a better future which will, for the first time, actually offer the right to a choice between different alternatives.

A useful point of reference here is the ambivalence of Gavin Kitching in his book, *Rethinking Socialism*.[6] Having previously argued convincingly that the struggle for socialism can only be a very long-term one, and that, in the meantime, socialist consciousness only has the economic space to develop under the material conditions created by a prosperous capitalism, he has to address the question of socialism and underdevelopment. The logic of his previous argument in the context of advanced capitalisms would and does lead him to doubt whether a marriage between a truly democratic socialism and underdevelopment is possible. However, he then dilutes this line of thought with some economistic reasoning, drawing attention to the material advantages of socialism on the periphery, although not without noting the often quoted experience in east Africa, where Kenya's free enterprise appears to have been more successful at raising living standards than Tanzania's socialism.

His basic – though economistic – reasoning, however, would certainly seem to be a perfectly possible line to take. Would human rights, complete intellectual freedom, and democratic participation in policy-making (which, it should be stressed, do not exist in Kenya) mean a great deal in the absence of an ability to satisfy even basic human needs, which the more successful state socialisms (of which Tanzania is not one) have shown themselves capable of doing on the periphery, while capitalism is only sowing increasing anarchy and destitution? Nicaragua has shown the world what can be achieved in a very short time, even in face of extreme pressure, once the bonds of capitalist exploitation have been broken. Moreover, this point can now be made more strongly, for the kind of socialist dogma which has been associated with dictatorship is on the retreat worldwide (in this sense there is some truth in Reagan's words), allowing greater pragmatism, albeit with risks attached, and better theory, opening up greater possibilities for more pluralistic, but no less effective, socialism. In turn this means that one can hope that the kind of civil society which Kitching sees as a prerequisite for real socialist democracy will emerge that much more quickly on the periphery *but after the revolution.*

In considering the other trade-offs it is important to reiterate that this is in order to identify the risks involved in different policy stances. This means that we are not concerned to conclude by generating the institutional characteristics of a particular 'feasible' socialism, as Nove is in his popular *Economics of Feasible Socialism*, although we shall enlarge issues which he either only touches on or addresses by way of anecdote.[7]

The principal trade-offs which emerge out of this study are contained, albeit crudely, in Figure 5.1 which lists broad policy stances along one axis and different performance criteria along the other. The policy stances do not, of course, cover all the possibilities involving combinations of, say, administrative and market allocation, but in any combination one of the stances will inevitably set the tone

Performance Criteria

Policy Stances	Producer power	Consumer power	Quantity of products	Availability of products	Quality of products	Full employment	Income inequality	Regional inequality	Autonomous civil society
Administrative allocation	?	–	+	–	–	+	+	+	–
Market allocation	?	+	?	+	+	–	–	–	+
Rapid industrialization	–	–	?	–	–	+	–	–	–
Collectivized agriculture	–	–	?	–	–	+	+	?	–
Peasant agriculture	?	+	+	+	+	–	–	–	+
Closed economy	?	–	+	–	–	+	+	+	–
Open economy	–	+	?	?	?	–	–	–	+
Vanguard party	–	–	+	?	?	+	+	+	–

Figure 5.1 A trade-off matrix

of the system which will therefore reflect the advantages and disadvantages with which it is associated. In the case of a combination of administrative and market allocation the system would either be predominantly demand-constrained, reflecting the domination of market allocation, or resource-constrained, reflecting the domination of administrative allocation. Moreover, all of the policy stances concern choices after the seizure of power. Thus while the stance projecting a vanguard party may not have been a choice in order actually to seize power, it can become so afterwards, as Yugoslavia demonstrated when the party opted for a kind of pluralism, withdrew from centre-stage, and changed its name (in 1952) to the League of Communists of Yugoslavia. In any case, behind our charted criteria for the political choices lies a complex interaction between political and economic factors.

The performance criteria only need elaboration in one important respect. This concerns our use of the concepts of producer power and consumer power, concepts which were used without elaboration earlier in the chapter. By producer power we are referring to the power which all producers are able to exercise over their incomes, their working environment, the nature of their product, and their working lives. By consumer power we are referring to the power which all consumers are able to exercise over the quantity, quality, and assortment of goods and services available to them. Both concepts are clearly equally important in a socialist society, because working people are both producers and consumers, and together they would seem to offer both more fundamental and less abstract yardsticks for gauging the democratic character of a society than simply discussing this question in terms of different institutional arrangements being associated with 'more', 'less', or 'real' democracy. Moreover, they hit at the heart of the contradiction embraced by the concept of 'workers' control'. If we reject the utopianism implicit in the term 'control', this must surely embrace attempts at control by workers (peasants etc.) as producers *and* as consumers. Unfortunately, because any conceivable non-utopian socialist society will exhibit a division of labour, these two ambitions will conflict with one another, as we have already seen and as we shall clarify further below. The implications of this contradiction provoked by the division of labour, by the fact that individual workers do not just consume their own product, are not generally addressed by those who congregate under the slogan of 'workers' control', which is therefore usually a synonym for a utopian producer power (which we have already dismissed), much to the detriment of the elaboration of credible and popular socialist alternatives.

Returning to Figure 5.1, each policy stance is marked by a plus or a minus against relevant performance criteria. Where the nuances are too great to apply such generalizations a question mark is used. Clearly, the two major policy stances which determine the economic character of the system and have a major influence on its political character are delineated by the choice between administrative allocation and market allocation. Administrative allocation is more effective in terms of achieving rapid increases in the quantity of products, securing full employment, and in tackling or controlling income and regional inequalities. The risks attached to it involve both a sacrifice of consumer power as suction affects the quality and availability of products, and a sacrifice of individual and group freedom of expression as the Leviathan state expropriates civil society. Shifting to market allocation has a positive impact on consumer power as the quality and availability of products improves and also provides political space for the development of a healthy civil society as control is decentralized. The risks attached to it involve the sacrifice of the ability to guarantee full employment and a decreased ability to control income and regional inequalities. The decreased ability to control income inequalities has serious implications because although the general availability and quality of products may increase, they would be rationed by money under a system of market allocation. The implications of both systems for producer power are rather ambiguous. On the one hand, the decentralization of decision-making associated with market allocation offers greater scope for producer participation but, as we have said, this is tempered by the market which can dictate objectives and undermine security of employment. Any attempt, initiated at the micro-level, to counter this threat to producer power by seeking to dominate particular markets will only, by increasing the scale of the organization, reduce the scope for effective producer participation. On the other hand, the highly centralized decision-making associated with administrative allocation offers little scope for effective producer participation but it does offer greater security of employment.

Rapid industrialization which is generally, but not exclusively, associated with administrative allocation merely serves to exacerbate the risks of that system – the priority given to investment and heavy industry has a further negative impact on consumer power, while producer power can also suffer serious abuse if full employment also embraces forced or directed labour. (These trends may be reinforced by necessary militarization.) As far as agricultural strategy is concerned, collectivization suffers from all the general risks of administrative allocation and may not even have the advantage of increasing the quantity of agricultural products, at least in the short term. Moreover, and in spite of guaranteed employment, the subordination of agriculture to industry and the alienation associated with collectivization can probably be said to have a negative impact on producer power compared with peasant agriculture based on owner-occupancy. Peasant agriculture shares all the advantages and risks of market allocation but, in addition, and stimulated by appropriate incentives, is likely to be the most effective vehicle for increasing the quantity of at least certain agricultural products. Moreover, in a country which is still predominantly rural, the maintenance of a prosperous peasantry is particularly important to the development of a healthy civil society.

While a closed economy or tightly controlled interaction with the world economy is generally part and parcel of a system of administrative allocation, and thus reinforces its positive and negative features, the same is not true for an open economy policy stance with respect to a system of market allocation. This is because an open economy invites exposure to much greater competitive pressure, which in turn means that the market may very seriously undermine the scope for the exercise of producer power offered by a system of market allocation. Moreover, the quantity and general availability of products may be adversely affected by balance of payments problems and an attendant foreign exchange constraint. If the products in question are producer goods this may also affect quality, if forced substitution becomes necessary. It is not therefore the case that a shift from a closed economy to an open economy stance parallels a shift from administrative allocation to market allocation, although on balance consumer power will probably be enhanced. On the other hand, an open economy, particularly in so far as it involves travel and the exchange of ideas and different experiences, is certainly a vital ingredient in the development of a healthy civil society.

Finally, the presence of a vanguard party, culminating in a one-party state, becomes very questionable in the aftermath of a seizure of power. It follows from our analysis that its antinomy would be a socialist civil society (freed, that is, from the old exploitation) in which citizens would have autonomous control of the decisions affecting their lives, and thus over the state apparatus. The trade-off between the two is expressed in Figure 5.1 above all in economic terms, and basically follows the pattern of administrative allocation and collectivized agriculture versus market allocation and peasant agriculture. This is logical, since the political forms in the last instance express the economic relations. Beyond this, the unity and mobilizational capacity which the vanguard party might be able to secure would have to be traded-off against its stifling of the avenues of individual and group expression in civil society, which is the lifeblood of a fully socialist project.

One possible alternative to the monopoly vanguard party, which is certainly fashionable, a multiparty, parliamentary-style system, political pluralism transplanted into a socialist society, is endorsed by authorities as diverse as Nove and Mandel. In fact both Nove and Mandel use similar arguments to prosecute their cases, in particular emphasizing the need for a diversity of political parties as the only effective vehicles for presenting alternatives to the populace (in Mandel's case throughout a hierarchy of workers' councils), of stimulating ideas and debate, in other words of promoting a healthy civil society.[8]

On the other hand, this viewpoint has to meet a strong challenge from the Yugoslav leader and theoretician, Edvard Kardelj, expressed cogently in his last testament to the Yugoslav people:

> The political system belonging to the era of bourgeois parliamentarism ... cannot serve a society of socialist self-management, and certainly not a society which was created by a popular revolution, like the Yugoslav society. In the present circumstances in Yugoslavia, such a system would put us far back into the past, to a situation of political struggle for political, or class, supremacy, i.e. to the relations and social antagonisms which caused the revolution in the first place. More than that it is totally incompatible with the organization of our society on the principle of self-management, based on *the pluralism of interests of self-managing subjects* and not on *the pluralism of parties, or their competition for the monopoly of political power.*[9]

Clearly Kardelj has a serious point to make – if power is vested directly in political parties then other forms of socialist democracy based on a diverse plurality of interest groups which directly reflect a wide spectrum of concerns from people in their different life-roles (at work, at home, living in a community, as members of trade-unions, as women, as members of ethnic minorities, etc.) are likely to be rendered impotent. And the idea of self-management pluralism does make the idea of socialist democracy both distinct and attractive. Indeed, it could be said to be a reconstruction of the concept of a socialist state by returning to the Marx of, for example, 'The Class Struggles in France' or the original Russian concept of soviets.

However, both views suffer from unadvertised defects which are in fact the mirror image of each other. Our two advocates of political pluralism evade the thorny question of whether there will be any constraints imposed on political activity, specifically will anti-socialist parties be allowed a platform to present their alternative to the populace? Nove implies that it will be open season for any political party, in turn raising the possibility that socialists may have to abdicate in favour of pro-capitalist forces. Mandel vaguely stipulates a requirement for 'working-class political parties', leaving aside by what procedure and by whom parties would be designated as 'working class'. On the other hand, for Kardelj and the Yugoslavs this problem is resolved by the continued existence of the League of Communists which guarantees the framework within which self-management pluralism will operate, but at the expense of political space for an organized, critical opposition.

While the incompatibility between monopoly vanguard parties and a healthy socialist civil society may be clear, the question of alternatives therefore leaves us ambivalent. As with the choice between administrative and market allocation, trade-offs seem to be involved. On the one hand, political pluralism may guarantee constructive and effective debate about alternatives, but it may also stifle other equally important and innovative forms of socialist democracy which enfranchise people in new ways, and it may even result in the restoration of capitalism. On the other hand, while a constrained political pluralism or self-management pluralism may offer guarantees against the restoration of capitalism, and in the latter case open up new and fertile extensions of socialist democracy, they may also inhibit both effective debate about alternatives and their implementation.

These, then, are the antinomies of socialism and underdevelopment. Evidently, any concept of democratic socialism implies that the trade-offs between the major policy stances which we have identified (as well as those which we may have missed) should be placed before the people so that they can weigh up the advantages which they wish to seek and the inevitable risks that they are prepared to take. This was not possible at the time of Marx and Lenin, but our experience since then, and progress in the field of communications, make it possible now.

PATTERNS OF THE IMMEDIATE FUTURE

If especially the last points made above are judged to belie our non-utopian intent, or to lie well into the future as a serious policy option, how are the patterns of the immediate future likely to present themselves? Given the conflicts and problems which we have analysed at length, how is the marriage between socialism and underdevelopment likely to work out in the short term?

Any answer must address two separate, if related, issues. First, how likely is it that we shall see many new marriages? Second, how are existing marriages going to work out?

The first question has already received some attention earlier in the chapter; here we only wish to crystallize some generalizations. Earlier we pointed out that out of the five categories of socialist seizure of power witnessed this century, four have been linked with non-repeatable events. This leaves the category where the form of intermediate integration has produced extended contradictions in a formally independent economy and in an international economy where advanced integration is becoming the dominant form, at least on a regional level (for example, the Pacific Basin). In turn this indicates that decisive seizures of power will become less likely, if only because the pool of intermediately integrated countries is diminishing or they are becoming 'basket cases' with almost total breakdown. As suggested earlier, situations in countries attempting to claim the status of advanced integration but not quite succeeding may lead to prolonged and complex socialist attempts. The Philippines comes most readily to mind here, with a process already initiated in the early 1970s.

However, this prognosis does not and really cannot take into account the new and unforeseen possibilities and schisms which will be opened up by an increasingly rapid and unchecked internationalization and re-internationalization of capital. The aspect of speed means that the status of, and living standards in any region of the world (including regions within the core of advanced capitalism) can be transformed almost overnight (by previous historical standards). Although it will not be so in every case (remembering Iran), the received ideas of socialism will continue to inspire movements involved in the consequent struggles for survival, even if these have to resort to existing state socialisms for practical support. On the other hand, it has to be clearly borne in mind that international capital is now reproducing a new sub-category of country as referred to above, places, above all in Africa, so poor that they have almost fallen off the edge of the US State Department's map of the world, places where the physical well-being of the people has been reduced below the level at which the mobilizing force of ideas can be expected to have much impact.

The suggestion that conjunctures and countries ripe for socialist seizures of power may well diminish is a controversial one, but it also draws the focus of our attention to what is, rather than to what might be, towards the prognosis for existing state socialist societies. Here the conclusions of our analysis are more helpful. First of all, we have rejected the notion that any new doctrine, any radically new and unforeseen system will come to the rescue. In turn this means that we are left with the existing antinomies of state socialism and underdevelopment, with trade-offs rather than a utopia. What does this amount to in concrete terms?

Already we have identified the compelling attraction of transition, not to but within state socialism. This means to stage three, to a decentralized, predominantly demand-constrained and politically more pluralistic self-managing economy, society and polity, a transition from stage two and perhaps in future cases directly from stage one. Indeed, as we write, the Soviet Union itself is adopting 'liberalization' measures, announcing the introduction of a new co-operative sector, the legalization of self-employment in small-scale services and manufacturing, the freeing of light industry from central planning direction over quantity and quality of output, and an end to the monopoly over foreign trade held by the Ministry of Foreign Trade. On the periphery Cuba and Viet Nam, for example, are attempting to grapple with the shortcomings of their rigidly orthodox systems.

All this, because it usually involves emphasis on the market and new individual liberties, is the cause of current ideological satisfaction in the White House. However, although as we have sought to demonstrate state socialist societies and the ideology of state socialism do face difficult problems, this is still misplaced. Today, first of all, the majority of socialists who have paused to reflect would agree that the market can and should play a useful role in a socialist society and would contend that this is not necessarily tantamount to the restoration of capitalism. The state versus the market is not therefore equivalent to socialism versus capitalism, and the increasing importance of the market in state socialist societies does not signify a victory for capitalism. Moreover, at a deeper level, many socialists are willing to appreciate the links between economic liberalization and individual liberties and to recognize that the latter are indispensable to a flourishing, socialist civil society. 'No state, no system and political party can bring man happiness' could have been written by Hayek or Friedman and mimicked by Reagan or Thatcher. So could, 'Only he who takes responsibility for his freedom can be free.' In fact both sentences were written by Edvard Kardelj, the Yugoslav communist, to whom we referred at an earlier point in this chapter.[10] In other words, liberalization could also enrich socialism to the lasting undoing of capitalism, rather than playing into the hands of capitalism to the lasting undoing of socialism.

Second, and on the other hand, it is not all one-way traffic in the contemporary world of state socialism. While for those countries new to it, the world of economic reform, decentralization, liberalization and the market may be one of unalloyed attractions, for those who have lived with it longer these can wear a little thin. Thus the 1980s have seen Yugoslavia carrying a huge debt burden and suffering phenomenal rates of inflation (predictable consequences of openness) compelling the reconsideration of re-centralization, at least as far as the major macro-economic aggregates are concerned. Thus, the trade-offs between state and market, between administrative allocation and market allocation are not mere abstractions but are embodied in living historical experience. We may well expect that the forces of liberalization will have to beat a retreat in new conjunctures.

In general terms, then, this leads us to view the immediate future of state socialism as lying between centralized collectivism and decentralized liberalization, oscillating or more likely lurching between them. Even if politics and populations will not be informed by intellectual arguments (one of our suppositions at the beginning of this section), experience will still force the same difficult choices. Further to this we can also add a possibility which has already been referred to in passing, namely, that some kind of 'convergence' may occur between the specifically state socialist societies which have been the principal focus of our attention and other socialist societies on the periphery which have not committed themselves to the Marxist–Leninist model (e.g. Nicaragua). This possibility arises as the former are drawn towards stage three via stage two and the latter, for various reasons, move from a stage one situation directly to stage three. In other words an economically and politically decentralized system, which is predominantly demand-constrained, may prove magnetic for a variety of radical social formations.

Finally, it also leads us to come to an entirely uncataclysmic view about the future of existing state socialist societies. Unless threatened by severe internal regional and/or ethnic conflict, their power blocs seem reasonably well placed to survive. Based on east European experience, at least, certain conditions can be postulated which in theory might lead to mass movements for radical change in state socialist societies. (Obviously we discount coups within the leadership, which in certain cases like Ethiopia, Benin, or the Congo may well still be military in form.) A basic necessity would seem to be a split within the power bloc, perhaps – though not necessarily – including some top figures, with a broader dissidence probably forming around a group of alienated intellectuals. These would have to have contacts with peasants and workers, since some measure of organization would be needed to support strikes and demonstrations at the moment of confrontation. Given the real demobilization and atomization of the mass of the population, some special circumstances would be required to ensure that many rallied behind the relatively few who could possibly be organized in advance. Probably the decisive conjuncture would come when measures were taken by the government to impose austerity in face of the continuing economic problems which we postulated in Chapter 3. Noting that it is Hungary in 1956, Czechoslovakia in 1968, and Poland in 1956, 1970, and 1980-1 which provide us with examples of such massive upswells from below suggests that there may be special features of the east European cases, above all anti-Russian nationalism and the influence of the Catholic church, which may not be present elsewhere.

Viewed, thus, in terms of the periphery as it now exists, the prognosis for future cases of mass upsurge seems gloomy. Looked at on the level of theory, it must be remembered that the social basis of power in these regimes is of a new kind. The new rulers are not a class in the generally understood sense. Their position is secured through their structural location within the party and/or state apparatus, and is ensured only by that. They have no independent power base outside it, in civil society. In that sense the system itself has priority over any social group, even those who direct it. If that is so, any hope of resisting the system and especially of radically changing it must be seen as slight. Such a struggle would be not just against a ruling group which was increasingly incapable of ensuring the regime's reproduction but all the complex underlying structures and their interpenetrations which define the regime. That immediately implies a revolutionary upsurge, and it is not easy to see how a move to this would be achieved from the piecemeal, atomized resistance which we have already described in Chapter 4.

Seen more politically, it may be suggested that there is unlikely to be any distinctive ideology around which mass oppositional forces can group. Other than preaching the restoration of capitalism (which paradoxically may achieve mass popularity if state socialist leaders do not learn some lessons), all that remains is an eclectic mixture which the power bloc can easily mimic as it lurches between centralism and decentralization, collectivism and individualism. (As it can also manipulate capitalist penetration as it grows in scope, and products and tastes from the capitalist world permeate the mass of the population.) So long as leaderships remain cohesive, distribute benefits to key elements like the armed forces and enough others to give them a base, and maintain the apparatuses of political control and security, the most that may be expected are mass movements around limited issues which may destabilize some regimes for a time.

This leaves us with the possibility of foreign intervention, perhaps in conjunction with the sort of regional or ethnic conflict referred to above. And that in turn brings us back to the fact that we are dealing with possibilities on a world scale, making what might happen to the state socialist systems, certainly in the long term, doubly unpredictable. As for the short term, we may expect, provided that humanity is spared nuclear and ecological disaster on a global scale, that the features and tendencies which have been analysed in this book will continue to work themselves out in fact well beyond the end of what might indeed be called the Century of Socialism and Underdevelopment.

Notes

1 SOCIALISM AND UNDERDEVELOPMENT

1   The term 'state socialist societies' is used subsequently as a blanket term to cover those societies which have arisen out of revolutions led by a party or movement influenced by what we shall call the 'received ideas of socialism'. It avoids the confusing use of just 'socialist' when referring to these societies while embracing one of the features which most of them have in common, namely, the central role assigned to the state in socialist transformation. The concepts elaborated in this book are used in two companion studies in which we investigate the political economy of two particular revolutions. One study is of Viet Nam (K. Post), the other of Yugoslavia (P. Wright). Our empirical and theoretical work has proceeded side by side, with each providing reciprocal inputs into the other. An issue faced in Post's work is not dealt with here, namely whether Maoist doctrine in China provided a real potential alternative. On this see the important discussion by P. Corrigan, H. Ramsay, and D. Sayer, in their *Socialist Construction and Marxist Theory*, London: Macmillan, 1978, and *For Mao*, London: Macmillan, 1979.
2   Those in Albania and Yugoslavia were not imported with the Red Army in 1944-5, as in Poland, Eastern Germany (perhaps better described, along with Czechoslovakia in 1948, as 'semi-developed'), Hungary, Rumania and Bulgaria, but these two were certainly 'underdeveloped'.
3   The most theoretically significant discussions of the Nicaraguan experience are to be found in Richard R. Fagen, Carmen Diana Deere, and Jose Luis Coraggio (eds) *Transition and Development*, New York: Monthly Review Press and Center for the Study of the Americas, 1986, which also contains some useful general pieces.
4   See L. Trotsky, *Permanent Revolution* and *Results and Prospects*, New York: Merit Publishers, 1969.
5   E. Mandel, 'Ten theses on the social and economic laws governing the society transitional between capitalism and socialism', *Critique* 3, 1974, 8.
6   T. Cliff, *State Capitalism in Russia*, London: Pluto Press, 1974, 175.
7   Here we draw particularly on the painstaking work by E. Preobrazhensky and B. Ollman. See E. Preobrazhensky, 'Socialist and communist

conceptions of socialism', *Vestnik Kommunisticheskoy akademii* 12, 1925, 19-75, and B. Ollman, 'Marx's vision of communism', *Critique* 8, Summer 1977, 4-41.

8   We say 'probably added' because some of these points, particularly (13), remained matters of controversy in 1917. By 1930 they were fully 'received'. Similarly, we do not believe that there were any real additions to the list after around 1930, because no new idea commanded such general acceptance. A good example is the doctrine of 'peaceful coexistence', evolved by the Soviet leadership from February 1956 onwards but never in their form accepted by the Chinese.

9   On the Second International and Lenin see the brief but penetrating remarks by Ernesto Laclau and Chantal Mouffe in 'Socialist strategy, where next?', *Marxism Today*, January 1981, 17-19.

10   It is appropriate here to acknowledge the value of part at least of the work of Corrigan, Ramsay, and Sayer. Their analysis of the origins and development of 'Bolshevism' is a most important one and runs parallel to ours, though we feel it to be rather too narrow in scope (see *Socialist Construction and Marxist Theory*, Chapters 1, 2, and 3). Moreover, we cannot accept their view of the thought of Mao Tse-tung as providing a sort of antidote and alternative to Bolshevism; rather, we see his ideas as very much the product of the attempt to carry out the socialist revolution and transformation in a peripheral capitalist country, a mixture, therefore, of Marxist–Leninist themes, pragmatism and populism, with a strong admixture of the need to justify ideologically his manoeuvres within a bureaucratic leadership. For further development of the opposing view see Corrigan, Ramsay, and Sayer, *For Mao*, op. cit.

11   As we have indicated, this review section of the chapter is by no means intended to be comprehensive – it simply picks out what we see as being the main paradigms, involved in the debate about the 'transition to socialism', and the main landmarks in that debate out of which we then begin to establish the framework of our own analysis. In turn this means that at this stage we do not consider those contributions which are more akin to (economistic) 'models' than paradigms, e.g. E. Preobrazhensky, *The New Economics*, Oxford: Oxford University Press, 1965, and E.V.K. Fitzgerald, 'Notes on the analysis of the small underdeveloped economy in transition', in R.R. Fagen, C.D. Deere, and J.L. Coraggio (eds) *Transition and Development*. Such contributions, we feel, are more appropriately addressed in the context of Chapter 3. For much fuller reviews of the debate in general see, for example, P. Bellis, *Marxism and the USSR*, London: Macmillan, 1979 and F. Feher, A. Heller, and G. Markus, *Dictatorship Over Needs*, Oxford: Basil Blackwell, 1983, Chapter 1.

12   See M. Dobb, *In Soviet Russia – Autumn 1930*, London, Modern Books, 1930, for a prominent example of romantic mesmerization.

13   On this last point see the perceptive essay by Rossana Rossanda, 'Revolutionary intellectuals and the Soviet Union', in R. Miliband and J. Saville (eds) *Socialist Register 1974*, London: Merlin Press, 1974, 21.

14   L. Trotsky, *The Revolution Betrayed*, New York: Merit Publishers, 1965, 47.

15   ibid., 112.
16   ibid., 113.
17   ibid., 248.
18   Mandel, 'Ten theses', 10. See also Chapter 3 of his *Revolutionary Marxism Today*, London: New Left Books, 1979.
19   'Ten theses', 9.
20   ibid., 6.
21   See E. Mandel, 'The nature of the Soviet state', *New Left Review*, 108, March-April 1978, 18, and also *Revolutionary Marxism Today*.
22   See Trotsky, *The Revolution Betrayed*, 175.
23   Mandel, 'The nature of the Soviet state', 36.
24   See Cliff, *State Capitalism*, 270 and 287.
25   This is not just the same as the bureaucracy being paid more than the value of its labour power. The value of labour power is that portion of total value which workers receive in the form of a wage. The difference between total value and the value of labour power is that portion of total value which is set aside for accumulation purposes. If the bureaucracy is exploiting the rest of the population, this therefore means that it is paid more than the total value which it produces: not only does it not make any contribution to accumulation, but it also encroaches on the value produced by the rest of the population. See Cliff's discussion of this point in *State Capitalism*, 80-1.
26   ibid., 166-7.
27   ibid., 181.
28   ibid., 182.
29   See C. Bettelheim, *Economic Calculation and Forms of Property*, London: Routledge & Kegan Paul, 1976. Bettelheim supplements his theoretical work with an empirical study of the Soviet Union in an attempt to demonstrate how it became 'state capitalist': see C. Bettelheim, *Class Struggles in the USSR: First Period: 1917-1923*, Hassocks: Harvester Press, 1976.
30   *Economic Calculation*, 98.
31   See C. Castoriadis, *La Société Bureaucratique 1 (Les rapports de production en Russie)* and *La Société Bureaucratique 2 (La révolution contre la bureaucracie)*, Paris: 10/18, 1973.
32   R. Bahro, 'The alternative in eastern Europe', *New Left Review* 106, November-December 1977, 9. See also, of course, his book of the same title, London: New Left Books, 1978.
33   Bahro article, 9.
34   ibid., 13.
35   Bahro's reason for rejecting these concepts is that the revolutionary terrain generated by the social structure of actually existing socialism lies more in the realm of *surplus* consciousness than alienated consciousness. We do not include a discussion of the meaning of surplus consciousness because it is not relevant to the main purpose of our review.
36   See M. Rakovski, 'Marxism and the analysis of soviet societies', *Capital and Class*, 1, Spring 1977, and *Towards an East European Marxism*, London: Allison & Busby, 1978. It should be noted that this author is in fact György Bence and János Kis: see the introductory note to Bence and

Kis, 'On being a Marxist: a Hungarian view', in R. Miliband and J. Saville (eds) *Socialist Register 1980*, London: Merlin Press, 1980.

37 'Marxism and the analysis of soviet societies', 85.

38 ibid., 91.

39 ibid., 100.

40 Feher, Heller, and Markus, *Dictatorship Over Needs*, 71.

41 ibid., 70

42 ibid., 70.

43 Incidentally, we selected companion case-studies other than the Soviet Union because we felt that the debate about the transition to socialism is focused too exclusively on the latter.

2 THE SEIZURE OF POWER

1 Examples of this 'modernization' are Russia, which sought 'great power' status; Thailand (Siam), where the grounds were laid for large-scale rice exports; the Ottoman empire, where the advent of the Young Turks, after earlier failures by the Sultans, held out hopes of a state which might help to stabilize the Middle East and above all hold back Russian expansion; Iran (Persia), where Tsarist ambitions were also a problem and some 'development' was needed to facilitate the production of oil, the new life-blood of industrial capitalism; and Ethiopia, which had less economic significance but consolidation of which under Menelik greatly helped Britain in containing and menacing the Mahdist state in the Sudan from the south, as the armies of Queen Victoria prepared to conquer from the north. All these states remained independent of direct colonial rule because of rivalry among the great powers; Italy's disastrous defeat by Menelik's army in 1896 showed what happened when a small colonial power moved out of its league. Japan is the most significant case, beginning modernization early, doing it most thoroughly (able to defeat Russia in the war of 1904-5), and basically keeping control of the whole process itself.

2 On this see Bill Warren's typically challenging posthumous work, *Imperialism: Pioneer of Capitalism*, London: New Left Books, 1980, especially Chapter 3.

3 For a full coverage, among other questions one would need to discuss the issue of whether the term 'peripheral' is itself satisfactory. If the advanced industrial countries can reproduce their privileged status only because the 'periphery' exists then, in terms of the world system as a whole, to call it such seems to strain at language. On the other hand, in terms of a distribution of power on a global scale, concept and word may be apt. Though we have some hesitation about using it at all, it may be taken that it is in the latter sense.

4 That does not imply, of course, that there would not have been poverty, starvation, disease, and social relations of exploitation without that expansion. For the most forceful statement of the view of active creation of underdevelopment see Walter Rodney, *How Europe Underdeveloped Africa*, London: Bogle L'Ouverture, 1972.

5 Reference may be made here to Immanuel Wallerstein's interesting study, *The Modern World System*, New York: Academic Press, 1974, which distinguishes two forms of spatial and economic organization emerging from the fifteenth century onwards, the 'periphery' and the 'external area' (see especially 301-2). Wallerstein has been subjected to considerable criticism. (For some of the most cogent see Robert Brenner, 'The origins of capitalist development: a critique of neo-Smithian Marxism', *New Left Review*, 104, July-August 1977, especially 29-33). We do not feel that the Wallerstein analytical frame and historical interpretation really hold up under the weight of cumulative criticism, but it is a stimulating approach.

6 Examples of countries which are far along in this transition are Argentina, Brazil, South Korea, and South Africa. Mexico has obviously begun it, and Iran under the Shah was trying to begin. It is worth noting further that the importance of the public sector in this sort of transition is a basis for 'state capitalism' in another variant, not as applied to the Soviet Union (though there are connections).

7 Russia had a relatively large manufacturing sector, but was still basically an exporter of agricultural raw materials and oil; Cuba was still dependent upon the export of a single crop, sugar, although sugar-milling (less so growing) was a highly capital-intensive enterprise in which some local capital had gained a foothold, and manufacturing was expanding.

8 The middle strata, it should be noted, do not constitute a class in themselves, since they do not have a distinct relationship to the means of production and control of labour power; in this they resemble most of all the working class, since they sell their labour power to live. On the other hand, their labour power serves different purposes in the production and realization of surplus value. Nor should they be merged with the petty bourgeoisie in one class, as most Marxists classify them, since they do not owe their living to even the petty property represented by tools, raw materials or a stock of trade goods. It should be recognized that their position and class status are complex and controversial: for further discussion see Ken Post, *Arise Ye Starvelings*, The Hague: Martinus Nijhoff, 1978, 98-103, and *Strike the Iron*, Atlantic Highlands, NJ: Humanities Press, 1981, vol. 1, 23-6.

9 From this point on, unless otherwise specified, this phrase will be used to cover the institutions, the power which they concentrate, and the legitimizing ideology associated with them, and the term 'state' to imply all five aspects.

10 See *NACLA'S Latin America and Empire Report*, special Nicaragua edition, X(2), February 1976, 18 and 22.

11 The seminal work here was Hamza Alavi, 'The state in post-colonial societies: Pakistan and Bangladesh', *New Left Review*, 74, July-August 1972.

12 'Extracts from the thesis on the Bolshevization of Communist Parties adopted at the Fifth ECCI Plenum', in Jane Degras (ed.), *The Communist International (1919-1943): Documents*, London: Oxford University Press, 1956- 65, vol. II, 190.

13 Though some countries, namely Yugoslavia, Albania, China, and

Kampuchea broke with the USSR *after* communists had won power there.

14 On this see Fernando Claudin, *The Communist Movement: From Comintern to Cominform*, Harmondsworth: Penguin, 1975, 260-5.

15 'Programme of the Communist International adopted at its Sixth Congress', in Jane Degras (ed.) *The Communist International*, vol. II, 538.

16 ibid., 539.

17 ibid. An example of this utopianism would have been Gandhi's doctrines in India.

18 'Programme of the Communist International', 539.

19 ibid., 540.

20 The key text is 'State and civil society', to be found in Quintin Hoare and Geoffrey Nowell Smith (ed. and trans.) *Selections from the Prison Notebooks of Antonio Gramsci*, London: Lawrence & Wishart, 1971; but see also 'Notes on Italian history' and 'The modern prince'. An important discussion is Perry Anderson's 'The antinomies of Antonio Gramsci', *New Left Review*, 100, November 1976-January 1977, and see also Anne Showstack Sassoon, *Gramsci's Politics*, London: Croom Helm, 1980, 193-204.

21 As almost always with Gramsci, this is basically a plausible interpretation of a number of scattered passages. It has to be remembered that he wrote the works used here in fragments and deliberately elliptically in order to disguise his real concerns from his gaolers.

22 There is an extensive coverage of this in Massimo Salvadori, *Karl Kautsky and the Socialist Revolution*, London: New Left Books, 1979, Chapters III-V.

23 Anderson, 'Antinomies', 70.

24 ibid.

25 ibid., 198, and 'Programme of the Communist International', 542.

26 'Programme', 542.

27 'Notes on Italian history', in Hoare and Nowell Smith, op.cit., 57-8, but following Anderson's translation, 'Antinomies', 45. It should be noted that there is an ambiguity concerning 'social group'; immediately before Gramsci was writing about political parties, but Anderson identifies this term as equivalent to workers. We give it a third meaning, more in line with Gramsci's concern with parties, that is a group of leaders.

28 Degras, vol. II, 506.

29 We owe the germs of this idea to Ernesto Laclau's treatment of 'interpellation' in his *Politics and Ideology in Marxist Theory*, London: New Left Books, 1977, though finding him in this instance more than usually difficult to follow. For that reason, and also because he is concerned only with advanced capitalist situations, we have tried to reformulate the ideas.

30 'The modern prince', in Hoare and Nowell Smith, op. cit., 181-2.

31 Laclau, *Politics and Ideology in Marxist Theory*, 110-11. For a critique see Nicos Mouzelis, 'Ideology and class politics: a critique of Ernesto Laclau', *New Left Review*, 112, November-December 1978.

32 Indeed, already before Lenin's statement Marxism as such had been

attacked by the anarchists, as a 'petty bourgeois' ideology specially directed towards securing their dictatorship over the proletariat.

33 Hoare and Nowell Smith, op. cit., 97, note.

34 See in particular his two works, 'The Intellectuals' and 'Notes on Italian History', in Hoare and Nowell Smith, op. cit., and the discussion in Sassoon, op. cit., 134-50.

35 'The intellectuals', Hoare and Nowell Smith, op. cit., 5.

36 ibid., 7.

37 ibid., 9.

38 ibid., 6.

39 On this see Hugh Thomas, *Cuba or the Pursuit of Freedom*, London: Eyre & Spottiswoode, 1971, 810-18.

40 'The modern prince', 168. For us there is some ambiguity in the phrase 'traditional policies', which could most obviously mean those of what we call the power bloc, but might refer to the revolutionary leadership itself. The general context of Gramsci's remarks was, of course, the debate within the ranks of the Second International and after it concerning the limited 'economist' struggle over immediate working-class interests and its progression towards the 'political' (revolutionary) struggle directed towards the seizure of state power. We do not take this as a central issue, primarily because we do not feel that there is an effective separation between economic and political struggle (see below).

41 For extended development and application of the concepts of conjuncture and conjunction, see Ken Post, *Strike the Iron*, op. cit.

42 Degras, vol. II, 522.

43 Through failing to maintain a sufficient presence in the more central areas and Bangkok, the party missed its chance in the period 1973-6, when it was the students, workers, and urban masses in general who had brought down the regime and used the opportunity of a bourgeois democratic government to begin to build a bloc with the peasants. The party in fact helped to thwart this by its attempts to move in and take control.

44 R. Debray, *Revolution in the Revolution?*, New York: Grove Press, 1967, 83-4.

45 R. Debray, *A Critique of Arms*, Harmondsworth: Penguin, 1977, vol. 1, 107.

46 This happened in Bolivia in 1967 to even as experienced a guerrilla commander as Ché Guevara; Debray earned a prison sentence for his marginal role in the same affair.

47 In his re-evaluation Debray comes back to the position that 'the *foco* as I envisaged it was no more nor less than one particular expression of the Party as defined in *What is to Be Done?*' (*Critique*, vol. 1, 169).

48 There is an important variant pattern. While the revolutionary bloc is still building, and before it can begin to manoeuvre itself effectively towards state power, a coup, usually by elements of the armed forces, may pre-empt the intended seizure and reform the power bloc in an attempt to stabilize the situation, even if for this the interests of elements of the dominant class have to be damaged by reforms. The main factor in determining whether or not this 'radical' turn is taken (contrasting Peru

in 1968 with Chile in 1973, for example) seems to be the current balance of class forces, and the social background and orientations of the officer corps.

3 STATE SOCIALIST ACCUMULATION: THE RESOURCE-CONSTRAINED ECONOMY

1 See N. Bukharin, *The Economics and Politics of the Transition Period*, London: Routledge & Kegan Paul, 1979, 57, and V.I. Lenin, *State and Revolution*, Peking: Foreign Languages Press, 1970.

2 J. Stalin, 'Economic problems of socialism in the USSR',in B. Franklin (ed.) *The Essential Stalin: Major Theoretical Writings 1905-52*, London: Croom Helm, 1973, 445-6.

3 W. Brus, *The Market in a Socialist Economy*, London: Routledge & Kegan Paul, 1972, 95.

4 N. Bukharin, op.cit., 147-8.

5 An elaboration of this point is beyond the scope of our enquiry. Suffice it to say that all kinds of political, institutional, and economic factors prevent the 'law of value' from operating. Among the latter would figure the fact that labour is not internationally mobile, a feature of the international market-place which is a cornerstone of the various theories of 'unequal' rather than equivalent exchange between countries. See, for example, O. Braun (with R. Brown and P. Wright), *International Trade and Imperialism*, Atlantic Heights, NJ: Humanities Press, 1984.

6 The concept of a 'resource-constrained economy' is borrowed from J. Kornai (see *Economics of Shortage*, Amsterdam: North Holland, 1980) but whereas his major concern is with the micro-economics of more 'mature' industrialized state socialist economies, we attempt to broaden the concept by adding macro-economic dimensions, particularly those associated with the industrialization process. We also give the idea of conflict a much higher profile. The concept of resource constraints has also been applied in macro-economic analysis to the problems of peripheral capitalist economies – to the so-called 'two-gap' model with its savings and foreign exchange constraints – but our usage is much less restricted and set within an entirely different context.

7 See Mao Tse-tung, *Selected Works*, Peking: Foreign Languages Press, vol. V, 1974.

8 See E.A. Preobrazhensky, 'Economic notes I – on the goods famine', in D. Filtzer (ed.) *The Crisis of Soviet Industrialization*, London: Macmillan, 1980.

9 See G. Irvin, 'Nicaragua: establishing the state as the centre of accumu-lation', *Cambridge Journal of Economics* 7(2), June 1983, 125-39, and E.V.K. Fitzgerald, 'The economics of the Revolution', in T.W. Walker (ed.) *Nicaragua in Revolution*, New York: Praeger, 1982.

10 It should be noted that we speak of 'original' accumulation, rather than following the customary misleading English usage, 'primitive'.

11 See E.A. Preobrazhensky, *The New Economics*, Oxford: Oxford University Press, 1965.

12   In this sense Preobrazhensky's view of the 'transition to socialism' suffers from the same defects as those which we subjected to criticism in Chapter 1:   state ownership, control and planning are simply equated with socialism.

13   See E.A. Preobrazhensky, 'Economic equilibrium in the system of the USSR', *The Crisis of Soviet Industrialization, op.cit.*, 187-90.

14   See V.I. Lenin, 'The development of capitalism in Russia', *Collected Works*, vol.3, London: Lawrence & Wishart, 1960.

15   See T. Shanin, *The Awkward Class: Political Sociology of Peasantry in a Developing Society, Russia 1910-1925*,Oxford: Clarendon Press, 1972.

16   See, for example, D. Warriner, 'Urban thinkers and peasant policy in Yugoslavia, 1918-19', *Slavonic and East European Review* 38, 1959.

17   These errors are usefully catalogued and discussed in M. Ellman, 'Agricultural productivity under socialism', *World Development* 9/10, 1981, 979-89.

18   The description of the collectivization of the chickens in a small Don village in M. Sholokov's *Virgin Soil Upturned*, Harmondsworth: Penguin, 1977, bears eloquent witness to this.

19   See M. Lewin, 'Taking grain', in C. Abramsky (ed.) *Essays in Honour of E.H. Carr*, London: Macmillan, 1974.

20   See M. Ellman, 'Did the agricultural surplus provide the resources for the increase in investment in the USSR during the First Five-Year Plan?', *Economic Journal* 85, December 1975.

21   Mao Tse-tung, *On the Correct Handling of Contradictions Among the People*, New York: New Century, 1957, 10.

22   In one of his essays Kalecki offered a theorem for pitting the future against the present but it still involves a coefficient measuring the strength of objections to reducing consumption in the short run – in other words, it still inevitably depends upon the choice of an appropriate discount rate. See M. Kalecki, 'Increasing the rate of growth of national income under conditions of an unlimited supply of labour', in his *Selected Essays on the Economic Growth of the Socialist and the Mixed Economy*, Cambridge: Cambridge University Press, 1972, 27-36.

23   Bukharin, *op.cit.*, Chapter 3.

24   Preobrazhensky, *The Crisis of Soviet Industrialization*, op.cit.

25   See J. Kornai, *Rush versus harmonic growth*, Amsterdam: North Holland, 1972, and B. Horvat, *Towards a Theory of the Planned Economy*, Belgrade: Yugoslav Institute of Economic Research, 1964.

26   See C. Rakovsky, 'The Five-Year Plan in crisis', *Critique* 13, 1981. Rakovsky's account is in sharp contrast to Maurice Dobb's romantic mesmerization with the First Five-Year Plan: see M.Dobb, *In Soviet Russia — Autumn 1930*, London: Modern Books, 1930.

27   See M. Kaldor, *The Baroque Arsenal*, London: Abacus,1983, 95.

28   *Source*: M. Kidron and D. Smith, *The War Atlas*, London: Pan, 1983.

29   See M. Kidron, *Western Capitalism since the War*, Harmondsworth: Pelican, 1970.

30   See especially D. Smith and R. Smith, *The Economics of Militarism*, London: Pluto Press, 1983; R. Smith, 'Military expenditure and capitalism', *Cambridge Journal of Economics* 1, (1), March 1977; and

'Military expenditure and investment in OECD countries', *Journal of Comparative Economics*, 1 (1), March 1980, and M. Kaldor, op.cit.,

31   'Baroque' is the term coined by M. Kaldor to describe decadent military technology: see M. Kaldor, *The Baroque Arsenal*, op.cit.

32   ibid., 95-6.

33   Net rather than gross investment is relevant because an allocation of investment for social capital caused by migration will be a deduction from surplus for replacement investment, i.e to replace social capital wasted in regions suffering from outward migration. Unemployment and underemployment building up in more developed regions as a result of migration will not represent an *additional* cost for the state: all that has changed is the location of unemployment and underemployment.

34   See M. Drulovic, *Self-Management on Trial*, Nottingham: Spokesman Books, 1978, Chapter 9.

35   See V. Dedijer, *The Battle Stalin Lost (Memoirs of Yugoslavia 1948-53)*, New York: Viking, 1970.

36   Fitzgerald makes this feature of the smaller state socialist economies the centrepiece of a didactic, Kaleckian model of their transition. Their complete lack of a capital goods sector and the consequent need to rely entirely on imports for such inputs provides the specific feature which distinguishes them from other cases – accumulation can only take place by engaging in foreign trade and the rate of accumulation then depends upon the success of that enterprise. See E.V.K Fitzgerald, 'Notes on the analysis of the small underdeveloped economy in transition', in R.R. Fagen, C.D. Deere & J.L. Coraggio (eds) *Transition and Development*, New York: Monthly Review Press, 1986.

37   See L. Huberman and P.M. Sweezy, *Socialism in Cuba*, New York: Modern Reader Paperbacks, 1969.

38   Cuba, of course, is not the only economy in the world to be subsidized in this way — in fact Israel is the most subsidized nation on earth, with grants amounting to about $10 million per day. See A. Kaletsky, 'Israel's economy: spinning in a vicious circle', *Financial Times*, 17 January 1984.

39   A. Gunder Frank, 'The political challenges of socialism and social movements in the world economic crisis', paper presented to International Conference on 'Has Socialism a Future?', Glasgow, April 1985.

40   Castoriadis's critique of Lenin's and Trotsky's paranoia about petty producers in the countryside is penetrating on this score. See C. Castoriadis, 'L'Exploitation de la paysannerie sous le capitalisme bureaucratique', *La Société Bureaucratique I*, Paris: 10/18, 283-312.

41   See P. Wright, *The State and Peasantry in Yugoslavia during the First Five-Year Plan*, Bradford Studies on Yugoslavia no. 10, University of Bradford Postgraduate School of Yugoslav Studies, 1986.

42   See, for example, M. Ellman, *Socialist Planning*, Cambridge: Cambridge University Press, 1979; A. Nove, *The Soviet Economic System*, London: George Allen & Unwin, 1977; and J Kornai, *Overcentralization in Economic Administration*, London: Oxford University Press, 1959.

43   Quotations cited in Kornai, *Economics of Shortage*, op.cit., 29 and 33.

44   This contrast with capitalism is probably overstated by Kornai: control over prices and privileged access to finance mean that large capitalist enterprises can be awash with 'slack budget constraints'.

45   Brus, op.cit., 77.

46   J. Kornai, *Economics of Shortage*, op.cit., 210.

47   Ibid., 200.

48   Moreover, it is important to be clear that a demand-constrained economy is not immune from arbitrariness – under demand-constrained contemporary capitalism profitability is just as likely to reflect chance factors (exchange rate movements, commodity price movements, etc.) and the exercise of market power (control over prices, predatory acquisition of other companies, etc.) as the internal 'efficiency' of a particular enterprise.

49   See Kornai, *Economics of Shortage*, op.cit., Chapter 7.

50   See P. Wright, *The Political Economy of the Yugoslav Revolution*, The Hague: Institute of Social Studies Occasional Paper no. 102, December 1985.

51   See P. Wright, *The State and the Peasantry in Yugoslavia*, op.cit.

4 THE POLITICS OF STATE SOCIALIST SOCIETIES

1   This line is not in itself original to us. See, for example, Ferenc Feher, Agnes Heller, and Gyorgy Markus, *Dictatorship over Needs*, Oxford: Basil Blackwell, 1983.

2   For discussions of the classical case see Andrew Watson, 'Introduction', in his *Mao Zedong and the Political Economy of the Border Regions*, Cambridge: Cambridge University Press, 1980, and Mark Selden, *The Yenan Way in Revolutionary China*, Cambridge, Mass.: Harvard University Press, 1971. For Yugoslavia see P. Wright, *The Political Economy of the Yugoslav Revolution*, The Hague: Institute of Social Studies Occasional Paper no. 102, December 1985.

3   For details on the ideological evolution and 'party-building' in Ethiopia, see Fred Halliday and Maxine Molyneux, *The Ethiopian Revolution*, London: Verso Editions, 1981, 135-45.

4   For a valiant attempt to make a case for popular control in the Soviet Union, see Albert Szymanski, *Is the Red Flag Flying?*, London: Zed Press, 1979.

5   Feher, Heller and Markus, op.cit., 86.

6   G. Konrad and I. Szelenyi *The Intellectuals on the Road to Class Power*, New York: Harcourt Jovanovich, 1979, 153.

7   Further on this see Richard F. Vidmer, 'Administrative science in the USSR: doctrinal constraints on inquiry', *Administration and Society* 12(1), May 1980.

8   See Carmelo Mesa-Largo, *The Economy of Socialist Cuba*, Albuquerque: University of New Mexico Press, 1981, 110-12.

9   For detailed studies of the two patterns see K. Post, *Revolution, Socialism and Nationalism in Viet Nam*, vols II and III, forthcoming.

10   The shift from moral incentives ('socialist competition', medals,

pennants, etc.) to material incentives, which usually occurs quite rapidly, is perhaps best analysed in the case of Cuba. For a summary discussion see Ricardo Carciofi, 'Cuba in the seventies', in G. White, R. Murray and C. White (eds) *Revolutionary Development in the Third World*, Brighton: Wheatsheaf, 1983, 201-5; and further B. Silverman (ed.) *Man and Socialism in Cuba*, New York: Atheneum, 1971; and Brian Pollitt, 'Moral and material incentives in socialist economic development', *Journal of Contemporary Asia* 7, 1977. A vivid portrayal of pressures on workers in an older system may be found in M. Haraszti, *Worker in a Workers' State*, Harmondsworth: Penguin, 1978.

11   Useful studies of different cases are Maxine Molyneux, *State Policies and the Position of Women Workers in the People's Democratic Republic of Yemen*, Geneva: International Labour Organization, 1981, and D. Davin, *Women-work: Women and the Party in Revolutionary China*, Oxford: Clarendon Press, 1976.

12   For an interesting discussion of this based on the older case of Hungary see I. Szelenyi, 'Social inequalities in state socialist redistributive economies', *International Journal of Comparative Sociology* XIX, March-June 1978.

13   It is this point in particular which marks our analysis off from that of Konrad and Szelenyi (*The Intellectuals on the Road to Class Power*, op. cit.), with which we otherwise have much in common. They seem ultimately unable to make the final break with Marxist–Leninist orthodoxy and move out of the conventional mould of class analysis. Conversely, they do not in fact offer an actual proof that either their 'intellectual class' or the 'ruling elite' which is its core (147) is related to the means of production in the same way as earlier dominant classes. For a critique along these lines see Jean L. Cohen, *Class and Civil Society*, Amherst: University of Massachusetts Press, 1982, 17-20, though this writer is further distanced from the Marxist tradition than we are.

14   Thus a survey of enterprises in three cities in the USSR in the late 1960s showed 44.9 per cent of specialists to be children of lower non-manual or specialist fathers, while another sample survey of scientists and engineers revealed that more than 70 percent were from non-manual families (Murray Yanowitch, *Social and Economic Inequality in the Soviet Union*, London: Martin Robertson, 1977, 109 (Table 4.2), and 113-14 (Table 4.4). A survey of 0.5 per cent of the economically active population in Poland in 1972 showed 68.3 per cent of sons (sic) of non-manual workers to be working in the same kind of jobs. In Hungary, in 1967, 53 per cent of top non-manual jobs were held by people from the same family background; 71 per cent had had non-manual grandfathers (David Lane, *The Socialist Industrial State*, London: George Allen & Unwin, 1976, 205-6 (Tables 13 and 14)).

5   TOWARDS A BALANCE SHEET

1   As reported in the *Financial Times* on 24 April 1986.

2   Karl Marx, *A Contribution to the Critique of Political Economy*,

Moscow: Progress Publishers, 1970.

3   J. Kornai discusses this approach in *Rush versus Harmonic Growth*, Amsterdam: North Holland, 1972.

4   For example, Ticktin's numerous articles in the journal *Critique* repeatedly stress that 'real' planning does not exist in the Soviet Union because effective democratic participation is absent – the implication and prescription being that 'real' planning could be introduced (were the right political conditions to be created) and that it would solve the fundamental problems of Soviet society.

5   A. Nove, 'Market socialism and its critics', *Political Economy and Soviet Socialism*, London: George Allen & Unwin, 128.

6   G. Kitching, *Rethinking Socialism*, London: Methuen, 1983

7   A. Nove, *The Economics of Feasible Socialism*, London: George Allen & Unwin, 1983.

8   ibid., 197–8, and E. Mandel, 'Self-management — dangers and possibilities', *International* 2(3), Winter/Spring 1975, 7-8.

9   E. Kardelj, *Democracy and Socialism*, London: The Summerfield Press, 1978, 34.

10   ibid., 17 and 235.

Index